DOING THINGS DIFFERENTLY

Tavistock Clinic Series

Margot Waddell & Jocelyn Catty (Series Editors)

Recent titles in the Tavistock Clinic Series

(for a full listing, please visit www.karnacbooks.com)

Addictive States of Mind, *edited by Marion Bower, Rob Hale, & Heather Wood*
Borderline Welfare: Feeling and Fear of Feeling in Modern Welfare, *by Andrew Cooper & Julian Lousada*
Childhood Depression: A Place for Psychotherapy, *edited by Judith Trowell, with Gillian Miles*
Consultations in Psychoanalytic Psychotherapy, *edited by R. Peter Hobson*
Contemporary Developments in Adult and Young Adult Therapy. The Work of the Tavistock and Portman Clinics, Vol. 1, *edited by Alessandra Lemma*
Couple Dynamics: Psychoanalytic Perspectives in Work with the Individual, the Couple, and the Group, *edited by Aleksandra Novakovic*
Creating New Families: Therapeutic Approaches to Fostering, Adoption, and Kinship Care, *edited by Jenny Kenrick, Caroline Lindsey, & Lorraine Tollemache*
Engaging with Complexity: Child & Adolescent Mental Health and Education, *edited by Rita Harris, Sue Rendall, & Sadegh Nashat*
Inside Lives: Psychoanalysis and the Growth of the Personality, *by Margot Waddell*
Living on the Border: Psychotic Processes in the Individual, the Couple, and the Group, *edited by David Bell & Aleksandra Novakovic*
Looking into Later Life: A Psychoanalytic Approach to Depression and Dementia in Old Age, *edited by Rachael Davenhill*
Making Room for Madness in Mental Health: The Psychoanalytic Understanding of Psychotic Communication, *by Marcus Evans*
Managing Vulnerability: The Underlying Dynamics of Systems of Care, *by Tim Dartington*
Oedipus and the Couple, *edited by Francis Grier*
Organization in the Mind: Psychoanalysis, Group Relations, and Organizational Consultancy, *by David Armstrong, edited by Robert French*
Reflecting on Reality: Psychotherapists at Work in Primary Care, *edited by John Launer, Sue Blake, & Dilys Daws*
Short-Term Psychoanalytic Psychotherapy for Adolescents with Depression: A Treatment Manual, *edited by Jocelyn Catty*
Sibling Matters: A Psychoanalytic, Developmental, and Systemic Approach, *edited by Debbie Hindle & Susan Sherwin-White*
Social Defences against Anxiety: Explorations in a Paradigm, *edited by David Armstrong & Michael Rustin*
Surviving Space: Papers on Infant Observation, *edited by Andrew Briggs*
The Anorexic Mind, *by Marilyn Lawrence*
The Groups Book. Psychoanalytic Group Therapy: Principles and Practice, *edited by Caroline Garland*
The Learning Relationship: Psychoanalytic Thinking in Education, *edited by Biddy Youell*
Thinking Space: Promoting Thinking about Race, Culture, and Diversity in Psychotherapy and Beyond, *edited by Frank Lowe*
Towards Belonging: Negotiating New Relationships for Adopted Children and Those in Care, *edited by Andrew Briggs*
Understanding Trauma: A Psychoanalytic Approach, *edited by Caroline Garland*
Waiting to Be Found: Papers on Children in Care, *edited by Andrew Briggs*
"What Can the Matter Be?": Therapeutic Interventions with Parents, Infants, and Young Children, *edited by Louise Emanuel & Elizabeth Bradley*
Work Discussion: Learning from Reflective Practice in Work with Children and Families, *edited by Margaret Rustin & Jonathan Bradley*
Working Below the Surface: The Emotional Life of Contemporary Organizations, *edited by Clare Huffington, David Armstrong, William Halton, Linda Hoyle, & Jane Pooley*
Young Child Observation: A Development in the Theory and Method of Infant Observation, *edited by Simonetta M. G. Adamo & Margaret Rustin*

DOING THINGS DIFFERENTLY

The Influence of Donald Meltzer on Psychoanalytic Theory and Practice

Edited by

Margaret Cohen & Alberto Hahn

KARNAC

First published in 2017 by
Karnac Books
118 Finchley Road
London NW3 5HT

British Library Cataloguing in Publication Data

A C.I.P. for this book is available from the British Library

ISBN: 978–1–78220–434–3

Edited, designed, and produced by Communication Crafts

Printed in Great Britain

www.karnacbooks.com

CONTENTS

SERIES EDITORS' PREFACE

Margot Waddell & Jocelyn Catty

Since it was founded in 1920, the Tavistock Clinic has developed a wide range of developmental approaches to mental health which have been strongly influenced by the ideas of psychoanalysis. It has also adopted systemic family therapy as a theoretical model and a clinical approach to family problems. The Clinic is now the largest training institution in Britain for mental health, providing postgraduate and qualifying courses in social work, psychology, psychiatry, and child, adolescent, and adult psychotherapy, as well as in nursing and primary care. It trains about 1,700 students each year in over 60 courses.

The Clinic's philosophy aims at promoting therapeutic methods in mental health. Its work is based on the clinical expertise that is also the basis of its consultancy and research activities. The aim of this Series is to make available to the reading public the clinical, theoretical, and research work that is most influential at the Tavistock Clinic. The Series sets out new approaches in the understanding and treatment of psychological disturbance in children, adolescents, and adults, both as individuals and in families.

It is a kind of publishers' lore that collections of conference papers seldom make a good book. *Doing Things Differently: The Influence of Donald Meltzer on Psychoanalytic Theory and Practice*, however, is in itself "different". As this conference proceeded and with no pre-planning, the papers submitted somehow arranged themselves into several quite distinctive threads in the development of Donald Meltzer's thought, whether in relation to young and latency-aged children, to adolescents, or to adults. In so doing, they further elaborated some of his most challenging and original concepts and built a coherent body of what that thought had inspired—something of immense suggestiveness.

The conference, held at the Tavistock Clinic in 2015, was convened by Alberto Hahn, Margaret Cohen, and Jonathan and Catrin Bradley to mark the 10th anniversary of Meltzer's death. It was an impressively international event, with contributions from North and South America and from several European countries as well as England, in particular from the Tavistock Clinic itself. All the participants knew Meltzer, and most had been supervised by him, in some cases over a period of several years. This made for a very powerfully positive atmosphere—a "work group", in Bion's terms—that also pervades the pages of this book in a very special and rare way.

Overall, one of the most striking and moving aspects of the book is that the chapters, in their very different ways, come together to express what could be called something like "the generation of meaning". They are testament to the space for the "co-creation of imaginative conjectures" that one contributor describes—a process at the heart of what Bion thought of as the growth of the mind, the developing a mind of one's own, so compelling and so enabling for the contributors as well as for all the readers. For threading their way through this book are countless examples, some fleeting, some deep and extended, of intellectual and psychic "growth", in the true sense of the word. Meltzer shared Bion's distinction between K and –K: the distinction between supposedly learning about the self and others, about life, even about psychoanalysis, through "cleverness or competitive ingenuity", and that which we can risk through our own experience. This latter is clearly voiced in one of the chapters in terms of, "if we could stop trying, then ideas would develop us". As we can see here, the *way* in which Meltzer taught and the actual *content* were inseparable: we hear of his wit and humour, his often surprising turns of mind and phrase, his surpassing originality, and, as the contributors here collectively attest, the presence of something as elusive as "clinical intuition", learned not through trying to define the indefinable but through the nature of the insights found here in the case material presented. Meltzer was opposed to what he described as any kind of "apostolic succession", and his approach to lecturing and supervision, the fruits of which are so apparent in the book, was, as he once said: "Does my way of seeing things help you to see them your way, only more clearly".

The chapters build upon his struggles to understand and to work with some of the most opaque areas of mental functioning. As is clear, the work is ever-evolving, always in a state of becoming. Some of Meltzer's collaborators were on the Tavistock staff at the time and some within the student body. Together, they shared the challenging puzzles of the Clinic's work with extremely disturbed young children, especially those on the autistic spectrum. The fruits of this collaboration are vividly expressed in the chapters on one- and two-dimensional mental functioning, for example—and dimensionality is indeed, on the whole, an immensely complex issue in psychic development generally.

Other chapters have expanded upon a concept that emerged much later in Meltzer's thinking: that of the "claustrum". Examples and clarifications are drawn not only from clinical cases but also from the wider culture of literature and film, in which the inner realities of the claustrum world are elaborated and described to enormous effect. Further light, both theoretical and clinical, is thrown on the meaning of the "aesthetic object", on dreaming, on latency and adolescence, on selective mutism, and on both having a mind of one's own and losing one's mind.

Overarching all is the stress on the immense significance of observation, directed as much towards the self as towards the other. Indeed, Meltzer himself stated that, "This power of observation, outward and inward, is the fountainhead of Bion's originality." These words could have applied with equal weight to Meltzer himself, also struggling, as he put it, "to find a conceptual framework for assembling meaningfully the masses of new observations". In our view, this capacity shines throughout these pages. In the present rather dark intellectual climate, one that tends to eschew painful or complex areas of thinking and is averse to not "knowing", to uncertainty, even to truth itself, we hope that *Doing Things Differently* may be something of a beacon.

ABOUT THE EDITORS AND CONTRIBUTORS

Louise Allnutt is the Lead Child and Adolescent Psychotherapist at an inner-city CAMHS, working with children with disabilities and other developmental difficulties. She supervises, teaches theory, and co-convenes the autism workshop on the Child Psychotherapy Training at the Tavistock Centre. Her clinical and research interests are centred on psychoanalytic approaches to understanding trauma and the development of early interventions for children at risk of autism.

Nubia Torres Calderón is a researcher and Associate Professor at the Psychology Department of the Universidad Javeriana in Bogota, Colombia. She is currently lecturing to pre- and postgraduates on the psychoanalytic emphasis in the Master's Degree in Clinical Psychology. She is a member of the Colombia Psychoanalytical Society and has worked for some three decades on research and intervention in cases of family abuse and projects for psychic development in community spaces in the city of Bogota.

Margaret Cohen is a child and adult psychotherapist in private practice in London. She worked in the Department of Psychological Medicine at Great Ormond Street and then in the Neo-Natal Intensive Care Unit and Paediatric Oncology at the Whittington Hospital, London. She has written about prematurity, among other subjects, and has taught at the Tavistock Clinic, the Anna Freud Clinic, and in Italy.

Jeffrey L. Eaton is a graduate and faculty member of the Northwestern Psychoanalytic Society and Institute and a member of the IPA. He is author of *A Fruitful Harvest: Essays after Bion* (2011). He has a particular interest in the treatment of autistic states and was the recipient of the 10th International Frances Tustin Memorial Lecture Prize in 2006.

Mary Fisher-Adams is a psychoanalyst with the British Psychoanalytic Association and is a training analyst for the Association of Child Psychotherapists. She edited the *Journal of the British Association for Psychotherapists* from 1999 to 2005. She works in private practice in London.

Alberto Hahn is a fellow of the British Psychoanalytical Society and works in private practice in London, teaches psychoanalysis at the Tavistock Clinic, and lectures abroad. He translated, from the Spanish, Leon Grinberg's *Introduction to the Work of Bion* (1977) and is the editor of *Sincerity and Other Works: Collected Papers of Donald Meltzer* (1994). He also edited, with Margaret Cohen, *Exploring the Work of Donald Meltzer: A Festschrift* (2000). He has written a number of clinical and theoretical papers, among them "Observation and Intuition in the Psychoanalytical Situation", "On Complaining", and "The Nature of the Object in the Claustrum".

Tara Harrison, following a career in opera, trained as a psychoanalytic psychotherapist at the London Centre for Psychotherapy, now part of the Psychoanalytic Psychotherapy Association. She works in private practice in London.

Didier Houzel is Professor Emeritus of Child and Adolescent Psychiatry at the University of Caen in France and a Full Member of the French Psychoanalytic Association. He was the recipient of the Sixth Annual International Frances Tustin Memorial Prize in 2002. He worked with several Kleinian psychoanalysts, including James Gammill in Paris, Donald Meltzer in London, and Frances Tustin in Amersham.

Jeanne Magagna received her doctorate from a joint programme of the University of East London and the Tavistock Clinic. Recently she has served as the Head of Psychotherapy Services at Great Ormond Street Hospital for Children, and as Consultant Psychotherapist at the Ellern Mede Centre for Eating Disorders. She started and headed, for many years, the Centro Studi Martha Harris Observation Courses, involving an MA from Tavistock Clinic and Child Psychotherapy Trainings, in Florence and Venice, Italy. Her professional interests include preventative work with infants, eating disorders, and self-harm. She has taught, either in person or by Skype, on most continents. Her publications include editing or jointly editing *Universals of Psychoanalysis in the Treatment of Psychotic and Borderline States* (1994); *The Silent Child: Communication without Words* (2102); *Intimate Transformations: Babies with their Families* (2005); *Understanding Your Nursery Age Child* (2014); *Psychotherapy with Families: An Analytic Approach* (1981); and *Creativity and Psychotic States in Exceptional People* (2015).

Suzanne Maiello is a child psychotherapist and adult analyst in private practice in Rome, a member of the ACP, and a founder member of the Italian Association of Psychoanalytic Child Psychotherapy (AIPPI). Donald Meltzer and Frances Tustin were among her teachers and supervisors. In 1997 she was the recipient of the First Annual International Frances Tustin Memorial Prize. She is the editor of *Gioco e linguaggio* (2012). Her English publications include *The Sound Object* (1995), *Prenatal Trauma and Autism* (2001/2015), *Song-and-Dance and Its Developments* (2000), and *Prenatal Experience of Containment* (2012).

David Mayers is a training and supervising therapist in the Psychoanalytic Psychotherapy Association and an honorary research fellow in Psychoanalytic Studies at the University of Kent. He has a special interest in the relations between the works of W. R. Bion and Samuel Beckett.

Cecilia Muñoz Vila is a psychologist at the National University of Colombia. She studied sociology in Santiago, Chile, in Münster, Germany, and at Cornell University, in the United States. She trained as a psychoanalyst and is member of the Colombia Psychoanalytical Society. She lectures regularly on the Master's Degree in Clinical Psychology at the Psychology Faculty of the Pontificia Universidad Javeriana and does research into the critical analysis of the media, the history of childhood, mourning in childhood, child abuse, and the abuse of women. She has written "The Old Ones—Testimony" (1984), "Childhood at the Beginning of the XX Century" (1991), "Requiem for the Dead Children" (2002, with Ximena Pachon), "Psychoanalytic Reflections" (2011), and "Psychoanalytic Clinic: Twelve Case Studies and Some Notes on Technique" (2014), among other publications.

Clara Nemas is a Senior Member of the Buenos Aires Psychoanalytic Association, an IPA Child and Adolescent Analyst, and a Member of the IPA China Committee. She is on the Editorial Board of the International Journal of Psychoanalysis and has published papers on Kleinian and neo-Kleinian theory and technique.

Maria Rhode is Emeritus Professor of Child Psychotherapy at the Tavistock Clinic and the University of East London. She trained at the Tavistock, where she was supervised by Donald Meltzer, and is a member of the Association of Child Psychotherapists and an Honorary Associate of the British Psychoanalytical Society. She has lectured and published widely, predominantly on childhood autism, and was awarded the Frances Tustin Memorial Prize in 1998. She is currently working on a pilot early intervention project for toddlers at risk of autism..

Margaret Rustin is a child, adolescent, and adult psychotherapist. She was head of Child Psychotherapy at the Tavistock Clinic from 1986 to 2009—a time during which it was possible to expand the training and to support many new trainings elsewhere. She continues to teach at the Clinic and in many other parts of the UK, Europe, and the wider world, and has a private practice in London. She has written on many psychoanalytic topics and has recently completed, with her husband Michael, *Reading Klein* (2017).

Pamela B. Sorensen is a child psychotherapist. She is the former director of the Under Fives Study Center at the University of Virginia, in the United States, and currently lives in Virginia, where she teaches Kleinian theory and provides case consultation.

Carlos Tabbia qualified in philosophy and psychology at Argentine universities and has a doctorate in psychology from Barcelona University in Spain. He is a founding member of the Barcelona Psychoanalytical Group and a training analyst of the Catalan Association of Psychoanalytical Psychotherapy (EFPP). He sees adult and adolescent patients in his private practice and is a lecturer and supervisor in Spain, Argentina, and Italy. He has published in psychoanalytic publications in Argentina, Great Britain, Brazil, Italy, and Spain.

Monica Vorchheimer is a training and supervisor analyst from the Buenos Aires Psychoanalytical Association (APdeBA), Argentina; she is a full member of the International Psychoanalytical Association and of the Latin American Psychoanalytic Federation, a member of the European Federation of Psychotherapy, and honorary member of the AAPPIPNA, Spain. She is a professor at the University Institute of Mental Health, of the Buenos Aires Psychoanalytical Association. She has been awarded the Bleger (1998) and Storni (2001) prizes by the Argentine Psychoanalytic Association and the Liberman prize (1999) by the Buenos Aires Psychoanalytic Association. She has a long experience of treating individual patients, families, and couples and has published various papers in Argentina and in Spain, where she has also worked as a psychoanalyst, supervising and teaching.

Meg Harris Williams is a writer and artist (www.artlit.info). Her books focus on the relation between psychoanalysis and literature, and include *Inspiration in Milton and Keats* (1982), *A Strange Way of Killing* (1987), *The Apprehension of Beauty* (with Donald Meltzer; 1988), *The Chamber of Maiden Thought* (with Margot Waddell; 1991), *Five Tales from Shakespeare* (for children; 1996), *The Vale of Soulmaking* (2005), *The Aesthetic Development* (2010), *Bion's Dream* (2010), and *The Becoming Room: Filming Bion's Memoir of the Future* (2016). She teaches and lectures widely in this country and abroad and is editor of the Harris Meltzer Trust (www.harris-meltzer-trust.org.uk).

DOING THINGS DIFFERENTLY

Introduction

Margaret Cohen & Alberto Hahn

In February 2015, the Donald Meltzer Development Fund organized an international conference at the Tavistock Clinic in London with the attendance of 120 participants. This conference was the response to a frequently expressed wish for a reunion in which Meltzer's ideas, teachings, and clinical insights could be pored over, where exchanges could be—as indeed they were—stimulating, and which could provide a place in which his work could be celebrated among colleagues from all over the world.

In organizing this conference, our motivations were several. We wanted to meet up with old friends and colleagues, but we were also aware that, whereas when we were training, Meltzer was a lively force in our thinking, people training now receive his teaching because it is implicit in so many of the older child psychotherapists' backgrounds. Furthermore, we realized that many of the papers came from people who had been supervised or taught by him.

Although there is systematic teaching of Meltzer's thought at the Tavistock Clinic, there is only an occasional mention of his work at the British Psychoanalytical Society, with no systematic reading. One of our motivations was therefore to set up an event that would interest the trainees and younger members of our profession. Also, from the beginning we wanted to continue the work of harvesting the rich crop that has come from his teaching and written work, and the papers presented at the conference bear witness to the fact that he remains a very lively force in our thinking.

The title of this conference, "A Mind of One's Own", proclaims a basic attitude of the psychoanalyst, who needs to rely on his—or her—own personal experience and capabilities, which, with the aid of his internal objects, allows him to engage with the distressed mind of his patients with a very personal brand of curiosity, commitment, and devotion. This job, which is isolating but never lonely, compels the practitioners to gather at meetings that take place regularly all over the world. These meetings provide an occasion for exchanging ideas, seeing ideological comrades, criticizing and discussing the finer points of individual bits of research that can be shared in a kaleidoscope of languages, and celebrating the work of one of the most original, creative, and much loved analysts in the United Kingdom.

We regret it was not possible to publish all the papers presented at the conference in this book, but editorial restrictions forced us to make some choices regarding the content and various lengths of the papers, in order to compile a faithful sample of the proceedings and to give you, the reader, an experience of the breadth of subjects that were being discussed. This book is a distillation of papers presented in the three-day programme of the conference and has been compiled to reflect a sequence of thinking that contains a true sense of development, of work in progress.

The enlightening scene-setting of our first chapter by Margaret Rustin is followed by three further chapters and one panel that deal with issues of dimensionality in primitive states of mind, with distinguished contributions from Maria Rhode (United Kingdom), Suzanne Maiello (Italy), Didier Houzel (France), Jeffrey Eaton (United States), and Louise Allnutt (United Kingdom). Directly related to dimensionality is the subject of isolation, which is examined in Carlos Tabbia's (Spain) chapter on adolescence. There then follows a most interesting study on the nature of clinical supervision by Clara Nemas (Argentina) and two clinical chapters on developmental issues by Monica Vorchheimer (Argentina) and Jeanne Magagna (United Kingdom). The topic of dreaming is addressed in Jeffrey Eaton's chapter, "The Second Life of Dreaming" and Meg Harris Williams (United Kingdom) contributes a theoretical chapter, "On Having Ideas; The Aesthetic Object and O". This takes us straight into the other important subject that was discussed at the conference—namely, the claustrum. Pamela Sorensen (United States) uses two films to address the "degrees of entrapment" of life or death in the claustrum, and Mary Fisher-Adams

(United Kingdom) presents a thorough study of James Joyce through his *Ulysses*, which is described as a claustrum world and how the fear and dread it can produce leads to a proleptic imagination that keeps the claustrum dweller imprisoned and paralysed. This is paired with a brief and brilliant critical commentary by David Mayers (United Kingdom) in his contribution, "Gaudete", which was delivered as a response to Fisher-Adams's paper at the conference. The third chapter on the claustrum is by Tara Harrison (United Kingdom) and contains a lively clinical example of a claustrum patient.

The final contribution from the conference shows the vicissitudes of claustrum patients, with a focus on battered women. This chapter, by Cecilia Muñoz Vila and Nubia Torres Calderón (Colombia), clearly shows the ultimate application of this diagnostic category to a seldom-addressed subject in the psychoanalytic literature: that of abused women and their abusers.

Over and over again, we are reminded of what fertile soil Meltzer's thought is and how it seems to enable and encourage practitioners to go on and have their own ideas.

CHAPTER ONE

Doing things differently: an appreciation of Donald Meltzer's contribution

Margaret Rustin

The title of this chapter is intended to draw attention to aspects of Donald Meltzer's ways of working which characterized his practice as a psychoanalyst and which, I think, are important in appreciating his originality. Of course, such observations arise from one's own particular perspective and may not be in accord with the recollections or understanding of others, and it is obvious that doing things differently—which I am interpreting, in part, as Meltzer's characteristic commitment to doing things in his own way—means that there will be conflicting views about whether such differences have a good outcome. This chapter is not going to address the institutional conflicts that were part of the historical picture—in fact, I am sure that I am quite ignorant of much of this history. Instead, I hope to describe things that I have observed both in the years of some personal contact with Meltzer and in reading his books and papers over time, things that have struck me as enlightening and interesting, or sometimes maddening and frustrating features of his work, and which arise from his personal style as a writer and analyst. Perhaps, also, I am going to be doing something rather different from other writers who address his ideas, since their focus is more usually on his clinical contributions.

The themes I want to follow are these: the central relevance of child analysis and the unity of child and adult analysis; the value of working in a clinical group with colleagues; the revision of psychoanalytic theory; joint research and writing projects; his discovery of infant observation; the commitment to a wider psychoanalytic culture; and the particular contribution to the Tavistock child psychotherapy training. As you can see, there are overlapping areas implied in this selection, and this is inevitable. I shall use examples from particular books and papers to try to demonstrate what I am getting at.

Let me start with a word about the British psychoanalytic context in which Meltzer was working during and following his years of analysis with Melanie Klein. This was a time when the discoveries of child analysis were greatly valued and when the interest in early mental development was closely linked to psychoanalytic research into serious mental illness. Child analysis and the efforts to analyse schizophrenic and other seriously disturbed patients by W. R. Bion, Herbert Rosenfeld, and Hanna Segal, among others, were taking place simultaneously, and, in some instances, analysts were involved in both these areas. It was also a time when the post-war development of the NHS gave hope that psychoanalytic ideas could influence community mental health in major ways, and the establishment of the Tavistock Child Psychotherapy training in 1948 was part of this. There were strong links between the group of mainly Kleinian analysts who were also trained as child analysts—for example, Isobel Menzies, Eleanor Wedeles, Doreen Weddell, and Athol Hughes—and the Tavistock training. Meltzer's lifelong interest in the continuities of psychic life, and his confidence that analytic techniques could encompass work with disturbed young children and the full range of adolescent and adult pathologies, grew very naturally from this fertile period of psychoanalytic exploration and simultaneous ambitious engagement with new institutional developments.

His unusual talent for and interest in theory-building combined with his original clinical imagination made for the powerful integration of theory and practice seen in *The Psychoanalytical Process* (1967). One of the particular features of his writing is that whereas the more standard form of communication in psychoanalysis is via individual scientific papers, and of course he wrote many such papers, it also came naturally to Meltzer to write books. Of course, these were sometimes based on a lecture series, but the fact is that a book-length piece of writing takes in a much wider horizon; this appealed to him, I think, because it involved following things through. Just as an analysis has a beginning, middle, and end, and requires substantial time for its development, so writing or reading a book is a process in time.

The Psychoanalytical Process is exemplary in rooting the ideas presented in clinical detail, and the chapter that describes the process in an individual session with a 4½-year-old girl seen in analysis from the age of 3 is a very powerful example of Meltzer's approach. The case was presented for detailed discussion in a seminar of child analysts and psychotherapists (reminding us, incidentally, of how closely these two groups worked together at that time), and the clinical material is presented in a carefully descriptive form, recording all the child's activities, verbalizations, facial expressions and so on, but, strikingly, including nothing at all about the countertransference impact on the analyst. Indeed, Meltzer is explicit in stating that he "leaves problems of countertransference aside as private to the supervisee". I think this method, even though it is clearly different from contemporary practice, where a group discussion of the clinician's feelings about the patient, and indeed contributions from other group members about their own emotional reaction, would be expected, draws attention to a fundamental idea underlying Meltzer's conception of psychoanalysis. This is that if the therapist is truly to be working at the appropriate depth to deal with the infantile transference, an analytic process also has to be ongoing for him or her, either in the form of continuing personal analysis or in the self-analysis that has to be the outcome of a good-enough analytic experience. The model of training as a psychoanalytic therapist which is based on personal analysis, clinical experience, and intensive supervision is thus seen also as the necessary cornerstone of an ongoing professional life. I think it is important to remind ourselves of this, because although professional bodies now demand evidence of continuing professional development (CPD) as part of continuing fitness to practise, the question of what this really requires of us is a serious one. The tremendous intensity of the training years is often seen as exhaustingly demanding, something from which people can crave a rest even if they are simultaneously aware of how much the quality of their clinical work is linked to that intensity. *The Psychoanalytical Process* makes a strong case that this level of engagement is integral to the capacity to continue to work psychoanalytically.

Meltzer uses the clinical material presented to clarify what he thought actually constituted psychoanalysis. From the patient's perspective, it is a question of the evolution of the unconscious in the context of the availability of a transference relationship. From the analyst, the contribution required is the provision and maintenance of the setting (that is, the psychoanalytic setting in the sense just discussed about the dedicated state of mind of the therapist in relation to the task) and a steady commitment to "working through", Freud's profound conceptual contribution to understanding the idea of process in psychoanalysis (1914g). Meltzer emphasizes that an adequate setting depends on "devotion" to the psychoanalytic method together with curiosity (a lively dose of the epistemophilic instinct, one might say) and argues that these two factors together sustain the tolerance of mental pain required of the psychoanalytic therapist. His discussion of "working through" differentiates two aspects of this process. The first is to do with the attempt to build up insight in the patient, which involves understanding the difference between infantile and adult modes of experience and acknowledging the distinctions between internal and external reality. The second concerns the modification of anxiety, following Klein's central emphasis on the interpretation of infantile anxieties, which Meltzer develops in the direction of the aim of psychoanalytic therapy being the growth of introjective identification with a thinking analytic mind, which can support the patient and prevent regression. This would be his understanding of what might constitute the "resilience" so beloved in contemporary discourse.

In *The Psychoanalytical Process,* Meltzer's conviction in the continuity and coherence of child and adult analysis is particularly vivid, and the developmental nature and function of analytic work is the central point. What is also impressive in the notes included in the appendices are the areas of theoretical work which he is exploring at the time and the hints of those to come. At this time, his thinking is, naturally, linked not only to Freud, Karl Abraham, Klein, and other predecessors, but also to his contemporary colleagues—Bion, Rosenfeld, Segal, Esther Bick, Roger Money-Kyrle, Betty Joseph, and Sidney Klein—whose work he cites in ways that illustrate the lively intellectual group-life of the Kleinians in that period. It also suggests just how much was lost when the dialogue between Meltzer and many of this talented generation of analysts came to a halt.

The enormous task he then took on to draw together his theoretical understanding of the Kleinian clinical approach and its roots in Freud's clinical papers, and to take his readers on into Bion's thinking, also marked the period in which his contribution to the Tavistock training was at its height. I remember rather clearly Mattie Harris speaking of her recognition of the gap between the clinical teaching offered to those of my generation in the late 1960s and the theoretical curriculum that accompanied that. When I enquired, truly puzzled about this, why we did not read Klein's *Narrative of a Child Analysis* (1961), she said something that amounted to "You wait!" The strengthening of the theory teaching that Meltzer's systematic lectures provided cannot be overestimated, and of course it massively influenced the curriculum of the observation course, the shape of which was gradually developing during the 1970s, as well as the theory teaching within the child psychotherapy training. What was so important about this for child psychotherapy was the way in which clinical practice was so clearly a present preoccupation in theory teaching done in this way, and the to-and-fro between child and adult analysis and theory and practice gave new potential for clinical experience in work with children to be theorized. I think we can be confident that the significant theoretical contributions later made by child psychotherapists—including, for example, Gianna Williams (1997), Maria Rhode (2013), and Ricky Emanuel (2001, 2012), who all shared this experience—grew from these roots.

Such possibilities were also closely linked to the impact of Bick's method of infant observation upon clinical practice (1964, 1968). The naturalistic observation of very early states of non-integration, the theory of the centrality of growth of a psychic skin, and the elaboration of second-skin defences were an important part of the work being done with autistic children by Meltzer and the group with which he worked so closely—presented in *Explorations in Autism* (Meltzer, Bremner, Hoxter, Weddell, & Wittenberg, 1972a, 1975)—and was also the background to Frances Tustin's work (Tustin, 1981). Just as in *The Psychoanalytical Process* the seminar group studying child analytic cases was the site for discovery, so in the autism book the shared discussion of the cases followed in such detail by the group was the heart of the project. Meltzer's capacity for theoretical writing was nourished by this contact with a rich range of cases which allowed him to delineate, again on a developmental model, the very particular forms of failed and alternative mental development which characterized autistic states of mind.

Meltzer's published work is full of creative collaborations—with Esther Bick, with Meg Harris Williams, with generations of analysts and child psychotherapy supervisees in England, Italy, Spain, and beyond, and with Mattie Harris. It is to a lengthy research paper (Meltzer, 1976b) written in conjunction with her that I want to turn to provide an example of why these co-operative efforts are so important.

The Paris-based OECD, a UN body, commissioned a report in the 1970s that would offer a psychoanalytically based theoretical model of the links between child, family, and community and serve as a basis for social-psychological research and, indeed, clinical research about forms of intervention (Meltzer, 1976b). The report has not been used as fully as its intent warrants, and it is not an easy document to digest, but I think the differentiation it describes between typologies of family culture remains provocative and enlightening.

The first section of the report outlines the central position of the concept of mental pain in psychoanalytic discourse: "Whose pain is it?" they write. This, of course, is the question we usually start with in any new referral, allied to the question of "Why now?" An elegant exposition of basic concepts—anxiety in its various forms, self, part-object, combined object, omnipotent phantasy, mechanisms of defence, and so on—follows. Because of the importance of Bion's definition of "learning from experience" and the crucial value given by Meltzer and Harris to such learning, there is a careful account of different, more limited or distorted and disturbed forms of learning. The life-space model is then introduced, with reference to the contribution of temperament, internal objects, adult and infantile elements in the personality, and family organization. Use is made of Bion's distinction between basic assumption and more reality-based "work-group" functioning, and of his 1970 description of the difference between commensal, symbiotic, parasitic, and paranoid orientations to define the nature of the links between family and community (Bion, 1961, 1970). Familiar themes such as the matter of relationship to time appear: timelessness, oscillating and circular time, which all undermine the awareness of linear time.

The breadth of application of these and many more familiar building blocks in thinking about family and community cultures is what is so striking in this report. One can imagine what a challenge it presented to the policymakers and researchers to whom it was, in part, directed; despite clear accounts in the report of unconscious phantasy, transference, and countertransference, without personal experience of psychoanalysis it is hard to imagine that they could grasp all these complexities. However, for clinicians there is a cornucopia of ideas. Meltzer's naturally theoretical psychoanalytic thinking and philosophical interests marry with Harris's literary background, her experience of infant observation, and her vast range of clinical experience with children and families at the Tavistock. The evocative finesse of the writing reminds us of their shared breadth of experience as both child and adult analysts. This conjunction is what makes for such a compelling shared focus on the internal and external world.

When they wrote this report, family therapy in the UK was just starting to develop. It would be a major but intellectually fascinating project to explore whether the ideas they proffer about family functioning might map onto the totally different discourses of family therapy in some ways, or whether the psychoanalytic recognition of the centrality of the unconscious makes for quite divergent perspectives. One could make a similar suggestion about the more recent but psychoanalytically much closer discipline of couple psychotherapy. Has this benefited from this earlier work? In James Fisher's writing about work with couples, we have an excellent example of the potential for imaginative integration (Fisher, 1999).

There is not space here for a full presentation of their typology of family cultures, but to remind us or whet the appetites of those unfamiliar with the report, I will pick out some examples. The structures described are being tested against the crucial functions that Meltzer and Harris ascribe to the family. These are set out as pairs:

» promoting love / promulgating hate
» promoting hope / sowing despair
» containing depressive pain / emanating (spreading) persecutory anxiety
» supporting thought, thinking / creating confusion.

The atmosphere evoked by each of these phrases also suggests to me that these categories are helpful and accurate descriptions we can use in pinpointing the valency of a clinical session. They refer to phenomena we can observe in the transference and countertransference and can also perceive in what we learn of our patients' internal and external experience, from lively dream material at one end of the spectrum to the most prosaic of sessions at the other.

The fundamental question is whether the family organization is promoting the development of each of its members according to their respective needs and potentials, and the same question can be asked of the wider community's relationship to the families within it. One can see that the model therefore has wide implications at a political level. For example, it could be said that recent and, tragically, ongoing events in Greece and, indeed, elsewhere in Europe confirm that austerity conditions imposed upon a society cause unacceptable levels of damage to family and individual development. As I find myself moving between the applicability of these ideas to both the analytic session and our experience as citizens, I think I am demonstrating why this paper has meant a lot to me.

The forms of family that Meltzer and Harris denote are:

- couple families, which Meltzer and Harris believe promote development through containment of dependence and anxiety;
- matriarchal or patriarchal families;
- gang families, in which, they suggest, negative identifications are predominant;
- reversed families (meaning when family values are in defiant opposition to more stable community values).

All of these non–couple-based families, in different ways, fail in the fundamental task of "bringing up" the children and supporting the growth of adult states of mind.

Holding these different family structures in mind may also enrich our work with parents. The importance of working with parents is much more readily acknowledged nowadays, including in the formal research literature, than it was before the 1970s. I give one example to indicate these possibilities.

I am thinking of a couple I heard about whose clever 7-year-old son, Adam, the older of two children, had considerable difficulties. He was offered individual therapy in the light of his striking immaturity, his extreme intolerance of his sister's very existence, and his own awareness of and longing for help in dealing with his paralysing anxiety when faced with any kind of choice.

As I heard, in supervision, about these parents, I could see that, although they were intellectually committed to talking things over together and to sharing responsibility for their children, both practically and emotionally, they did not really manage to come together in a way that contained their son's massive infantile outbursts. Neither they, nor he, felt that they could cope with his level of dependence and unpredictable waves of anxiety, and he would become wholly despairing in his collapsed melt-downs. They felt humiliated and persecuted by this repeated scenario, particularly when it was enacted in full public view, and also very angry when they felt it was aimed at their efforts to provide good experiences for him and resulted in these being spoilt.

At the beginning of the work, the father viewed the sessions not as involving thinking about his own contribution to the unhappy family situation, but as oriented to the therapist's conveying his understanding of their son. This was allied to the implication that it was the mother's upset that should be attended to: she was the one who could not cope with Adam, whereas he could come in and calm things down. Mother's difficult family background, in contrast to his own, was suggested as the reason for her vulnerability to becoming overwhelmed, and she agreed with this. Gradually, this somewhat grandiose paternalistic stance—the patriarchal family, as described by Meltzer and Harris, including the harshly scathing and belittling scolding of Adam, and the denigration of his wife—began to show cracks. The criticism of the other adults in Adam's life who were not felt to be good enough at their jobs—including his teacher, cricket coach, and babysitter—gave way to a realization that these others were offering the boy a great deal of support and that the view of things that only he as the father of the family really knew what was what and could be relied upon was a distorted one. At this point the work with the couple felt quite different, in that both now seemed more on a level with each other and both were able to voice their worries and despondency about their frequent failures to contain the children. As the unbalanced dynamic between mother and father shifted, it was also interesting to note that the younger sister began to feature differently, not only as the victim of her brother's aggression and greed for space, but as having her own difficulties in being so easily able to set him up to be in the wrong.

The transference manifestation of all this was an initial idealization of their therapist in which he was seen as possessing something akin to patriarchal authority and omnipotence. I think he was probably also secretly feared for the harsh criticism that was forestalled by concealing the extent of their helplessness and rage in the face of Adam's distress. Later came some of the secret denigration, behind a polite exterior, of anything offered by anyone else, and a difficulty in attending sessions regularly. However, it was possible for the therapist to speak to the couple about the impact it had when there were longer periods of time between sessions, whether planned or unplanned, and for them to see that these tended to coincide with an escalation of trouble in the family. This awareness that these meetings had some meaning for them led to the shift I have briefly described. The couple of parent worker and child therapist—not always an easy one to hold together—can, of course, be a potent representation of the couple functioning to which one hopes parents may aspire, and this was both an area of potential splitting and of its modification in this case.

There are natural connections between the work on family functioning and Meltzer's major study, "Sincerity" (1971), in which he uses three of Harold Pinter's early plays to tackle the topic of truthful emotionality and its perversions. As some readers will know, I too have felt inspired by dramatic texts to explore their meaning psychoanalytically, and no doubt this is one reason I am drawn to mention this remarkable essay (Rustin & Rustin, 2002). But there is another link to be made with the OECD report I have just been describing, for in both of these pieces of work it is clear that Meltzer believes in the potential for a psychoanalytic contribution to understanding society and culture as well as in the responsibility of analysts to use their knowledge to write for a wider public than the still tiny British psychoanalytic world of 1970. Very little publication outside the specialist journals had yet taken place at that time. The value he gave to the original Imago group, which included philosophers, art historians, and others, and its later revival, which mirrored this interdisciplinary approach, also, I suggest, arose from his belief that psychoanalysis had much to receive from elsewhere, as well as much to offer, the potential commensal link noted by Bion. There is an obvious symmetry between this idea about where growth comes from and Meltzer's clinical emphasis on our necessary dependence on allowing our internal parental objects to enjoy intercourse in their own private space. Noticing these recurring elements in his thought has helped me to have more of a sense of the whole. Initial reading of any of his books or papers usually involved, for me, an experience of not understanding a good deal of what was being said, and this feeling of ignorance, combined with one's awareness of the sophistication and complexity of his clinical thinking and his large range of reference to philosophy and literature, can have the effect of making one feel excluded rather than invited to think further. Those of us who were privileged to have personal contact with him were encouraged to find that he could make it clear, in his wry way, that he did not see himself as superior to us struggling ones far beneath him.

There are touching words at the end of the Pinter essay as he formulates his sense of what it has meant to him to do this very detailed work on Pinter's text:

> I do, therefore, in retrospect, think that the method of investigation, of testing upon works of art some of the subtle impressions regarding the emotional atmosphere of human relations drawn from the consulting-room and daily life—this unusual method has been a fruitful one. I feel more convinced that this particular aspect of atmosphere created by fluctuations in sincerity and its corollary, intimacy, throws a useful light on the processes by which understanding grows—or fails to grow—between people. I find my conception of sincerity, phenomenologically, sharpened for use in observation of myself and others. I feel a greater tolerance of failures of sincerity in

> others and particularly a sympathy for those caught in unsincerity. I can understand why sincerity is so powerfully attractive, for good and evil, in the eminent joyousness of the complete person and the charisma of the psychopath. [Meltzer, 1971, p. 284]

Meltzer's enjoyment of the exploration of many areas of cultural life was, I think, very important in fertilizing his theoretical imagination, as he acknowledged so directly in these words. One simple instance of this is a delightful short paper, entitled "Positive and Negative Forms" (1970), in which he describes a variety of forms of mental space. These are building blocks in his conception of the geography of the mind, a construction that he found so helpful in his thinking. That word "geography" brings to our minds both the physical spaces of our external world and the ways in which man lives within this, his cultivation of and assaults on nature—the human geography of cities, travel, political boundaries, war and conflict, and so on—and the geography of the natural world we and other living creatures inhabit. This proved an apt model for the description of the inner world. In this paper, Meltzer writes about internal and external space and what is to be found within each domain. In a few pages of vivid examples from dream material in which buildings are central, he shows how these can be differentiated and how different areas of the internal maternal body can be discerned, and he hints at how intrusive phantasies can create confusion between inside and outside and self and object, a theme to be developed later more fully in his book *The Claustrum* (1992a).

I was reminded of some vivid recent material from an 11-year-old girl presented to me in a seminar as I re-read this 1970 paper. Meltzer says that it is from adult patients that he mostly learned to think about the meaning of space, but here is a small contribution from child psychotherapy:

> Lucy, the girl described to me, spoke one day of how she had had an individual music lesson at the end of the day, thus managing to avoid a disliked final class lesson. The music department was in the basement of her school, but her form room was right at the top, so in preparing to leave school and come to her session she had to go up to collect her belongings. On the way to the tube station, she realized she had forgotten her purse and Oyster card, so she ran back to look for them. She located the card, though not the purse, and then hurried back to the station, managing to arrive only seven minutes late for her session. The time was filled with complaints and real misery about how hungry and thirsty she was,

> because she had had no time or money to buy her usual snack. Her dry mouth and her empty tummy filled her mind, and she made her discomfort seem absolutely visceral. Her therapist felt it was really hard not to offer at least a drink of water. This was a post-weekend session not long after a holiday break, so the therapist spoke to her about how painful it was to find that what she wanted was not within her reach. This led to more details about the lost purse. Lucy wondered at first about it having been stolen, but because they had previously been able to work on her paranoid fear of things being stolen from her, which in reality were things she herself had lost, her main idea was that she had left it in the lunch room. She then explained that she had chosen the" extra" choice at lunch, one not covered by the already-paid-for dish of the day, and in fact she found she hated it and therefore hardly touched it, hence now being terribly hungry, and hence having had to take out her purse to pay for it. "If only", she said, in an infinite regress, "if only I had had the ordinary lunch, I wouldn't have lost my purse, I wouldn't have been late in arriving here", and so on. More associations about things she loses or damages followed this.

I think we have here a picture of how the evasion of being an ordinary one in the group of children, and being able to be aware of being one of the whole family of patients, is brought about. Lucy tries repeatedly to make special individual arrangements. These take her down to the basement, to the one-to-one music lesson where her music is what is listened to. When she goes up to the top and rejoins the others, she becomes aware of feeling empty and hungry. One might say she is flooded by painful infantile feelings, but her resentment about having to wait and to share interferes with her looking after herself properly and further deprives her of what she needs. Here the inner spaces of the school with their different emotional significances to her, and the journey which reminds her of having to come from outside to her session, all combine to bring her in touch with a serious problem she and her therapist are working on.

The sequel to this was interesting: the next day, when she had no session, particular circumstances at school enabled her to see herself as very special indeed. The following day she felt too ill to go to school (a totally exceptional thing for her) but well enough to come and tell her therapist about the triumph of the day before! This had almost obliterated any memory of what had happened earlier in the week, but not quite. The real pain of this child's confrontation with the emptiness of her efforts to escape reality, both internal and external, became starkly visible in her recognition as the session proceeded that the ease of not having to get up in the morning and go to school and instead to stay luxuriously at home in bed also meant that she was bored and lonely, missing her friends, and dying to get to school tomorrow, just as she had been very keen to get to her session despite exceptionally nasty weather. She was, in fact, both provocative and persuasive in her delighted seductive tricks to ensure that she continue to occupy a princess position, and her therapist struggled to resist colluding with this. Her sessions in earlier years were absolutely filled with princesses and their amazing wardrobes and the undoubted superiority of various imaginary realms. At times it was tempting to shoot her down, and both therapist and supervisor could feel this desire to puncture Lucy's narcissism harshly. But giving in to this pressure would doubtless have served to make her redouble her efforts to protect herself from a very cruel and superior superego, of which we got an occasional glimpse in her extreme anxiety about being in quite ordinary trouble with adults.

Now, to return to the 1970 paper about mental space: it is fascinating to find that Meltzer's final example is from architecture itself, in the form of an architect patient's description of his planned building. This vignette provides us with a glimpse into the workings of Meltzer's clinical imagination: he sees the building the patient describes as showing him the shape of his patient's inner world, and simultaneously he alerts us, his readers, to view the buildings of our external world anew. He reminds us that a sensitive appreciation of both natural and man-made worlds, as of the riches of art and literature, is what makes for an imaginative response to the language of the unconscious. While a grasp of theory and technique is needed for good analytic work, it is surely clear that psychoanalytic education should embrace a serious engagement with much that is studied in other disciplines, particularly the arts and humanities, if it is to flourish.

Meltzer's interest in so many spheres of human endeavour is, of course, linked to his enjoyment of collaborative work, including his work with non-clinicians. One of the ideas implicit in his model of atelier training was that an atelier could have more porous boundaries than the clinical trainings within professional training bodies and thus could benefit from freer intellectual interdisciplinary dialogue, as in the Imago group I mentioned earlier. Certainly, it was explicit that he favoured non-traditional scientific backgrounds as a good basis for psychoanalytic training.

Now this preference for fluidity involved a fair degree of dislike of almost any institution, which he mostly saw as in part damaging the very things they were supposed to be sustaining. However, his long partnership with Mattie Harris included a division of labour in which she continued to build an institution—namely the Tavistock child psychotherapy training and, more broadly, the child psychotherapy discipline as a whole—while he made a major contribution in devoting himself to a long period of intellectual work presented at the Tavistock. The lectures he gave on Freud's clinical papers, on Richard week-by-week, and, later, on Bion—the work that came together as *The Kleinian Development* (1978)—are testament to very detailed and careful reading of the texts he discussed. While one of the limitations of some of his writing is the paucity of scholarly cross-references which can help the reader orient him/herself to the argument, in this work, he could not have been more precise. Remembering this period of his teaching and the later similar structure of the presentation of *Dream-Life* (1983), I wonder if the Tavistock context, which allowed for more open audiences (current and past child psychotherapy students, staff, and interested others) at these lectures, was helpful to him. In other words, was there, perhaps, a fruitful conjunction between the kind of group Meltzer wanted his ideas to reach and the one available at the Tavistock, which served to support very sustained and rigorous efforts on his part? The devotion to child analysis, which the study of Richard demanded, found a home among child psychotherapists, who continued thereafter to give pride of place to psychoanalytic writing in which clinical experience was the basis for theorization.

Meltzer had many original ideas, and wrote a great deal. In this chapter I have selected some of those that, I think, have proved most influential, while recognizing that there are others that I could have chosen. To conclude, I offer a brief summary.

I give pride of place to his elaboration of the concreteness of the child's internal world and of the relationships between the internal objects of phantasy. Closely linked to this is the emphasis on the lifelong interaction between infantile and more mature aspects of the personality—the baby and child in the adolescent, all of these in the adult, and none of these defined by chronological age but the nature of their relationship to reality. The way in which adult mental functioning can be seen at times in a young child is one of the wonders of work with children, and the light thrown on work with adults—if one can be alive to the many ages within the patient—is immense. How can one understand the significance of holiday breaks in clinical work unless one can see, in the mind's eye, the baby put down after a feed? How to make sense of the existential anxiety and confusion of identity stirred by the awareness of there being more than just one patient unless we think of what we learn in infant observation about the terrifying loss of identity involved for a young child when a new baby appears? "Who am I if I am not mother's baby?" is a shattering question. Meltzer's sensitivity to these early terrors, which were so much at the heart of his close collaboration with Esther Bick, has influenced technique greatly and engenders the capacity for analytic kindness in the face of the depth of infantile dependence that is evoked by the transference relationship (Meltzer, 1960).

Alongside these broad themes is the interest in dimensionality and its special importance in working with autistic children and autistic phenomena. The particular early development seen, I believe, in autistic children with their vulnerability to too-early depressive anxiety (too early for them to manage, that is) is also linked with his later revised model of child development and the introduction of the concept of aesthetic conflict. Here he suggests a pre–paranoid-schizoid phase in which the pain of the early encounter with mother is what pushes the infant into a more schizoid state as a defence against the too-muchness of the beginning of life outside the womb (Meltzer & Harris Williams, 1988).

I think we do see some babies in infant observation or everyday life of whom this description rings true, and we certainly encounter similar moments in clinical work, but I would suggest that the range of states of being and states of mind at the start of life is quite considerable. One account of the beginnings of life is not likely to encompass the complexity we might reasonably expect.

The distinction between different forms of identification—projective, introjective, intrusive, adhesive—to which Meltzer devoted much attention remains vital, and this takes us to the investigation of claustrophobic anxieties and the phenomena of the claustrum (Meltzer, 1992a). In supervision of child psychotherapy with the many quite disturbed children now seen in clinics, this is, I believe, alongside the idea of the "gathering" of the transference, the single most useful of Meltzer's concepts. I find myself explaining his theory to bewildered therapists who are suffering the experience of being with a child who seems inside something while they remain irrelevant outsiders. His technical suggestions about how to find a position from which one can make useful observations, muse aloud, make contact with a child who feels inside his or her object have often proved useful. Of similar clinical value is the paper about temperature and distance (1976c), which I have always felt to have a background in infant observation as it brings alive the extreme vulnerabilities of the baby self and the responsibilities of the therapist to respect these.

I should like to finish by expressing the hope that continuing engagement with Meltzer's ideas will provoke fresh lines of inquiry in psychoanalysis today. It is painful to see that his isolation from most of the psychoanalytic community in Britain during the later years of his life has led to the neglect of many of his contributions. I think, in parallel, that it is painful to see that his own enrichment through dialogue with other creative analytic thinkers in the UK was cut short. I am heartened that, in more recent years, this division of ways seems less absolute. The greater internationalism of psychoanalytic thought may be creating new sets of connections and can, perhaps, undo damaging splits, and there may be less need for new generations to repeat the divisions and ruptures of their predecessors, although this will always be a risk.

Another factor that I think may be proving helpful is that the increasing scholarly potential within child psychotherapy, in which the clinical doctorate development has played an important part, does demand proper attention to the literature of the field. It has been a pleasure to read some of the completed theses and note the theoretical exploration and integration taking place. What I think we must aim at is a culture that values work in progress, and what we must hope for is that the desire for development, rather than nostalgic regressive impulses, will dominate.

Note

This chapter is based on a version previously published in the *Journal of Child Psychotherapy, Vol. 42* (No. 1, 2016), pp. 4–17.

CHAPTER TWO

The relevance of Donald Meltzer's concept of nipple-penis confusion to selective mutism and the capacity to produce language

Maria Rhode

My aim in this chapter is to explore the bearing of Donald Meltzer's concept of nipple-penis confusion, firstly on selective mutism, and secondly on the articulation of words. I suggest that this concept has great explanatory power, as it seems to be capable of subsuming phenomena that Meltzer (1986a) described in connection with the Theatre of the Mouth as well as the traumatic experiences that can be implicated in selective mutism. It also provides a framework for linking these two areas to the child's character.

I begin by outlining the concept of nipple-penis confusion and then refer to Meltzer's proposed conditions for language development, supplementing this by discussing the child's ability to take psychological ownership of the organs of the mouth. This is necessary for the production of speech and is a process that Frances Tustin's work on autistic children's experience of the mouth allows us to understand to some extent. I shall distinguish different ways in which the paternal part-object can be implicated in traumatic experiences, as these often seem to be the trigger for selective mutism, and contrast various identifications that seem to influence how children may respond to such experiences. I shall also suggest that it may be useful to extend some of Meltzer's formulations on the motives in play in nipple-penis confusion by considering its manifestations on these more primitive levels of trauma and adhesive identification.

Meltzer referred to the concept of nipple-penis confusion from his early writings onwards: it belongs, I think, in the lineage of Melanie Klein's statement that the secure internalization of the first good object can be interfered with if the paternal part-object is too much in the foreground too early in life (Klein, 1932).[1] In *The Psycho-analytical Process* (1967), he mentions "the zonal confusions such as nipple=penis=tongue" in the context of the attempt "to seduce the object into [a] mutual idealisation and closed system of mutual gratification" (p. 30)—that is, in the context of eliminating the distinction between the feeding relationship and adult sexuality. In a 1974 paper on "The Role of Pregenital Confusions in Erotomania", he reports the treatment of a woman patient who dreamt that "she and another woman were in rivalry for her lover, lying in bed on either side of him. She was horrified to see that both had dark erect penises instead of nipples [. . . her mother's nipples are in fact dark . . . and had been erect . . .]" (p. 332). Meltzer saw the confusion as the patient's response to weaning, in which "she was now turning away from the breast to the father's penis and entering into a fierce competition for control and possession of that object, thus invoking a confusion between nipple-in-mouth and penis-in-vagina to obviate the experience of weaning and relinquishment". In *Sexual States of Mind* (1973b), a patient's dream is understood as showing that "the penis and breast . . . are united as a combined object" (p. 118). The nipple-penis "is interested in the little boy's mouth and bottom, and becomes the homosexual penis when it leaves the breast". Along similar lines, he writes in *The Apprehension of Beauty:* "Splitting of the nipple-penis from the breast, which generates an eroticized penis and an envious breast-with-a-hole, seems to be the most serious impediment to development; while the paranoid distrust secondary to the confusion penis-feces-nipple which results in the malignant nipple undermines mental health" (Meltzer & Harris Williams, 1988, p. 62). There are further references to the nipple-penis confusion in *Adolescence* (Meltzer & Harris, 2011) and, no doubt, others that I am not aware of.[2] In supervision he often referred to it, usually in the context of the baby's phantasies about whose presence inside the breast was implied by the protruding nipple.

As I understand it, these formulations concern a level of development at which weaning is a painful event that the child may refuse to accept, but not an existential catastrophe in which parts of the mouth are felt to be lost. This (adhesive) level is, however, important for the understanding of children who may have achieved adequate symbolic capacity, but not the psychological ownership of their mouth that is necessary for voiced, articulate speech. I would like to suggest that extending the reach of Meltzer's concept of nipple-penis confusion so that it encompasses that level can be fruitful in attempting to understand some selective mutes as well as the fluctuating capacity for correct articulation, and in locating both within the wider context of characterological conflicts.

Meltzer did not himself write about that aspect of the experience of the nipple that is central to the child's acquisition of psychological ownership of the various parts of the mouth, with all the implications that this has for the capacity to produce articulate speech. Winnicott (1963) first pointed out that the realization of being separate from the mother, occurring before the infant had developed the equipment to deal with loss, could mean that "certain aspects of the mouth disappear[ed] from the infant's point of view along with the mother and the breast", whereas the same loss later on would be confined to "a loss of object without this added element of a loss of part of the subject" (p. 222). Tustin (1966, 1972b) showed that it was specifically the loss of the sensations generated by the nipple that led to the (illusory) loss of an essential part of the mouth: her little patient John was amazed that the "red button", as he called the nipple, was not part of him but "[*grew*] on the breast". Tustin (1986b) subsequently wrote that the child with autism had the experience of a breast that was broken and, because his mouth was equated with the breast, felt that his mouth was broken also. This is a much more concrete level than Meltzer's formulation concerning the envious breast-with-a-hole that is formed when the breast and nipple-penis are separated; but both statements imply that development—whether it is a matter of bodily integrity or emotional stability—is compromised or does not take place where it is felt to be at the expense of the mother figure.

In his chapter on mutism in *Explorations in Autism,* Meltzer (1975d) focused on five factors that he thought were necessary for the production of language. These included "the capacity to form dream thoughts suitable for transformation into language" (p. 193), the identification with speaking figures, and the desire to communicate with other human beings who are recognized as separate. Such factors are concerned with the child's object relations. But Meltzer also mentioned vocalization, which is necessary if the capacity for language is to show itself as speech. He proposed that children with autism could remain mute even when they had moved towards three-dimensionality and when projection and introjection were playing an increasing role, because "pre-genital oedipal jealousy interferes with the verbal coition of internal objects, rendering them separate and silent" (p. 205). I suggest later that the concept of nipple-penis confusion provides a way of approaching this issue of "the interference with verbal coition" on the concrete level of the organs involved.

Some children understand language well and can read and write fluently but do not feel that the organs of their mouth are theirs to use. Morton Gernsbacher (2005) has called this "oral dyspraxia". For example, Tito Mukhopadhyay, beginning when he was eight (Mukhopadhyay, 2000), has written a series of books in which he describes in sensitive, lyrical detail both his relationship to other people and his imaginative construction of the world. And yet he continued to present as a classical severe autistic who never really acquired a voice. Tellingly, one of his books is called *How Can I Talk If My Lips Don't Move?* (Mukhopadhyay, 2008).

Selective mutes are capable of "moving their lips" in specific situations and in the presence of particular people, but are quite incapable of doing so with others. For this reason, they provide the perfect example of the importance of strictly emotional factors in the production of language. Non-analytic authors have described selective mutism as a social phobia and have recommended a gradual and progressive de-sensitization strategy. A traumatic incident can often be the triggering factor, as it was with many victims of "shell-shock" in the First World War. Judith Trowell and Israel Kolvin (1995) have carried out an unpublished retrospective study in which adults who had been selectively mute as children were interviewed and assessed on a variety of instruments. These adults ranged from those functioning normally, through those with a neurotic character structure, to a few who were schizophrenic: clearly, selective mutism in childhood does not imply a single pathway (though Jeanne Magagna, 2012a, 2012b, has suggested that early problems with language development always point to an impaired "bridge" between child and parents). But every one of the interviewees stressed how overwhelmingly helpless they had felt as children—a very different perspective from that of the adults surrounding selective mutes, who tend to feel helpless themselves and to see the child as controlling, withholding, and extremely powerful. Writing from a psychoanalytic perspective, Weininger (1992) has emphasized selectively mute children's fear of their own aggression, particularly on the anal level, while Staehle (2007) has stressed the importance of traumatic separation and Truckle (2006) that of trauma more generally.[3] My own anecdotal impression is that these children often show the same intense, primitive bodily anxieties that we meet with in children on the autistic spectrum—including a terror of falling, of spilling out, and of losing parts of the body—though the length of time during which such anxieties occupy the foreground of the child's experience may vary enormously.

Trauma of various kinds can be construed as though it were mediated by the paternal element, which may be either intrusive or ineffective. For example, Britton (1989) proposes that where the mother refuses the child's essential projected communications, the child may cling to the mother in order to survive and may instead ascribe to the father the function of blocking these communications. This concerns relational trauma. In Tustin's "illusory trauma" of losing part of the mouth (Tustin, 1994), it is the hard, masculine, sensation-generating nipple that is felt to be torn away, so that the child's mouth is left with a hole in it. Where the child is intruded into by sensory impingements, it can feel that loud noises, for example, are equated with a masculine figure who comes between the child and the mother figure (this was the case for a boy with autism I treated who would cover his ears if a man came towards us as we went through a door; Rhode, 2004). Where a catastrophic event has occurred in external reality, this can feel as though the boundary between the child's inner world and outside events had become too permeable and needed reinforcing (Britton, 1994)—as though that aspect of the paternal function that separates the child from the mother, and internal reality from external reality, were not working properly. This means that external reality can seem as though it were simply the child's reflection, which makes it too dangerous to engage with. Velleda Cecchi (1990), for example, describes the case of Marella, a normal 2½-year-old girl whose parents were "disappeared" by the Argentinian secret police in the middle of the night and who was found cowering, wet, soiled, and mute, in a state of autistic withdrawal from which she emerged only gradually during analysis. Cecchi conceptualizes this, persuasively in my view, as the need to withdraw from an external world that seemed unable to withstand the child's worst impulses.

Findings such as these make it plausible that the relationship to the nipple-penis should be an important issue in children with selective mutism, given that a traumatic event often triggers their symptom and that they typically experience extreme helplessness. The child's own identifications will obviously play a central part in shaping this relationship. For example, I have discussed elsewhere (Rhode, 2004) two boys with autism who had each suffered serious trauma and whose material was very similar, but who responded quite differently to treatment. An important factor seemed to be the mothers' relationship with their own respective internal fathers. The first boy, who had a supportive maternal grandfather as well as a predominantly depressive attitude, dealt with his fear of doing damage by equating himself with his very damaged mother. His chief anxiety seemed to concern being separated from a maternal figure by the intrusion of a paternal element: in that sense, he had some conception of a good object and he did very well in therapy. The second child's mother had an ambivalent relationship to her internal father. This child's main fear was of being engulfed: he had no concept of a good object, and his progress was disappointing. He identified with a hard, traumatizing phallic element that showed itself, among other ways, in the loud, vibrating noise he produced when he was anxious. The following vignette, from the treatment of a different child, illustrates how an identification with a traumatizing aggressor can play out specifically in the area of speech:

> Anthony, a boy with quite severe autism whom I began to work with when he was 6 years old, was able to speak in his own voice at certain crucial junctures in his therapy (Rhode, 1999). On occasion he could even speak poetically, hard though that was to believe or remember as it was so totally out of keeping with his habitual mad grimaces. Sometimes these grimaces were accompanied by fragments of words; sometimes he remained mute. If he did speak in sentences, it was not in his own voice, but in a repertoire of voices belonging to a number of characters—notably the cruel man-eating giant in *Jack and the Beanstalk*.
>
> Anthony often lay under the couch growling menacingly as though he were the giant. On one particular occasion, he retired under the couch clutching at his genitals. I said that perhaps he needed to be sure they would remain part of him, so he became a dangerous giant who made frightening noises from under the couch. He immediately came out of his hiding place: he looked straight at me, which very rarely happened, and said, "Will-ll-ll-lly—noise". His voice as he said this was exceptionally resonant, and he moved his tongue energetically from side to side in his mouth.

Interestingly, Anthony's tongue inside his mouth seems to be equated with the giant's genital inside a maternal space as well as with his own body under the couch. It is understandable that such confused identifications—and, in Meltzer's terms, the equation of tongue and nipple-penis within a context of violence—should lead to problems in using the mouth consistently in line with its proper purpose as an organ for the production of speech.

I would now like to illustrate some of these points with vignettes concerning two boys with varying degrees of selective mutism. Both had suffered serious trauma, and both seemed to equate talking with concretely taking the nipple-penis out of the maternal object. They also both showed a predominantly depressive orientation, and their mutism seemed to be based on their identification with damaged parental figures rather than on persecution by an "envious breast-with-a-hole".

Ricardo: the healing power of a strong father figure

Ricardo was a young adolescent I heard about from a South American colleague some years ago. At that time, Ricardo had recovered from selective mutism and was speaking fluently and with gusto: it was hard to believe that he had spent more than half his life completely silent.

> When Ricardo was just entering latency, he witnessed a serious attack on one of his aunts who had surprised a burglar. Very fortunately, she recovered from her injuries, but the violence was vicious and must have been extremely frightening. Coincidentally, Ricardo's father died prematurely at about the same time, leaving his mother bereft. Ricardo stopped speaking, and he did not begin again for years. At that point, a family friend who acted as a father surrogate and had shown himself to be a caring and reliably protective figure let Ricardo know very forcefully that he was no longer prepared to tolerate his not speaking. Ricardo began to speak normally again virtually at once; his referral for treatment was in connection with his general development, not with his mutism, which did not in fact arise as a theme in the therapy. However, I was very struck when my colleague told me about an incident in which the boy drew an elaborate and very potent-looking erect cobra, which he cut out and hid in one of the desk drawers. These were equipped with prominent wooden knobs with which Ricardo liked to fiddle while opening and shutting the drawers, so that the constellation of the snake behind the knob seemed a convincing representation of the nipple-penis. He responded with pleasure and amusement when my colleague commented on what a sexy snake this seemed to be.

I would hypothesize that the traumatic attack on a woman that Ricardo had witnessed, together with his father's premature death at about the same time, must have been a catastrophic intrusion into the resolution of his Oedipus complex. More specifically, it would have conveyed the message that any normal oedipal competitiveness and assertiveness would have the cataclysmic consequence either of killing his father or of summoning up murderous strangers. He did not regress to the extent of Mariela, the little girl whom Velleda Cecchi (1990) described; Ricardo was a few years older at the time of the double trauma, and his reality sense as well as his speech would have been better consolidated. He did, however, spend the following years in a state of mutism and substantial withdrawal, in which he may have been identified both with his dead, mute father and with his overwhelmed, depressed mother. My guess is that the male family friend's combination of care and assertiveness made him feel that it was safe to show the masculine qualities that the developmental thrust of adolescence was in any case strengthening, secure in the knowledge that there would still be a healthy snake hidden inside the maternal object with which his own tongue could legitimately be seen to be identified. I want to emphasize again that the concept of nipple-penis can account both for intrusive trauma to the child and also for damage to a mother who has lost something vital. Ricardo's snake behind the nipple-knob seems an example of a well-balanced constellation in which the father-element supports the mother, and hence the child, without intruding.

Harry: growth that leaves a hole in the breast

Harry, a 5-year-old boy who never spoke at school and whom I saw for assessment, similarly seemed frightened that he could take the nipple-penis out of the mother figure, with disastrous consequences.

> He wanted to do a drawing but felt unable to help himself to one of the felt-tipped pens in a pencil case. When I wondered whether he was worried about leaving a gap in the pencil case if he did so, he managed to extract a pen and drew a house. First, he said that there was a ghost in the house; next, that there was nothing inside it. He then became confused and said that there was no one *out*side the house. Harry had been 2 years old when his father died suddenly, leaving his mother desolate, like Ricardo's.

I understood the fact that there was no one *out*side the house as pointing to his own identification with his dead father, who should have been *in*side. As far as his mutism was concerned, we could say that his voiceless or tongueless mouth was identified with a mother-house that contained no nipple-penis, and that Harry was frightened that it was his activity and initiative that had removed the nipple-penis from the breast. Again like Ricardo, this child was transformed when a man came into his mother's life.

I want to repeat that neither of these boys seemed to be relating to the nipple-penis in a way that was hostile to the maternal breast-object, and that both showed a considerable degree of depressive feeling.[4] This is likely to be important in terms of who it is that the child predominantly identifies with—whether with the damaged parental figure or, like Anthony, with the traumatizing giant. I shall return to this question later.

The nipple-penis and problems surrounding articulation

So far, I have tried to explore what the concept of the nipple-penis may contribute to our understanding of selectively mute children in relation to phantasies concerning the possession of the tongue or the voice. I will now discuss several consecutive sessions with 6-year-old Andrew in order to trace Meltzer's proposed sequence of nipple=penis=faeces in connection with Andrew's capacity for correct, articulated pronunciation.

> Andrew, who was seen non-intensively, had earlier shown some features suggestive of autism. He did not, in fact, receive a diagnosis, and he came to take obvious pleasure in communicating vocally, even going so far as to provide me with useful clues when his pronunciation meant that I had trouble understanding him. However, even in latency he continued to speak in sentences in which the words were divided into syllables, but in which the consonants were often left unpronounced[5]. Sounds such as "D" and "T" seemed to present particular problems—sounds, that is, that involve touching the roof of the mouth with the tongue—though I knew that he was capable of pronouncing them correctly as I had heard him do so. But this was inconsistent: he produced these sounds at some times but not at others, and even the division of his

words into syllables was sometimes blurred, so that his sentences could deteriorate into an inchoate jumble. Often this happened in the context of his tearing up paper, manipulating plasticine, or spreading the contents of his box or his own snot around the room. This kind of behaviour struck me as an anally based move that was meant to blur differences, and I thought of the accompanying blurring of Andrew's speech as an example of Meltzer's Theatre of the Mouth (1986a) in which the structure of his words and sentences reflected the structure of his internal figures. My conviction grew when, over several sessions, the deterioration of Andrew's words came together with play sequences in which he stuck his open mouth to its reflection in the mirror while spreading saliva over the mirror's surface and the furniture in the room. I understood this as an attempt to mark the mirror and furniture with his own body fluids—to assert his bodily continuity with them and me—while at the same time establishing a narcissistic, adhesive partnership with his own reflection. This pointedly excluded anything like a nipple-function that could have served as a boundary between his mouth and the breast or bottle.

A few sessions later, Andrew accidentally broke the bulb inside a metal wall lamp by fiddling with it so that it fell on the floor. He was obviously shocked. I said that I thought he had not meant this to happen, even though perhaps he sometimes thought that he should be able to fiddle with anything, particularly with things inside other objects that might feel to him like people who managed to have a place inside me. He repeated "Broken" several times and wanted a "man" to replace the bulb immediately.

At the beginning of the following session, we had to wait together outside until the caretaker let us in. After some of his customary attacks on the physical integrity of the room (he always seemed reassured when I could prevent these from getting out of hand), Andrew staged what looked like a primal scene with two large cars and one little one. Sometimes the little car was the excluded one, sometimes one of the large cars was, and Andrew kept swapping over which car represented him and which represented his father. At the end of this sequence, he indicated that he was one of the large cars, while "Daddy" was the little one. Then, turning to the lamp, he gestured as though asking whether there was a new bulb. I said that it hadn't yet been replaced, and that perhaps this

> made him feel worried. "Broken," he said, "I broke it" (notice the correct syntax and pronunciation). I agreed that he had, though I repeated that I thought he hadn't meant to and had been shocked when it happened.
>
> Andrew now fitted his mouth around the rim of the lamp, and produced considerable quantities of saliva that spread over the lamp's surface. Then he repeated, "broken" and fiddled with his mouth, his chin, and particularly his tongue. I said that he was worried about breaking the bulb inside the lamp, and that now, if his mouth wasn't joined up to the lamp or to me by means of his own spit, he seemed to feel that his tongue and chin were broken too, and it was hard to speak properly. He responded with some more fingering of his chin and the organs of his mouth.
>
> He then curled up on the couch and whispered "Mummy" in a tiny baby voice, pretending to be a baby who was crying. I said that he was showing me a baby who was missing his mummy and was feeling very sad. Towards the end of the session, he became absorbed in switching the lights off and being able to switch them back on, saying, "Dark". I said how important it was to feel he could stop things being dark inside me. In a later session, he fingered his mouth while doing this, and I said that he needed to make the light come back on: that if my eyes seemed dark, perhaps it made him feel his mouth was broken.

I would like to emphasize several points. First, I think that encountering the firm paternal boundary of a closed door that was then opened by a helpful (male) caretaker probably reassured Andrew considerably about his omnipotent capacity to destroy rivals. This would have been particularly important after he broke the light bulb without at that moment meaning to. Feeling reassured that it was safe to engage in oedipal rivalry (as in the game with the cars) probably contributed to his ability to produce correct syntax and pronunciation, as though, like Ricardo and Harry, he needed an intact breast with an undamaged nipple in order to feel that his mouth was unbroken and that he could make proper use of his tongue. The material about the lights suggests a link between maternal depression (which he seemed to interpret as the consequence of his own capacity to break the Daddy–nipple–light-bulb) and his variable ability to speak correctly. I would see this as an example, on the concrete level of tongue=nipple-penis, of Meltzer's proposal that problems concerning vocalization can be linked to an interference with the "verbal coition" of parent figures.

> Andrew's sadness and depressive concern were followed in the very next session by a major negative therapeutic reaction. For the whole 50 minutes, he relentlessly attacked the room, particularly "Daddy-like" elements like the door-stop protruding from a wall. His articulation was very deteriorated: it was only after some time that I thought I could recognize the words "In my bum" amid the incomprehensible jargon in which unrecognizable syllables flowed into each other. When I repeated the phrase, he began to pronounce it more clearly. We appear to be witnessing Meltzer's proposed sequence in which the nipple is confused with the penis, which in turn is confused with faeces in the bottom within a context of general deterioration (here, specifically in relation to language). In the following session, Andrew referred (in his idiosyncratic pronunciation) to daytime and night-time, and said that he would sleep in his mother's room or in mine. He then fingered the lamp again and said clearly, "I broke it". Again, straightforward oedipal rivalries seemed to imply catastrophic consequences.
>
> Like Meltzer's (1974) erotomanic patient, Andrew then seemed to turn to a fierce competition for the penis in a genital context. Lying upside down on the couch, he presented me with his bottom and sang a favourite song in a muffled voice that obscured the separateness of the words: "My name's Isabel, dance with me/ On a Tuesday morning" (he had no session on Tuesdays, but had often indicated that he should). I said that he was being a girl, Isabel, inviting my husband's penis to come out of me and into his bottom, so that there should be no one in his way. Forcefully and articulately, he asserted, "Boy!"

Andrew's material seems to me to illustrate clearly, in relation to language, the tongue–nipple-penis–faeces confusions that Meltzer delineated. I think, however, that, like Riccardo and Harry, he was fending off an unbearable depressive fear about the state of a maternal figure rather than just the pain of weaning: his syntax and articulation temporarily became normal when he could feel reassured about the Daddy-nipple's ability to survive his oedipal attacks and my capacity to follow some of his tricky behaviour. Thinking about such material in relation to nipple-penis confusion has the important advantage of linking concrete experiences concerning the organs of the mouth to aspects of the child's developing character.

Concluding remarks

To sum up my argument: I have tried to illustrate the power of Meltzer's nipple-penis confusion as a conceptual tool in the attempt to understand two cases of selective mutism as well as the way in which the clarity of one child's pronunciation varied with his state of mind.[6] Meltzer's original formulation applied, I suggest, to a level of experience where weaning might be a source of pain that the child rebelled against, with various characterological consequences. In contrast, the children I discuss seem to be preoccupied with the loss of the nipple as an existential catastrophe, as delineated by Frances Tustin, and I think that it is useful to extend Meltzer's concept so that it includes this adhesive level. This allows concrete experiences in the mouth to be linked with such ideas as "the verbal coition of internal objects" and to be situated within the context of the child's developing character. I have also proposed that the concept of the nipple-penis can encompass the fact that trauma of one kind or another, which is often a trigger of selective mutism, can be construed as being mediated by the paternal function.[7]

The rivalrous appropriation of the nipple-penis (as Meltzer described it and as shown in Andrew's material) can be contrasted with the identification with damaged parental figures (as with Ricardo and Harry). The question of whether the child identifies with a damaged parent or with a phallic aggressor appeared to be linked in two autistic children with the degree to which of the mother's own internal father was supportive and could serve as a "buttress" (S. Klein, 1980; Houzel, 2001) to the maternal function. This may well apply to differing identifications in selectively mute children.

Juliet Mitchell, who has stressed the identification with a dead mother figure in mute, shell-shocked soldiers of the First World War (Mitchell, 1996), has also reminded us that the hysterical aphonia with which Freud's patient Dora came to treatment is often overlooked (Mitchell, 1998). She points out that it returned temporarily after the end of treatment and suggests that Dora was identified with a dead father who was therefore mute: "in Dora's dream, it is her mother who writes to Dora in Dora's dream-absence, telling her daughter that she can come home, as her father is dead" (p. 129). In fact, Dora's second episode of aphonia came on after she had seen Herr K knocked over by a carriage—an obvious parallel to Ricardo. This implies, I think, that descriptions on the level of the nipple-penis can be relevant to patients such as hysterics whose functioning is apparently much more advanced than that of many children with selective mutism. Again, it is the degree to which Meltzer's concept is capable of unifying many different phenomena, conditions, and levels of experience that makes it so useful.

Notes

1. Klein thought that premature erotization led to a harmful confusion between oral and genital experience and, indeed, to confusion more generally (Klein, 1957, pp. 195, 197–198). A body of literature exists on the relationship between the male and female elements of the primitive combined object, which falls beyond the scope of this chapter. This literature includes S. Klein's suggestion that the baby first experiences the masculine element as a necessary support to the feminine element before it comes to be seen as an intrusion into the mother–baby couple (S. Klein, 1980). Similarly, Houzel (2001) has emphasized the necessary "buttressing" function of the masculine nipple; he differentiates the "nipple link", which he thinks is operative "proximally", from the "penis link", which operates over longer distances. Birksted-Breen (1996) distinguishes between the narcissistic phallus and the "penis as link", which provides triangulation and promotes the structuring of mental space, while I have suggested (Rhode, 2000) that primal, essential splitting can be interfered with when it is confused with damage to the developmentally necessary early conjunction of male and female elements.

2. Lubbe (2011) has posted a helpful review of Kleinian and post-Kleinian theories of sexuality.

3. Since the paper on which this chapter is based was first written, Pozzi Monzo, Micotti, & Rashid (2015) have published an account of selective mutism that includes individual and family approaches as well as a literature review.

4. In contrast, I have heard from a colleague about a girl who seemed concerned to hide her capacity for speech as well as her interest in sexual matters—themes that appeared together in her sessions—as though trying to avoid retaliation by her female therapist, who was also pointedly excluded from the child's close relationship with her father.

5. This is a feature that I have seen in a number of children; Geneviève Haag (2004) has called it *"démutisation en voyelles"* [demutization in vowels].

6. Carlos Tamm (2014) has recently documented the parallel between the capacity of two boys with autistic or psychotic features to use language correctly and the nature of their "mental landscape".

7. It can also encompass cases in which words are felt to be produced by objects inside the mother (by babies as well as by a father), whose existence the child wishes to suppress by magical means (Rhode, 2013): these are beyond the scope of this chapter.

CHAPTER THREE

Point–line–surface–space: on Donald Meltzer's concept of one- and two-dimensional mental functioning in autistic states

Suzanne Maiello

> "In the early days, there was great pleasure in doing what my teachers taught me to do and finding out that they were right. . . . But then . . . there comes a time when you cast off from the pier and into the open sea and are on your own . . ."
>
> Donald Meltzer, "A Review of My Writings" (2000)

Dimensionality and the human mind: Edwin A. Abbott and Donald Meltzer

Towards the end of the nineteenth century, Edwin A. Abbott published a satirical narrative with the title *Flatland—A Romance of Many Dimensions* (1884). This modest little book did not achieve great success at the time. It was discovered almost forty years later after Einstein's formulation of the theory of relativity and the introduction of the concept of *time* as the fourth dimension of three-dimensional space. The story is about a two-dimensional world referred to as Flatland. Its inhabitants are geometric shapes. The main character is a square. He receives the visit of a sphere who takes him to three-dimensional Spaceland. The revelations of Spaceland open the Flatlander's mind to new and unexplored lands. His research is oriented both forwards towards increasing dimensions, and backwards to Lineland and Pointland.

After his initiation into the third dimension, the native Flatlander explores in his dreams the one-dimensional and even a-dimensional world. The one-dimensional country of Lineland is inhabited by a "multitude of small Straight Lines . . . of the nature of lustrous points—all moving to and fro in one and the same Straight Line" (p. 54).[1] For the Linelander, "the Straight Line . . . constituted the whole of the world, and indeed the whole of Space. Not being able either to move or to see, save in his Straight Line, he had no conception of anything out of it. . . . Outside his World, or Line, all was a blank to him; nay, not even a blank, for a blank implies Space; say, rather, all was non-existent" (p. 55).

Eventually, Abbott's dream-explorer is taken to Pointland, "the Abyss of No dimensions" (p. 92), whose sole inhabitant is a point:

> That Point is . . . confined to the non-dimensional Gulf. He is himself his own World, his own Universe; of any other than himself he can form no conception; he knows not Length, nor Breadth, nor Height, for he has had no experience of them; he has no cognizance even of the number Two; nor has he a thought of Plurality; for he is himself his One and All, being really Nothing. [p. 92]

Abbott was a philosopher and mathematician, not a clinician, but his was a free, critical, and creative mind. When he published *Flatland*, he did not intend to write a psychological treaty. At that time, Freud had not yet developed his interest in psychopathological phenomena, but it seems that thoughts around the functioning of the human mind were in the air.

Donald Meltzer does not seem to have come across Abbott's *Flatland*. He never refers to this satirical little book. Although the intentions of the two authors were different, there are striking similarities in their descriptions of the functioning of the mind in terms of dimensionality: they both explore the narrowing effects of two-dimensional mental functioning and the ultimate breakdown of mental dimensionality altogether. Today, Abbott's description of Pointland evokes the notion of the astronomic black hole, which had yet to be discovered when he wrote his *Romance of Many Dimensions*. An astronomic black hole is described as what remains after the catastrophic breakdown of a dying star with great mass. Space-time collapses over the star which then disappears from our universe (Kaufmann, 1977). In Abbott's prophetic vision, Pointland is close to this absolute unthinkable nothingness.

Autistic mental functioning seems very close to that of the inhabitants of two-dimensional Flatland and one-dimensional Lineland, and autistic children even seem to know about the ultimate a-dimensional nothingness of Pointland. Their existential terrors are linked to this kind of absolute void. Tustin's little patient John referred explicitly to a black hole in his mouth when the red button (the nipple) was gone (1972a). Can we imagine that these children's one- or two-dimensional mental functioning represents a retreat from dangers threatening them from both sides? On the one hand, the endless falling into the a-dimensional abyss of the black hole, and, on the other, the threat of annihilation anxieties which would accompany the emotional experience of separateness implicit in three-dimensional mental functioning. The two extremes seem to meet, blocking the child in his or her internal Flatland or Lineland.

Abbott and Meltzer in dialogue

Abbott wrote at the time that the Flatlanders cannot see properly, they have only one eye, and eye and mouth are one and the same organ. (In autistic two-dimensional functioning, there is no binocular vision, and the centre of the original trauma, which led to the breakdown of the primary three-dimensional mental disposition, seems to be located in the mouth). The author writes that, in Flatland, shapes "move freely about, on or in the surface, but without the power of rising above or sinking below it, very much like shadows" (1884, p. 4). Meltzer describes this state as "being on one side or the other of a paper-thin object" (1975b, p. 226), which is in "effect an object without an inside" (1975e, p. 18).

In Abbott's *Flatland,* life is monotonous; symmetry and regularity are the guarantees of safety. In Meltzer's *Explorations in Autism,* "Circumstances which threaten this *changelessness* would tend to be experienced as break-down of surfaces . . ." (1975b, p. 225, emphasis added). Abbott's Flatlanders—the author actually refers to the female inhabitants of Flatland, but this would open a socio-historic parenthesis, which is beyond our immediate concern—are "wholly devoid of *brainpower,* and have neither *reflection, judgment* nor *forethought,* and hardly any *memory*" (1884, p. 15, emphasis added).

According to Meltzer, two-dimensional functioning perceives and appreciates only

> . . . the surface qualities of objects, but its aims will necessarily be curtailed by an impoverished imagination, . . . The reason for this limitation of *thought* and *imagination* would reside in the lack of an internal space within the mind in which phantasy as trial action, and therefore experimental thought, could take place. Furthermore,

> the self which was living in a two-dimensional world would be impaired both in *memory* and *desire*, or *foresight*, for the same reason . . . it would be unable to conceive of *enduring change*, and therefore of *development*—or *cessation*. [1975b, p. 225, emphasis added]

Meltzer introduced the notion of the dimensionality of mental life in *Explorations in Autism* (Meltzer et al., 1975). It is a concept that we could not do without today, an open metaphor that embodies and gives shape to the mystery of mental functioning and, at the same time, invites us to expand and explore its intrinsic potentialities. The notion of the dimensionality of the mind develops the spatial representation of Klein's *internal world* with its *objects* and is akin to Bion's concept of *container/contained.* Meltzer maintains that, in normal development, "the feeling of being adequately contained is a precondition for the experience of being a continent container . . ." (1975b, p. 226). His notion of dimensionality has a solid clinical base in work with autistic children who have lost precisely the potential of three-dimensional mental functioning, which is the *conditio sine qua non* both for the experience of separation and separateness, with its wide range of intense emotions, and for the development of symbolic thinking.

The clinical material and the drawings of an autistic child demonstrate this little boy's initial two- and even one-dimensional mental functioning, as well as his struggle, supported by the sensitivity and firmness of his psychotherapist, to move towards the third dimension of the mind with its threats, its dangers, its surprises, and its frightening, painful, enlivening, and passionate emotional potential.

An autistic child's struggle to emerge from a two- and one-dimensional world

Emilio,[2] a highly intelligent child with a diagnosis of autistic spectrum disorder, began his three-times-a-week psychotherapy at the age of 4½ years. He was verbal, but used language almost only echolalically, repeating the same words or short sentences endlessly with a high-pitched mechanical tone of voice that flattened any possible emerging meaning.

Emilio was the first child of a young couple. The pregnancy was normal, but during labour, according to the mother, "the baby was sleeping, did not want to come out and had to be pulled out with a vacuum extractor". He sucked the breast voraciously, which scared the mother at the beginning. From birth he slept in the parents' bed with the nipple in his mouth. At age 6 months, the mother tried to introduce spoon-feeding, which Emilio refused. From that time, the baby would close or avert his eyes and cover his ears if anybody approached him. Around that time, mother had to resume work. Every morning, she took the local train with baby Emilio on her lap. The mother left him with her parents, who lived almost an hour away, and brought him back home on the same train in the evening.

When he was 15 months old, mother decided that it was time to wean him, but she seemed unable to imagine how to manage this change. So, she covered her nipples with Band-Aids. From one day to another, the potentially ever-present breast became a *no-access* breast. Emilio touched the Band-Aid strips and said, "Bua–bua" ("sore–sore"), but after a week the breast seemed "gone" from the child's memory, and Emilio did not search for it again.

It was only when he started nursery school, at the age of 3, that the parents began to worry seriously about his development. Emilio was withdrawn; he did not play with other children, he flapped his hands, and his speech was echolalic. For one year, Emilio had two-weekly sessions of psychomotor therapy. After a follow-up consultation, the clinic suggested psychotherapy.

From the beginning of his life, Emilio seemed to have experienced the nipple as an integral part of his mouth. Had he managed to exclude any awareness of differences between presence and absence, and any perception of otherness from his experience? When partial weaning was started, Emilio covered his eyes and ears, obliterating the distance senses—sight and hearing—that open the mind to undeniable three-dimensional experiences in the external world. He may have clung to the exciting tactile sensation of the nipple-in-the-mouth, which still continued at night. It is possible that he had shut out any awareness of the existence of in-betweenness in the dimensions of both space and time and had withdrawn into a pathological delusion of uninterrupted adhesive union with the mother:

> In an attempt to re-establish the primary situation of *flowing-over-at-oneness*, which had been agonisingly disturbed by experiences of sensuous disconnection from a sensation-giving "mother" who had been experienced as part of the body, auto-sensual reactions are set in train which bring about the delusion of fusion with a sensation-object. [Tustin, 1981, p. 22]

When Emilio entered the therapy room for the first time, he acknowledged neither the separation from his parents nor the therapist's presence. His behaviour was robotic and so was his speech, yet, in that very first session, he was able to represent the catastrophe of the breakdown of his potentially three-dimensional mental container: he made a rudimentary archway with building blocks, which he called "bridge". He then took another block, said "choo-choo", and moved the train perpendicular to the archway. It could easily have passed underneath and crossed over to the other side, but the train hit one of the pillars, thus causing the archway to collapse and bury it under the blocks. The therapist commented what had happened, and Emilio repeated over and over again, "train make bridge fall, all broken", while he endlessly reproduced the scene.

The monotonous, ritualized repetition of the same action and words, which had been meaningful initially, was an aspect of Emilio's obsessive autistic protection manoeuvres, thanks to which he tried to blot out the emotional impact of and contact with the catastrophe of the dimensional breakdown. Meltzer writes about the crucial importance of the awareness and capacity to conceive of orifices for three-dimensional mental development. Emilio's archway was both a boundary, which created a spatial structure on the flat table surface, and an opening. His vocal "choo-choo" announced the train's original intention to move through that opening which connected the two sides of the wall. Meltzer writes in his comment to Shirley Hoxter's little patient Piffie: "The nipple, which is required as a go-*between* [between] the baby's mouth and the content of the breast, in itself implies separateness as well as 'togetherness'" (Meltzer et al., 1975, p. 176, emphasis added).

For Emilio, crossing the threshold of the archway had not been possible. It would have entailed the experience of three-dimensional space, with its limits and differentiations and therefore the experience of otherness. But he had set the scene. This was prognostically encouraging. The archway and the train could be seen as a representation of the traumatic experience of the tearing apart of the baby's mouth and the mother's nipple, which had contributed to the breakdown of three-dimensional mental functioning.

Two- and one-dimensional mental functioning and the breakdown of the differentiation of shapes

Emilio's first drawing (Figure 3.1), which he produced after four months of psychotherapy, bears witness not only to the catastrophe of the collapse of the third dimension, but also to the breakdown of the functional differentiation of shapes and the notion of dimensionality altogether.

FIGURE 3.1

> Emilio first drew a small blue square at the bottom of the sheet, then a large pink shape, a "bubble". Around the bubble, were knobs, which he called "clicks", and various other protruding shapes. On the upper side of the bubble, he added a larger blue bulge, which he called "shoulder", and to the left a big long purple protrusion, which looked like a tongue, but he said that it was a "throat".

Emilio had a notion of the body parts that he had drawn, but neither their position nor their shape had a consistent formal identity nor felt meaningful. What he drew were part-objects, unrelated both to one another and to the body of the bubble. The clicks look like sticking-out nipples—might they correspond to Tustin's patient John's buttons?—over which Emilio may have needed command. The sticking-out shoulder corresponds, more or less, to its anatomic shape, but with the tongue-shaped throat everything seemed to have become more confused: there had been a breakdown of differentiation between the convexity of tongue and nipple, and the concavity of mouth and throat. With this drawing, Emilio seemed to have found a way of representing an even deeper level of the primary catastrophe that he had shown with the archway and the train, where what had collapsed had been "only" the potential of three-dimensional mental functioning.

In this drawing, the breakdown seemed to have occurred at an even more primitive mental depth. If nipple and mouth become confused in their basic difference of shape in space—convexity versus concavity—the catastrophe seems to reach almost cosmic dimensions, the star being swallowed in a black hole and disappearing from the very universe of what is conceivable. Emilio's confusion at this level not only involved basic graphic shapes, but had a linguistic counterpart, which showed his intelligence and sensitivity in the middle of the dimensional and formal confusion. At first, Emilio had used the correct Italian word for shoulder, "*spalla*", and had pronounced it correctly, but then he changed the sound of the word to "*smalla*" (which has no meaning). "Spalla" has a hard daddy sound, "smalla" has a mummy-softness to it. If we try to transfer the shift of sound into English, "shoulder" might have become "zmoulder". Was there something dangerous in the hardness of sticking-out bits? Had there been a flicker of awareness of differences in both visual shape and sound shape, which had to be confused again immediately in order to avoid once more the threatening awareness of differences in the mouth-nipple configuration?

At this point, Emilio turned the drawing upside down. The shoulder and the throat, as well as the neighbouring protrusions and clicks, which had stuck out from the upper part of the (pink) bubble are now hanging down from its lower part. Everything is upside down.

> Emilio added two long thin (reddish) shapes to the drawing, which pointed downwards to the low edge of the sheet of paper, without reaching it (Figure 3.2). To explain what they were, he said "*reggi, reggi*". "*Reggere*" means to support, bear, hold, sustain. The child had felt that the big pink bubble seemed no longer able to sustain itself, but it was unlikely that those two fragile added supports would really be strong enough to carry its weight.

The breakdown of the differentiation between convex and concave shapes revealed the depth of the topographic confusion in the child's mind, which went deeper than the mere breakdown of the third dimension. It was as if the spatial category of dimensionality itself, with its structuring function, had broken down, leading to what we might call an a-dimensional world of shapeless shapes. In normal experience, different shapes have specific functions in the encounter between mouth and breast at the part-object level. They acquire a stable meaning in a three-dimensional mental configuration, thanks to the acknowledgement of betweenness, which allows for the experience of an encounter, a reunion, between the empty concave mouth

FIGURE 3.2

that searches for the convex nipple to fill the empty space and create the condition for the arrival of the nourishing milk.

Emilio's upside-down drawing showed not only his spatial confusion, but also conveyed his dawning feelings of utter helplessness, which the omnipotent illusion of the initial magical clicks was no longer able to keep at bay. The drawing of the following session seems to confirm this (Figure 3.3).

It is black to begin with. No soft pastel colours any more. Emilio produced a shape reminiscent of the pink bubble. The little blue square of the first drawing was now replaced by a sharp black prick. Emilio

FIGURE 3.3

started colouring the inside of the bubble, but soon gave up. The haphazard black scribbles seem to say something about the child's utter disorientation and hopelessness.

There were no clicks any more, only the sheer weight of primary depression that Emilio had shown in the first assessment session with the bridge that had collapsed under the impact of the train and buried it under its broken parts. Could Emilio's experience of catastrophe even be linked back to mother's anxiety around the voracity of her new-born baby? A ferocious predator meeting a fragile bubble-breast resulting in the breakdown of the baby's primary experience of dimensionality? Or even further back to the birth scene, with the mother imagining that the baby was sleeping and did not want to be born? Tustin (1994) writes about autistic disorder in terms of a two-stage pathology, the unbearability of separation being the second stage of a preceding state of undue adhesive unity.

The long walk towards the experience of three-dimensional space and containment

About one year into therapy, Emilio started building two intersecting railway tracks with flat building-blocks, forming a cross shape on the play table (Figure 3. 4). The cross structures space, becoming the basis of a coordinate system through which every single point in space can be reliably identified. Tustin (1981) underlines that the appearance of a cross-shape in the clinical material of an autistic child is, literally, a crucial moment in the child's psychic development:

> Many . . . children have shown me the importance of the stage when they use a vertical line to intersect a horizontal one. . . . As straight lines are brought together to intersect each other, the child begins to bring together basic sensuous contraries . . . [pp. 156–157]

Emilio seemed to know that this was where a reparation of the catastrophe needed to begin. He placed two "trains", which consisted of one thicker building-block each, on the two arms of the cross. Each train moved on its own track. No crashes occurred at the cross point, because the two trains never moved simultaneously, but there were no encounters either. The trains were identical, but Emilio accepted to identify them as the Emilio-train and the Francesca-train, respectively. One day, his train was about to fall off at the far end of his rail. Emilio was precipitated into a state of panic. The terror of endless falling into bottomless space, which had been counteracted by transforming the

FIGURE 3.4

world into a Flatland-surface or a Lineland-line, hit the child once more with annihilating intensity.

In the next session, Emilio's experience of being suspended at the rim of the abyss at the end of his rail may have induced him to build two shelters at the two ends, one for each train (Figure 3.5).

For the first time, Emilio had produced a three-dimensional object with an inside: the basic shape of a container and, in Virginia Woolf's

FIGURE 3.5

terms, of "a room of one's own" (1929). Emilio had a long way to go, but it looked as if the preconception of a third dimension of the mind had revealed itself and become imaginable and representable. The shelters had doors, which were sometimes open and sometimes closed. The trains could be either inside or outside. The very experience of the opening and closing of a door (or sphincter) entails a momentary awareness of an inside differentiated from an outside. Meltzer does not hesitate to assert that, with the discovery of body orifices, "the entire view-of-the-world rises to a new level of complexity, the three-dimensional one of objects, and by identification, the self, as containing potential spaces. . . . The potentiality of a . . . container can only be realized once the sphincter-function has become effective" (1975b, p. 226).

With this arrangement, Emilio had, in fact, set the scene for the first tentative experiences of existing and moving in three-dimensional space and, at the same time, of existing as a separate being. There were two trains and two shelters. When his anxiety grew, especially when a holiday was approaching, he would put the shelters right at the cross point, so that they touched each other at one corner, and the doors were tightly closed to prevent the trains from coming out. The original unbearable annihilation anxieties, which had brought about the autistic two- or one-dimensionalization of Emilio's immature mind at the beginning of his life, could now be experienced and tolerated for brief moments as separation anxieties that he survived as long as he was safely enclosed in the womb-like shelter.

But the day came when being shut in the shelter became, in itself, a source of anxiety. Weeks later, Emilio built only one shelter, put the train inside, and closed the door tightly. The therapist's perception in the countertransference was that of being enclosed and suffocating inside a coffin. When she asked Emilio what the train was doing in there, he said "Dark . . . sleep". He looked at the closed shelter for some time and then said in a whisper: "Train . . . scared." The shelter no longer had a protective function, but had become a prison, a *claustrum* (Meltzer, 1992a). Projective identification had started functioning, mental three-dimensionality was dawning. Emilio opened the door, took out the train, and stroked it lightly with his finger. The formerly enwombed train had been born from the darkness and had encountered Emilio's tender, comforting maternal presence. The once sought-for continuity of an undifferentiated primal union had become a frightening prison. Emotions could be felt and had been expressed in human language.

The rail-cross, the trains, and the shelters were arranged in every single session over many months in an almost identical configuration, but occasionally with minimal variations. There were also endless stand-stills and, again and again, the risk of stereotyped repetitions that denied meaning to what had been represented, with the child's mind withdrawing from the communication with his therapist and from his train and rail-cross activities. In those moments, he escaped physically to the window and stood there, sometimes for most of the session time, lost in an unreachable no-man's land. From the window, he could see the local trains arriving, stopping at the nearby station, and moving on again. He seemed to lull himself and to dissolve in their sound and repetitive motion, to-and-fro, in both directions. No contacts, no crossings. There was an addictive quality to his withdrawal at the window. The therapist was reminded of the time when, from the age of 9 months, and for almost a year, Emilio had been taken on daily train journeys with his mother. At that time, his autistic manoeuvres may have allowed him to shut out the experience of separation from his mother, who left him with his grandparents for the day; he would take refuge in the rocking continuity of a delusional sensuous union, enveloping himself in the sounds, noises, and vibratory rhythms of the moving train.

The movement of change was slow but eventually undeniable. Physical three-dimensionality had become part of Emilio's experience; the shelters offered a reliable protective function, the trains occasionally met at the cross point, and the opening and closing of the shelter doors, with the trains going in and coming out, had brought about basic differentiations in Emilio's mental configuration. The scene was set for the discovery of the vicissitudes around traumatic experiences in the mouth and oral aggression, which, as suggested by Tustin, are invariably connected in some ways with autistic withdrawal. The first intentional representations and the first moments of pretend play appeared in Emilio's activities.

The emergence of oral aggression

Emilio's parents reported that he had become increasingly fussy about food. In his sessions, at that time, he had discovered and started using the cooking utensils, which were part of the material in his box:

> He took the kitchen-pot and made the gesture and the hissing sound of lighting the gas flame under the pot. He put the little

> mummy-figure in the pot and "cooked" her. When she was "done", he gave the doll to the therapist to eat, but warned her that the mummy was very hot and would burn her mouth. He also cooked the children, including the baby, and occasionally banged the mummy doll on the table with rage. He took a piece of string that had represented a strip of Band-Aid in an earlier session and tied it around the boy-doll's neck, saying that his neck or his throat (it was not clear) was sore.

After a long time, the child seemed to have taken up the confused and confusing throat/tongue issue of his first drawing again, but at a new, emotionally more intense and meaningful level. At this point, "an internal space within the mind" seemed to have developed in the child, "in which phantasy as trial action, and therefore experimental thought, could take place (Meltzer, 1975b, p. 225). During this "cannibalistic" kitchen period, in which mothers and babies alike were cooked and eaten, Emilio had become able to project his emerging, burning-hot, oral phantasies into the therapist, who was made to feel the scorching emotions connected with his abrupt weaning at the age of 15 months. From one day to another, mother's nipples, which had filled his passionately sucking mouth since he was born, were gone. By that time, he must have had a mouth full of teeth. Was he terrified that his voracious mouth had bitten off mother's nipples? At the sight of the Band-Aid strips on her breasts, Emilio had said at the time that they were sore. The disappearance of the nipples had caused the abrupt rupture of the baby's highly eroticized delusional continuity of the breast-mouth connection, leaving him with the "black hole with the nasty prick" feeling in his mouth. Had the sight of those mutilated flattened breasts, which had lost their powerful, dark protruding part, contributed to the final breakdown of the third dimension in the child's mind, a process that had started much earlier, at the latest at the time of partial weaning when the baby covered his eyes and ears when approached by a person perceived in his or her *otherness*?

There must have been a mixture of unbearable pain, despair, and guilt, which entailed not only the breakdown of any differentiation between mouth and nipple, but at the deepest levels of spatial experience, the collapse of the preconception of the encounter of opposed and complementary concave and convex shapes. Mother's nipples and the child's mouth may have disappeared in one cosmic existential wound, a great black hole.

The orientation in space and the projection of three-dimensional visions

A new period began during which Emilio produced a long series of drawings in which he represented a duck family. These drawings bear witness to his new-found capacity to move in linear motion and to conceive of structured three-dimensional space, which he was able to project on paper.

He had made great progress in the use of and orientation in space, and his graphic figurative capacity was surprising, although stereotyped aspects persisted and were expressed in the endless repetition of almost identical stamp-like duck drawings. Three of these have been chosen to show the gradual transformations that occurred in his use and subdivision of space, which led to further differentiations and the emergence of new contents. It is important also to note Emilio's new capacities in the use of colours. Not only is his way of colouring more vigorous, but the sea is as blue as it is in the illustrations and he is careful in respecting contours. Above the surface, he colours with black pencil only, but under the waterline there is a meaningful emotional progression from the uncoloured white drowned duckling to the alive orange fish and finally the multicolored aggressive sharks.

> In the first drawing (Figure 3.6), Emilio began by outlining the big duck's beak, then he drew its head, eye, neck, and body. Next came a duckling. The child was pleased with what he had produced and said, "mummy and son". Two more ducklings followed in a row and, finally, a fourth one was added underneath the mummy

FIGURE 3.6

> duck. Only then did he notice that he had not drawn the waterline. He drew it from left to right, in the direction of the ducks' swimming motion. The line began at a low level and moved upwards towards the birds with the clear intention of supporting their bodies. However, he did not quite succeed in his intention, and the ducks remained floating above the water line. Emilio noticed this and vigorously filled the gap between the ducks and the water with black pencil. He clearly wanted them to be supported by the water line. Pointing to the fourth duckling, he said that that one was "under water" and added "eyes burning". (Was the experience of the distance between him and the mother duck too painful to be looked at? Or did he simply remember summer holidays and the salty sea water? In either case, there was a mental association.) He coloured the water carefully, paying attention to the contours of the under-water-duckling. When the therapist asked him, having intuitively grasped that Emilio's new capacity for orientation in space allowed new meanings to emerge, if that duckling had fallen into the water, Emilio replied: "Drowned."

This was Emilio's first figurative drawing. It has an unmistakable stereotyped quality, typical of the drawings of autistic children, which suggests a kind of mechanical two-dimensional cartoon-learning of repeatable shapes, perhaps the graphic equivalent of echolalia. The therapist imagined that the drawing reproduced shapes that Emilio had seen or drawn before, but some elements were connected with his dawning experience of existing in real space. Top and bottom are distinct. A line separates the air from the water, which has to sustain the ducks. They are swimming, moving in space, from left to right. The drowned duckling is not in a row with the others but separated from the mother duck by the waterline—"under water", as Emilio said himself. He does give the impression of beginning to be in touch with the fear of dying related to the separation from the mother at a part-object level, which has now become thinkable, and he is able to represent this by projecting his death anxiety into the drowned duckling, without the representation escalating into *nameless dread* any more (Bion, 1962a).

Emilio had started drawing the mother duck from the beak, which was somewhere high up. Could that beak be connected with the unreachability of mother's breasts after the abrupt weaning, and with his very first drawing—the knobs and clicks that were stuck on the surface of the pink bubble? At the time, those protrusions had lost their function in the tongue-shaped throat, which revealed the general confusion between convex and concave shapes. Of course ducks, like all birds, are confusing, because their nipple-shaped beak is their mouth. It seemed, however, that now the child was ready to explore this puzzling issue.

He had re-evoked his weaning experience, which had been the object of his intense cooking activities. In the following two drawings, he explored oral issues at an increasingly higher representational level. For months, he had produced a countless number of duck drawings. Repetition often led to a loss of meaning, but over time, important changes did occur. This showed that the unconscious mental processes that had been set in motion during moments in which three-dimensional functioning of the mind was becoming more bearable continued to develop in the child's internal world. Oral phantasies came to the fore again with more and more urgency and needed to be represented in his later duck drawings.

> The first thing Emilio did this time was to trace the waterline, which was straighter and less hesitant than in the first drawing. Space was clearly divided horizontally into an upper and a lower part. There were again five ducks, the big mother and four ducklings (Figure 3.7). On the whole, they looked more solid than in the initial drawings, and their bodies were in contact with the water. Their necks were coloured in black and the mother's neck, in particular, was quite big. Emilio added little wings to each duck, but there was not enough space for the last duckling of the row. Its

FIGURE 3.7

> body was nothing but a tiny annex to its black throat, and it looked rather miserable. It seemed to be lagging behind and was not really part of the family. From its position, it could not see the mother duck properly, because the duckling in front of it was too big.
>
> But in this drawing Emilio added a new element: two little fish swimming under the surface. Their shape and colour reminded me of Nemo, the cartoon fish who gets lost in the ocean after its mother's death but is found in the end by its father. Both little fish in the drawing have a big round eye with a clearly drawn pupil and an eyebrow and, under the eye, a smaller, uncoloured circle. Emilio explained that this was the mouth. The eyes are quite elaborated, and the mouth is empty. This drawing, too, was replicated almost identically for many sessions.

Under the water, where in the first drawing there had been a drowned duckling, there were now two colourful living fish. Did Emilio gradually come to life? And did two-ness become more and more thinkable? Were there signs of the primary split, of a primary differentiation whose first signs had appeared with the intersected train rails and had developed further with the horizontal line on the paper, which structured space by separating the upper from the lower part? Separation and differentiation seemed no longer to coincide inevitably with trauma and death. The duck family above the water line is rather stereotyped, guaranteeing possibly an illusion of continuity, but in the under-water-world new elements became visible. Fish have no beaks. They have mouths like people. In this drawing the mouths are empty. But the eyes are quite elaborate. New explorations became possible as shown in the last of the chosen duck drawings (Figure 3.8).

> This time, Emilio moved the water-line higher up on the page. Was this intentional? Did he have a project for which he needed more space in the under-water-world? The ducks seem to have lost some of their importance. They look rather undifferentiated in their black-and-whiteness, except for the mother's long, seductive eye-lashes. The fourth duckling, which looked lost and poorly in the previous drawing, is more like the others and seems to be part of the group of siblings. At the same time, the distance between the ducklings and the mother has increased. Here again, there are two fish under the water. They are bigger and much more colourful and more differentiated than in the previous drawing. For the

FIGURE 3.8

first time, their mouths are not empty, but coloured in red and protruding from their faces. Emilio said that they were wicked monster-fish. They ganged up to attack the mummy-duck from underneath and wanted to eat her. They were sharks, Emilio said, "mother and son, a big shark and a small shark". He then drew a green and a red circle in front of the open mouths of the two fish. These circles were lanterns, he explained. (In a parent meeting, the therapist was told that he had been to the zoo and had been impressed by so-called lantern fish, which have a large luminous spot on top of their head.) In his drawing, Emilio had moved the "lanterns" down from their heads and placed them in front of their mouths. Was it there that something had to be illuminated? He commented that the bulging red shapes that emerged from the mouths were "the tongue".

The lanterns in front of the fish mouths reminded me of a patient of mine, an autistic little boy, whose material Meltzer supervised in the late 1970s. When the child began to have some idea of an inside distinct from an outside, he began to draw tunnels which he coloured in black. One day, he drew a human figure inside the tunnel and explained that the man was *"l'operaio della luce"* (the light workman). His job had been to hold up a yellow lamp to help people see in the darkness.

Emilio seemed to need an extra light to support his search for clarity about the internal space in the fishes' mouths. On the water surface of Emilio's drawing, a peaceful duck family was swimming in a row.

But under that surface, a very different, but more genuine internal world began to be representable: voracious sharks, mother and son, were conspiring against the unsuspecting duck mother. Emilio had developed an internal world with internal objects, which could interact with each other. The primary split allowed for idealization and denigration, and for a vengeful alliance against the formerly idealized, but emotionally indifferent duck mother.

There was a story with a dramatic plot. But this was only part of it. Thanks to the fish lanterns' illuminating function, Emilio could begin to explore and sort out the confusions caused by the breakdown of three-dimensionality in his traumatized baby mind. Now he could observe and notice the difference between concave and convex objects and also acknowledge their different locations and functions. The lantern was placed so that it could illuminate the oral cavity, the tongue in the mouth and the implicit teeth of the mother–child couple of sharks. The acknowledgement of the difference between tongue and nipple—the two similar protruding shapes that were confused initially at the part-object level—became the object of a realistic quest once Emilio had realized that the fullness of the tongue could not replace the emptiness caused by the disappearance of the nipple. In fact, the mother-son gang of sharks was about to attack the unsuspecting duck mother from underneath. She did not know, but the shark mother-and-son knew and had a plan.

The deceptive idea of the oneness of mouth, tongue, and nipple, which had protected Emilio from the catastrophic experience of his weaning, could be abandoned and his oral rage overtly directed towards the maternal object. Oral aggression, hitherto submerged, could now come to the surface, not only in his representation of cruel oral phantasies in the cannibalistic kitchen scenes, but also, at a more abstract level, in his drawings and in the accompanying meaningful verbal narrative.

In conclusion

The core of autistic one- and two-dimensional mental functioning lies in the inability to conceive of separation and separateness. But the dream of a primal one-ness must be abandoned for two-ness to become possible. Two-ness implies an internal migration: it implies leaving behind, at the most primary level, what Meltzer has called the *"romantic object"*. This migration is the prerequisite for the emergence of a space/time between self and other. It is this very *betweenness* that contains the germ of three-dimensionality, with the possibility to set in motion both projective and introjective identification and to abandon the pathological terrorized clinging to two-dimensional imitative adhesiveness or to one- or a-dimensional thoughtlessness. This process is the prerequisite for the emergence of *a mind of one's own*, with its potential for creative thinking and, at the same time, for the discovery of new "enriched objects, which the very *relinquishment* makes attainable" (Meltzer & Harris Williams, 1988, p. 27).

Notes

1. All page numbers for quotations from *Flatland* refer to the version available online at www.feedbooks.com

2. I thank Emilio's psychotherapist, Francesca Bevilacqua, Rome, for allowing me to discuss her patient's material and drawings.

CHAPTER FOUR

Autism reconsidered

Donald Meltzer's concept of dimensionality in clinical work with autistic patients

Suzanne Maiello

At the age of 8 years, Donald Meltzer accompanied his parents on a trip to Europe. The young boy was deeply impressed by the beauty of historical buildings on the old continent and wanted to become an architect. Later, as a psychoanalytic thinker, Meltzer continued to use his gift for spatial design by conceptualizing and interpreting psychic phenomena at the meta-psychological level in terms of dimensionality. Following on from Klein's notion of an internal world inhabited by internal objects and, later, Bion's concept of *container/contained*, the scene was set for the emergence, in 1967 (well before *Explorations in Autism*) of Meltzer's spatial notions of the *geography of the mind*, of *geographical and zonal confusions*, and, later, of the *compartments of the internal object* and the *claustrum*.

In *Explorations in Autism*, the idea of *dimensionality* of mental functioning became the central notion from which Meltzer's theoretical formulations were to spring and expand. He introduced the chapter on "Dimensionality as a Parameter of Mental Functioning" by stating:

> It is of interest with regard to the psycho-analytical method that altered views of life-space found expression in the interpretative work long before they came as theoretical realizations. [1975b, p. 223]

Has psychoanalytic theory not always grown out of the experience of pioneering clinicians, which allowed it to expand and deepen earlier conceptualizations, and sometimes outgrow them? In *Explorations in Autism,* the reports of psychoanalytic work with autistic children by members of the research group *precede* Meltzer's conceptual formulations on the reduction of three-dimensional mental functioning to two- and even one-dimensional states. Years later, he linked this back to Klein's "Notes on Some Schizoid Mechanisms" (1946) when he wrote: "It was largely by the extrapolation of her implicit model of the mind that we developed such concepts as dimensionality, dismantling of the senses . . ." (1986b, p. 122). Our attempts to imagine and describe invisible mental processes inevitably require the use of metaphor. Meltzer's metaphor of the dimensionality of the mind has become a ground plan with enormous creative potential. It was never meant to be viewed as a static, saturated concept, but invited and continues to invite further developments, such as the exploration of the effects of psychic movement, which implies the experience of both limits and direction in the spatial dimension and of both finitude and rhythmicity in the temporal dimension.

An important theoretical issue is whether or not Meltzer views one- and two-dimensional mental functioning as stages of normal early psychic development, to which there would be a regression in autistic pathology; or, alternatively, whether one- and two-dimensionality represent massive defensive strategies to ward off the inevitable emotional turbulence connected with a primary potential for proto-mental three-dimensional functioning. This would include the experience of *space, time, and relatedness,* without which there can be no thinking and, to anticipate Meltzer's later formulations, no *aesthetic experience* of the beauty of the world (Meltzer & Harris Williams, 1988).

In two-dimensional autistic functioning, in which objects are "experienced as inseparable from the sensual qualities that can be apprehended of their surfaces, a conception of the self must necessarily be limited. . . . The reason for this limitation of thought and imagination would reside in the lack of an internal space within the mind in which phantasy as trial action, and therefore experimental thought, could take place" (Meltzer, 1975b, p. 225). This is Meltzer's implicit answer to my query. Let us just evoke the emotional intensity of a newborn baby's first encounter with the breast, his search for the nipple, his mouth's passionate latching to it, pulling it inside, and his vigorous sucking which calls for the milk that he never had before.

What happens in the Theatre of the Mouth (Meltzer, 1986b), long before the baby starts lalling and babbling? The milk enters the oral space on one side and is swallowed on the other. A *sphincter* function is implicitly present. A primary rhythm develops. The lips organize themselves around the nipple to form a tight circle, but then there is the dynamic inward pull. The act of sucking itself can be described as a realization of a preconception of three-dimensional functioning. Incorporation is the physical precursor and counterpart of introjection. Esther Bick describes the experience of the "nipple in the mouth as the optimal object" capable of "holding the parts of the personality together" (1968/1987, p. 115), a kind of forerunner, we might say, of an internalized psychic backbone.

Meltzer's concept of *dimensionality* of the mind, with its double aspect of space and time, is not only a creative metaphor of normal mental functioning, but represents a precious tool for a deeper understanding of autistic states. Three brief clinical examples of autistic children may bring to life specific aspects of one- and two-dimensional autistic functioning and describe the existential struggle of these children when they begin to face their three-dimensional psycho-physical potential and experience the intensity of the emotions from which they had protected themselves with their autistic manoeuvres.

Tommaso: the discovery of linear movement and three-dimensional space

Tommaso[1] was a severely autistic 4-year-old child without language when he began psychotherapy. He spent the first months of his treatment running aimlessly around the room. At some point, however, the corridor that led from the waiting room to the therapy room became a meaningful space of transition. The child began to experience *between-ness*. He wanted the therapist to walk beside him, but he allowed her to do so at her own pace. Differences began to be noticed and accepted. During the sessions, he started hiding behind an armchair and then re-emerge, and he spent months engaged with repeatedly placing a small box inside a larger box and taking it out again. One day, he discovered the reflection of his face on the window pane. He had *seen* it for a brief moment, although he blurred his image immediately with saliva.

> One day, he was lying on the floor at the therapist's feet, looking towards a corner of the room. He then crawled to that corner. Lying on his back, his eyes moved upwards from the floor, all the way to the ceiling, along the line where the two walls meet, and then followed the horizontal lines along the ceiling. Suddenly, he turned on his stomach, made masturbatory movements and then got to his feet. He stood there motionless, his eyes lost, while his urine began to form a puddle on the floor.

Tommaso's autistic defences had diminished. He began to experience the concreteness of physical three-dimensional space, and possibly for a moment of himself existing in that space, when he actively explored the boundaries of the room. But the emotional experience was overwhelming, and his fragile psychic container broke down again. His eyes got lost in space while his self liquefied, his body froze, and he disappeared in a one-dimensional nowhere.

This session, however, was to represent a turning point in Tommaso's therapy. For the months to come, he used a small stick to "measure" the therapy room in all its dimensions and directions, again and again. The Latin "*dimensio*" means "extension", and the term includes the activity of measuring. The stick helped the child to get some realistic and no-longer omnipotent control over external space. His measuring activity was not a stereotypical repetition any more, but an exploration which he could allow to become a mental experience. Only a few months later he began to form and utter his first words in the inner space of the Theatre of the Mouth.

Rosetta: the dimension of time—from endlessness to finitude, from dismantling to rhythmic coordination

Rosetta began three-times-a-week psychotherapy just before the age of 5 years. Her verbal language was echolalic. In the fourth year of our work, she began to be aware of the alternation of presence and absence. The reality of rhythmically structured time began to dawn upon the little girl's mind. The alternation of *yes-days*, when she came to therapy, and *no-days*, when she did not, could be acknowledged. When differences can be experienced, three-dimensional mental functioning is on the way, as a conquest, but also as a threat of renewed existential catastrophe. The little girl's material shows her struggle to overcome the autistic need for sameness but, at the same time, the ever-lurking temptation to deny endings and dismantle consensuality, in order to prevent the catastrophe of the emergence of overwhelming emotions.

Rosetta was 8, and was going to school, when she began to sing nursery rhymes in the session and needed me to sing them with her. She no longer used our unison to obliterate separateness, but to reinforce her capacity to bear it. She particularly liked a rhythmical song about the days of the week, which were named in sequence and accompanied by clapping. This is how she learned to count. Her learning process was imbued with emotional turmoil around presence and absence, meeting and parting, beginnings and endings. She had known the names of numbers before, but in the past these had rarely been connected with the here-and-now experience of reality. She would start to count real objects, but then lost touch with them, continuing her counting until she would lose herself in the high range of senseless numbers. Stopping would have represented a boundary, an ending, including the end of the one-dimensional illusion of infinite continuity and sameness, where all-ness and nothingness coincide.

In the entrance hall of my office there are five spotlights in a row. During that same period, Rosetta noticed them for the first time. She started counting them: one, two, three, . . . and raised her fingers as we walked to the therapy room. However, at the end of the corridor she noticed that the last number that she had pronounced did not correspond to the number of her raised fingers. There had been no shared rhythm between voice and hand. When she noticed the discrepancy, she used to give up.

Meltzer writes: "It seems likely that . . . the first leaps of imagination were of a myth-making variety, enacted in song-and-dance" (1986a, p. 184). When Rosetta first tried to count the spotlights, there was no connection yet at the level of song-and-dance between her "singing" voice and her "dancing" fingers. However, something in Rosetta needed to explore this most primitive proto-symbolic myth-making level of three-dimensional mental functioning. At this point in time, dismantling was no longer an unconsciously sought-for strategy against consensuality, but was experienced as a failure. The day came when Rosetta's voice and fingers met in a shared rhythm: the vocal *five* coincided with the raised five fingers of her open hand. She was beaming. She took my hand to lift both our arms in triumph, and we had to sing Beethoven's *Ode to Joy* together.

João: a haphazard mental topography[2]

In one- and two-dimensional mental functioning, shapes are both reversible in their formal configuration and unreliable as to their position in space. Autistic children often seem to ignore the basic physical laws of gravity. They may walk on tiptoes and feel to be floating in unstructured space, where not only does nothing have volume or boundaries, but where up and down, front and back, left and right are interchangeable. Meltzer illustrates the two-dimensional mental functioning of an autistic little boy by describing his drawing of a house with a door on one side of the sheet, and another house with a door in the same position on the other side of the sheet:

> . . . the child demonstrated his experience of a two-dimensional object: when you enter by the front door you simultaneously exit by the rear door of a different object. It is in effect an object without an inside. [1975e, p. 18]

Front and back coincide.

A drawing by an autistic child will illustrate the interchangeability of spatial vertices in this child's mind: up/down, left/right, as well as the indifferentiation of shapes themselves—convexity/concavity, and the haphazard quality of movement in and through space. Nothing is grounded anywhere. Every potential space-structuring and meaning-conveying shape or movement is reversible. Since there is no mental container, there is no meaningful memory and, therefore, no base for anticipatory phantasy or expectation.

João was born prematurely and spent the first three weeks of his life in an intensive care unit. He was not breast-fed. He vomited after feeds and underwent gastric surgery shortly after his arrival home. At the beginning of his five-times-a-week treatment, he was 2 years old. He had no verbal language and seemed fused with his mother's body. From the age of 4, he started to produce drawings which were replicated endlessly throughout the sessions. At the beginning, they were just scribbles. Later, some became more structured. The child was powerfully attracted by the steep, high mountains that rise from the city of Rio de Janeiro: the Corcovado with the Christ figure on top, and the Sugar Loaf. João used to repeat their names and draw their shapes endlessly. Figure 4.1 is the last of an endless series of identical drawings produced during one session. João was now 9 years old.

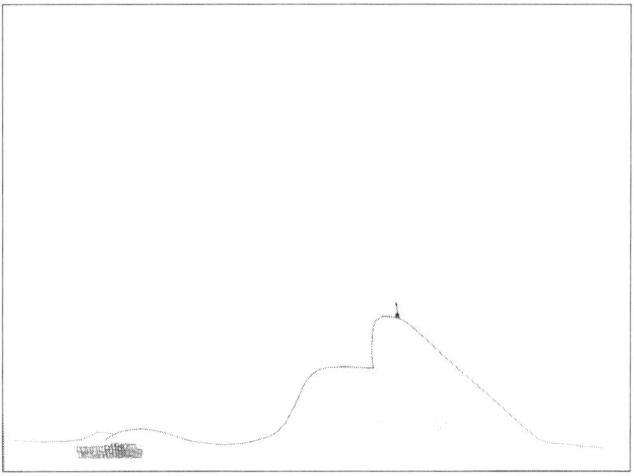

FIGURE 4.1

João first drew the outline of the Corcovado mountain, with a tiny vertical pole on a little pedestal on top, representing the statue of Christ, and a town, a tight cluster of buildings, at the low end on the left, underneath the mountain outline. He then turned the sheet around by 180° and drew another mountain line (Figure 4.2).

It was again the Corcovado, this time without the statue. João then drew the Gávea stone, a large rock in that neighbourhood of Rio de

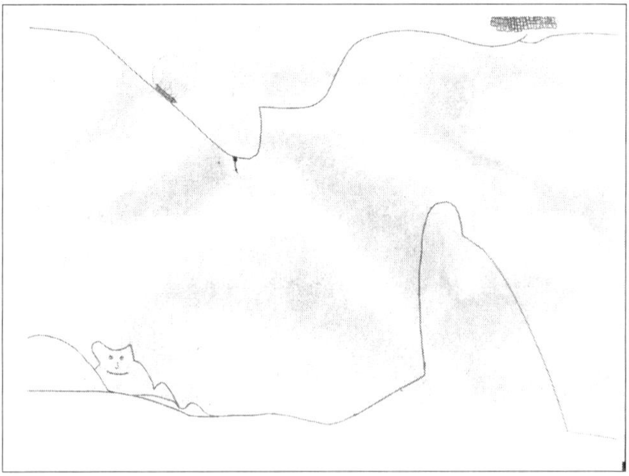

FIGURE 4.2

Janeiro, with natural geological formations that look like eyes, nose and mouth. Maintaining the sheet of paper in this second position, João now drew a roller coaster which ran downhill on the steep slope of the first Corcovado, which was now upside down. Thin lines on the vehicle represented the arms held up by excited people.

Comment

Considering the drawing in its first position: there is a steep, high mountain shape with a rounded top and a short vertical line pointing upwards. It seems difficult to reach that top. (In reality there is a cogwheel train that goes up.) João's town is a cluster of stone blocks, which lies under the horizon. At the part-object level, might we wonder whether at the deepest depths of this child's unconscious mind there could be a surviving preconception of an unreachable breast and nipple, of which he had experienced no positive realizations. As a baby, he had vomited the milk contained in the bottle that had replaced the absent breast.

Considering the inverted drawing: the animal-like shape is a petrified creature that adheres tightly to "mother earth". There is no nipple on this second mountain, but, according to the child, it is the Corcovado again. A roller-coaster runs down the steep (inverted) slope of the first Corcovado. What would have been uphill in the first position of the sheet of paper is now downhill. The saving nipple of the first mountain is unreachable once more, this time because it is buried under the inverted horizon line. What is visible of the people on the roller coaster are just the very thin lines of their arms rising up in excitement. There are no passages, no openings leading from one side to another, no orifices with their both separating and connecting function. The awareness of orifices, as Meltzer suggests, ushers in three-dimensional mental functioning.

If we tentatively turn the sheet back to its original position (which João did not do), the Gávea stone is upside down and stuck to what is now the skyline (Figure 4.3). Perhaps he is at risk of falling off? The second Corcovado is no longer a mountain, but has turned into a deep pit. And the roller-coaster on the first Corcovado would now be hanging over an abyss, with the people head down, at risk of hurtling into nothingness, unless they were glued, from underneath, onto the surface of the slope.

João seems to represent dramatically the non-orientation and the disorientation of his movements in space. He tries to protect himself

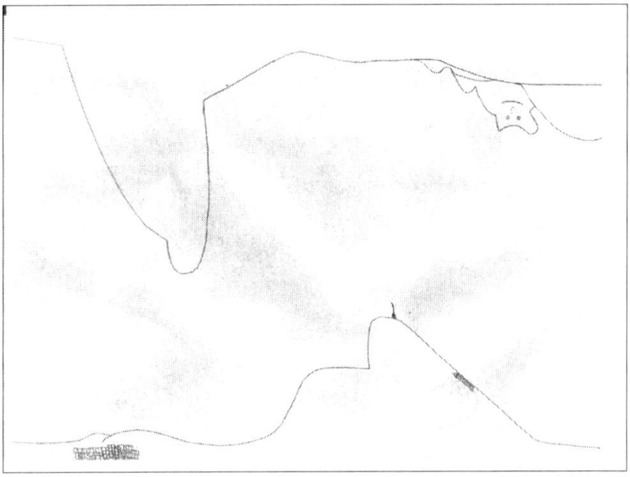

FIGURE 4.3

from devastating precipitation and annihilation anxieties with the mental autistic strategy of two-dimensionalization; a mountain and an abyss become interchangeable, and every experience is flattened and loses its potential emotional meaning. His material shows the crucial role of dimensionality, not only in terms of the normal primary need to feel one's existence as a defined psycho-physical entity in space and time, but also in terms of a reliable spatio-temporal orientation, which includes the capacity for linear movement (up or down, left or right), the differentiation of convex and concave shapes, as well as the acknowledgement of the force of gravity.

For object constancy and links between objects to develop, there must be a minimal awareness of selfness differentiated from otherness. In one- and two-dimensional mental functioning, there is no inner space available to contain internal objects. Endless repetition is meant to replace introjection, and petrification represents another fruitless attempt to gain control over the world at the cost of shutting out any human emotion and any living relationship.

Concluding remarks

Meltzer's meta-psychological metaphor of the dimensionality of the mind is a precious legacy, which not only maintains its meaningfulness forty years after the publication of *Explorations in Autism*, but, being an unsaturated concept with much wider implications, maintains its full creative potential in view of further developments. In particular, the general concept of mental dimensionality becomes an invaluable Ariadne's thread for those who are prepared to enter and seek orientation in the one- and two-dimensional sensual world of autistic minds.

Notes

1. I thank Patrizia Ercolani for permission to present some considerations on her patient's clinical material.

2. I thank Marisa Helena Monteiro for allowing me to present some considerations on an aspect of her patient's material.

Does the meta-psychological concept of dimensionality refer to a geometrical or a topological model?

Didier Houzel

The scientific exploration of a domain of experience supposes the possibility of locating this domain within a space whose internal structure can be described. Such an approach was rendered impossible within the field of psychic phenomena by Cartesian dualism for almost two centuries. Descartes (1641) opposes the biological body—which he defines as an "extended substance", that is to say, occupying a space and, thus, capable of being explored scientifically—and the non-extended soul, which occupies no space and, consequently, escapes any form of scientific study. A century later, Kant still affirmed that the soul was indivisible. At the very most, he admitted a temporal dimension in the internal sense but rejected any possibility of a "science of the soul":

> The theory of the soul can never become anything more than an historical doctrine of nature, and, as such, a natural doctrine of inner sense which is as systematic as possible, that is, a natural doctrine of the soul, but not a science of the soul . . . [1787, 4:470–471]

Admittedly, critiques of these dualistic points of view, which ruled out *a priori* any possible psychology, were rapidly formulated: Leibniz (1714) for Descartes, Herbart (1824) for Kant. Nonetheless, it is true that the scientific study of the human mind had to wait until the second half of the nineteenth century to begin to see the light of day. How are subjective phenomena to be inscribed within an extended space whose contours and internal structure can be studied? It is my contention that the adventure began with the book of the great Aristotelian philosopher, Franz Brentano, entitled *Psychology from an Empirical Standpoint*, published in 1874, a time when Freud regularly followed Brentano's seminars. I am not going to dwell on the work of this author, but I would like to cite two hypotheses that he makes which, it seems to me, deeply influenced Freud in his exploration of the mind: the first is that, if subjective experience appears to us in its immediateness and disappears almost immediately from our conscious awareness without our being able to grasp it and explore it more deeply, this same experience can reappear in memories where it acquires temporal and spatial qualities that allow us to situate it and to explore it. Freud would recall this proposition when he said, in 1893, that the hysteric essentially suffers from reminiscences (Freud, 1893a). Brentano's second hypothesis, from which I think Freud drew inspiration, is that psychic phenomena are characterized by their intentionality, thus distinguishing them from physical phenomena, which respond to a causality. This notion of intentionality can be found in Freud's work in "cathexis", but this time extended beyond conscious phenomena to the preconscious and unconscious.

Freud based his study of the mind on a topography, from the Greek word *topos* signifying "place". We are all familiar with the two topographies that he proposed: the first, conscious/preconscious/unconscious; and the second, Id/Ego/Superego. It is the Freudian topographies that are at the origin of the concept of psychic space. It seems that Bion (1965) was the first to utilize the term "space" to describe the psychic world, although for Donald Meltzer the notion of inner space had been presented implicitly in the work of Melanie Klein. Bion speaks of *space for thinking* and *emotional space* (1965, 1970).

Meltzer's model of dimensionality

I propose now to examine Meltzer's model founded on the geometrical notion of *dimensionality*, before considering to what extent topology can help us to gain a better understanding of what happens in the world of autism to which Meltzer applies this notion of dimensionality.

Watching Meltzer listen to clinical material, one sensed that he was exploring a landscape aroused in his own internal psychic space. His way of thinking referred chiefly to a spatial model, in direct line from Freud, who described the psyche as a tripartite space and Melanie Klein, who described the infant's unconscious phantasies as scenarios taking place upon the stage of the mother's body, a space containing desirable or threatening objects. But, for Meltzer, the spatial model is more than a metaphor: the mental space is a real space, governed by other laws than those governing physical space; a true space where you can move around and discover unknown and unexpected recesses.

Several meta-psychological concepts stem from Meltzer's exploration of psychic space: the geography of phantasy, the compartments of the internal mother, and the dimensionality of mental functioning. My particular focus is on the latter. I question the use Meltzer made of it in *Explorations in Autism*. Meltzer describes a bi-dimensional functioning in an autistic child as follows:

> The child cannot for any length of time experience the distinction between being inside and being outside the object. Looking into the therapist's eyes can be immediately transformed into looking outside of the window. But the moment of triumph over (say) the birds in the garden as the excluded outside-babies, immediately turns into enraged fist-shaking and banging the head on the window, and then to burrowing and banging the head on the therapist's chest. The outside-babies have suddenly turned into the triumphant inside-babies, and triumph of the child turns to puzzled rage.
>
> One child showed us the answer in a single stroke of creative intensity. For months he had drawn doors and gates, usually with complex wrought-iron grills. Then gradually rather Victorian gothic houses took shape. One day he painstakingly drew an ornate house seen from the front on one side of the page, a house in Northwood, while on the other side he drew a back view of a pub in Southend. Thus the child demonstrated his experience of a two-dimensional object; when you enter by the front door you simultaneously exit by the rear door of a different object. It is in effect an object without an inside. [Meltzer, 1975e, p. 18]

The problem is that, in a bi-dimensional space, you cannot enter or exit by a door: you cannot go across a surface. It is very difficult to imagine life in a bi-dimensional space, in which there are only lines, semi-lines, and segments of line. The novelist Edwin A. Abbott (1884) described such a world in his wonderful short story *Flatland.*

Although I acknowledged that Meltzer's spatial metaphor was highly relevant to understanding the subjective experience of our patients, I thought it necessary to investigate the psychic process beneath these metaphors.

Soon after reading Meltzer's description, I read a paper by two mathematicians, Thurston and Weeks, about what they called tri-dimensional manifolds ("manifold" designates here a generalization of the notion of surface whatever the number of dimensions). They described a special manifold called a "three-torus". To build a three-torus, you must take a cube and stick its superior face to its inferior one and its right face to its left one. In fact, it is not possible to achieve such a building process in our three-dimensional Euclidian space. It is possible only in four-dimensional space. It is not a problem for a mathematician, however, to use his imagination to project himself into a space with any number of dimensions. In a three-torus, life is as follows:

> Look at the back wall and the line of sight passes through that wall and returns from the opposite point on the front wall. What you see is a copy of yourself from behind. Look to the right and you see a copy of yourself from the left; look down at the floor and you see the top of your head. [Thurston & Weeks, 1984, p. 108]

It is strikingly similar to Meltzer's description of the autistic bi-dimensional space, but the model is different. Meltzer's is a geometrical model based upon the concept of dimension: the child constructs his or her internal world by successive additions of one spatial dimension to another; time makes up the fourth dimension. By contrast, the three-torus model is a topological one based on the concept of orientability and non-orientability.

A topological model based on orientability and non-orientability

Topology is the mathematical discipline that studies the bijective and bicontinuous transformations that are known as "homeomorphisms". Bijective signifies that, between the elements of two sets, there is a one-to-one correspondence; each point of one of them corresponds to one point, and one point only, of the other, and vice-versa; bicontinuous signifies that the transformation occurs without tearing or sticking.

Orientability means that a Cartesian-coordinate system remains unchanged on the surface (manifold), whatever the displacement it is submitted to. When the coordinate system changes, the surface (manifold) is called non-orientable:

> An abstract surface (i.e. a two-dimensional manifold) is orientable if a consistent concept of clockwise rotation can be defined on the surface in a continuous manner. That is to say that a loop going around one way on the surface can never be continuously deformed (without overlapping itself) to a loop going around the opposite way. [Wikipedia: orientability]

The more common non-orientable manifolds are the *Moebius strip*, the *Klein bottle*, and the *projective plane*.

I have noticed that some patients become disorientated when there has been a discontinuity in the psychoanalytic frame and may, for example, experience difficulty finding their car after a session. Working with autistic children has inspired me to hypothesize a non-orientability or a loss of orientability of psychic space, which I hope to illustrate with the following extracts from my work with an autistic boy.

A clinical illustration

Cyril's analysis began when he was 3 years old. For the first two years, I saw him three times per week; then, when he was 5, this increased to four weekly sessions. He had been diagnosed with autism. Cyril is the elder of two boys: his brother is two years younger. His parents are from a cultured background: his father is in an intellectual profession, while his mother had been in higher education but, currently, does not work. A deformity of the uterus made her pregnancies difficult, and she only conceived Cyril after three miscarriages. This pregnancy was a time of great anxiety, during which she stayed mainly resting in bed, and the baby moved very little *in utero*. Her impression was that, by remaining very still, he was protecting himself from the uterine contractions that she experienced as being threatening to him, given the very little space that he had. So, from the beginning, she found it extremely difficult to conceive of herself as a good container for her baby and even sensed herself as a threat from which he had to protect himself.

Cyril was a quiet baby. His sleep soon settled into a regular pattern. He was breast-fed for six weeks, but this was very brusquely interrupted due to an infection of the mother's breast. Nothing was noticed at the time of this sudden weaning. Cyril's motor development was delayed: he only sat up when he was a year old and did not walk until he was 22 months old.

Mother's second pregnancy began when Cyril was 15 months old. Complications during the final trimester threatened to provoke a premature birth, so she remained in bed until being hospitalized for the last month.

Cyril's parents first became concerned by his delayed motor development, but they soon worried about his failure to develop language.

In addition, they noted behaviours that they described as "strange". Cyril would bang his head against the floor or against the wall, and he would rock backwards and forwards. At around 20 months, his parents felt that he was withdrawing from the world, that he was "in his own bubble"; his interests were limited, for example opening and closing doors and listening to music; he did not develop any symbolic play; and he would take an adult's hand to obtain what he wanted and did not point.

Rather rapidly, after a few sessions, Cyril was able to pay attention to my presence and communicate with me emotionally. It seems that he had opened his mental space. A non-orientable space is always twisted on itself. Opening such a space is like removing this twist. To make it concrete I will use the metaphor of a boomerang: the encounter between a preconception and its object looks like a boomerang reaching its target. If the boomerang misses its target, it returns to its starting point, describing a curve twisted on itself. According to my hypothesis, the possibility of creating an inner space does not depend upon a constructivist process adding one dimension after the other. Rather, it depends upon finding an adequate object that fits with the preconception, giving meaning and orientation to the unconscious expectation it entails.

Work with autistic children reveals a huge gap between the moment a preconception emerges and the moment it reaches its target in the transference. This gap is filled with terrors and persecutors, like the "nasty prick" little John described to Tustin when emerging from his autistic encapsulation.

As soon as he had opened his inner world, Cyril encountered these terrors. The first was a terror of spilling out, as if opening his internal space threatened the loss of everything it contained; Cyril would scatter everything he could find in the therapy room—pencils, paper, toys—all over the place. However, quite quickly, he wanted to bring things together and control the containers. In particular, he became interested in the boxes of modelling clay and the lids that covered these boxes. Shortly after this, he uttered the first word I ever heard him pronounce: "lid".

Second, Cyril had to face the terror of what Tustin called "the nest of babies":

> In this phase, when the child is beginning to be able to bear the awareness of a clear distinction between himself and other people, there invariably develops a fantasy which I have come to call the

> "nest of babies" fantasy. This is associated with the notion that there are "special babies" who are given "special food". [Tustin, 1972a, pp. 177–178]

After our first summer holiday break, Cyril inaugurated a new activity: he emptied his box of toys, threw away the pens and paper from the table where I had put them, climbed triumphantly onto this table and from there onto my lap, and exclaimed "big, big, big". I first interpreted this as his wish to grow into a big boy coming to see me and drawing support from me. But then I realized that he was expressing rivalry with the objects he had thrown away, representing the rival babies who (in his view) had stayed with me all through the long summer break. In a subsequent session, this aspect became clearer, as the following extract shows:

> Cyril threw the pens to the floor, then played with the water, attempting to flood the whole room, in spite of my forbidding him to do so. Then he threw all the sheets of paper from the little table to the floor, and climbed onto the table saying in a triumphant tone of voice "Grown up". From there, he climbed onto my lap, then back to the table. He picked up the pens, gave them to me to hold for him, then threw them back onto the floor. With one of the pens, he drew several long lines on some sheets of paper, saying they were "little cats". He then threw these sheets of paper to the floor and went through the whole sequence again: climbing onto the table, then onto my lap, then back to the table. He also made as if to bite me.

Cyril then had to face the paternal figure as a powerful rival—the biggest baby, said Tustin—who threatened to separate him definitively from the maternal figure. One day he arrived slightly early and saw me walk in accompanied by a woman. Once in the therapy room, he seemed furious, asking, "Why was there a lady? Where did the lady go?" Then he told me, "You know, I could break your feet, your legs, your knees?" all the way up to my head and my hair.

During the following years Cyril's fantasies evolved into more and more orientable scenarios, but with two kinds of preoccupation according to the direction of the action. On a horizontal axis, the question was this: how might he find the right way to join me in the transference? He expressed this through fantasies of the route he might follow with the taxi driver who drove him to the clinic: which way out of the ring road did they have to choose? How could they avoid traffic jams or accidents caused by other cars crashing into the back of the taxi? I interpreted these fantasies in the transference as connected to his mother's second pregnancy and his little brother's birth which he had felt as a violent intrusion in his maternal containing object (the taxi). When he had such a fantasy he called for a policeman to recover his own space in his containing object. The policeman seemed to represent a good paternal protective figure.

On a vertical axis, the question was this: how could he slide down from the top to the bottom, but not too fast and without too much anxiety? To illustrate this, he used the scenario of sliding on a toboggan in a swimming pool, which made me think of a precipitated birth. Cyril put lights at the top of the toboggan to force people to wait before sliding. I link this fantasy with an adult patient's account of being at the birth of his children: he noticed that, during the delivery, it was necessary to slow down the progression of the baby's head to prevent the risk of a perineal tear. I interpreted this as the reclamation of a protective paternal figure in the transference to prevent the psychoanalytic process, which resembles a kind of birth, from going too fast and roughly. The patient replied that sometimes he felt lost in a huge space, without knowing which direction he might follow. I understood Cyril's scenario in the same way: he needed to reclaim a good paternal object to help him get out of the maternal womb in order to be born and to grow up without destroying his maternal container (the perineal tear) or falling endlessly through space. I suppose that the orientability of the psychic space relies both on the paternal elements of the container and on the child's identification with a paternal figure. By contrast, non-orientability could be a defence against the primitive agonies the child has to face when leaving the womb.

Conclusion

One of the most original features of Meltzer's work is its spatial reference. He describes the psychic world in terms of spaces and the different states of mind as linked to a shift from one space to another. This spatial reference leads him to describe autism as a state with no differentiation between an inner world an outer world. Absence of differentiation hinders any possibility for projection outside or introjection inside any external object and the chance of communication with it. To describe this state of mind, Meltzer uses a geometrical model based on the concept of dimensionality. But scrutinizing his clinical illustrations of this model, one might think that a topological model would better suit clinical work with autistic children or with patients having an autistic enclave. The topological concept of non-orientability allows for the description of spaces—whatever their dimension—in which there can be no differentiation between interior and exterior.

In his introduction to *Explorations in Autism*, Meltzer writes:

> In fact it will soon be clear to a discerning reader that we are in the business of locating problems rather than of solving them. This is probably really the fundamental truth about the human sciences in general and psycho-analysis in particular. Thus we believe we have located some very mysterious phenomena of the mind by recognizing them operative in very condensed form in the children treated. [Meltzer, 1975c, pp. 4–5]

It seems to me that, by emphasizing this locating function of psychoanalysis, Meltzer introduces the issue of a topological model of mental apparatus. Topology was first called by Leibniz *analysis situs,* which means analysis of the location of the elements studied in mathematics. Autistic children teach us that we have first to clarify the problem of location if we are to help them develop their own psychic space.

A response

Jeffrey L. Eaton

Forty years ago, in *Explorations in Autism*, Donald Meltzer offered eloquent testimony to the complexity of autistic experience (Meltzer et al., 1975). His keen formulations remain as valuable today as when introduced in 1975. It was his capacity to capture and describe *complexity* that I want briefly to highlight as a context for the specific developments offered by Suzanne Maiello and Didier Houzel.

With his colleagues, Meltzer noted a number of specific features about the children with whom they worked, including the child's often high intelligence; the factor of speed (they were fast to register and slow to process experience); their openness to sensation (Meltzer characterized it as "naked to the wind"; 1975e, p. 9); their sensitivity to the therapist's state of mind; and, finally, a primitive permeability to the emotions of others.

Meltzer also described other features, including what he called "an uncompromising possessiveness of the maternal object" (1975e, p. 10), hyper-sensuousness, and a hatred of transience, leading to a feeling of being persecuted by the awareness of time. All of these observations, and many others that I have not noted here, help to clarify the autistic and post-autistic states as witnessed in analytic experience with children who are often difficult to comprehend. With these features in mind, one can better appreciate the rich contributions of Maiello and Houzel regarding the specific theme of psychic dimensionality that is a particular instance of the complexity Meltzer started to investigate.

Maiello describes analytic work with three children—Tommaso, Rosetta, and João—while Houzel brings the story of Cyril. All of these are beautifully observed cases. Maiello introduces a particular theme that captures my imagination: she sees the creative extension of Meltzer's concept of psychic dimensionality in what she calls the "exploration of the effects of psychic movement".

Henry David Thoreau wrote in his *Journal* that "All perception of truth is the detection of an analogy; we reason from our hands to our head" (2009, p. 76). This certainly seems true for Tommaso, whom Maiello movingly describes as using "a small stick to 'measure' the therapy room in all its dimensions and directions, again and again". She goes on to say that, "His measuring activity was not a stereotypical repetition any more, but an exploration which he could allow to become a mental experience. Only a few months later he began to form and utter his first words in the inner space of the Theatre of the Mouth."

I return to the idea of the Theatre of the Mouth at the end of my remarks. Now I want to draw attention to Maiello's suggestion that we attune ourselves to the themes of movement in space and time. What can attention to the child's actual movement and behaviour indicate about his or her relationship to psychic space and time? This focus on movement is particularly important for the way that psychic realizations can arise from a body physically exploring in space and time.

Maeillo suggests that investigating space reveals elements of direction and limit, while attention to movement in time involves finitude and rhythm. To this we might add the idea of cause and effect. Investigating primitive notions about cause and effect reveals themes of arbitrary or random happenings versus sequential and constantly conjoined events. When we add together the experiences of space, time, and cause and effect, we begin to get a sense of the child's orientation versus disorientation in the creation of his or her picture of the world.

Deepening familiarity with the concept of dimensionality and its extension into the observation of *psychic movement in time and space* creatively enlarges the therapist's capacity to begin to observe and imagine the complexity of an autistic child's *construction of experience*. With these concepts, it becomes more plausible to track how this complexity evolves through the influence of contact with the analyst's attention, emotion, and imaginative capacity for interpretation.

According to Maiello, "Meltzer's metaphor of the dimensionality of the mind has become a ground plan with enormous creative potential. It was never meant to be viewed as a static, saturated concept, but invited and continues to invite further developments." I think we can imagine how psychic movement has different qualities in one, two, and three dimensions. One of the most important questions might be, why is the child afraid to move at all? How much of the child's activity is designed to control or inhibit movement and its unknown or anticipated consequences? Further exploration of Houzel's (2014) concept of "precipitation anxiety" could prove fruitful in this context.

The capacity to imagine different countries of the mind that are created by different forms of psychic movement may be difficult for those who have not been immersed in work with autistic or psychotic children. Houzel brings a challenging and extremely interesting point of view when he asks us to consider the difference between a flat bi-dimensional world of surfaces and that which mathematicians Thurston and Weeks call "tri-dimensional manifolds". Houzel quotes an often-evoked vignette of Meltzer's (1975e):

> The child cannot for any length of time experience the distinction between being inside and being outside the object. Looking into the therapist's eyes can be immediately transformed into looking outside of the window. But the moment of triumph over (say) the birds in the garden as the excluded outside-babies, immediately turns into enraged fist-shaking and banging the head on the window, and then to burrowing and banging the head on the therapist's chest. The outside-babies have suddenly turned into the triumphant inside-babies, and triumph of the child turns to puzzled rage.

This is highly condensed material and the particular details are very important. Meltzer continues:

> One child showed us the answer in a single stroke of creative intensity. For months he had drawn doors and gates, usually with complex wrought-iron grills. Then gradually rather Victorian gothic houses took shape. One day he painstakingly drew an ornate house seen from the front on one side of the page, a house in Northwood, while on the other side he drew a back view of a pub in Southend. Thus the child demonstrated his experience of a two-dimensional object; when you enter by the front door you simultaneously exit by the rear door of a different object. It is in effect an object without an inside. [Meltzer, 1975e, p. 18]

Houzel takes issue with the conclusion that this describes an object without an inside. In working with autistic states, one does encounter descriptions of flat, adhesive states that are without an inside and that seem to present purely sensation-dominated surfaces. This vignette, however, does not seem like a good example, because, as Houzel points out, you cannot *enter* a two-dimensional space. There is no door to a surface or a plane.

We should take such facts literally. Meltzer emphasized the concreteness of psychic reality. If you take the drawing literally, the child gives much attention to doors and gates. These figures are drawn over and over for months. If one looks at sameness, then one may feel there is a repetition. If one looks at novelty, then one may feel that something is being constructed, something is trying to be realized.

What kind of complex space allows the passage from a house in Northwood to a pub in Southend? Is this an object without an inside? Alternatively, can it be seen as an object with such a complex inside space that it cannot be easily mapped or represented? I have observed in my work with autistic children the ubiquitous presence of "portals" (doors and gates) in many children's material, which suggests the challenge of managing experience both within and between very complex spaces.

To describe the extraordinarily complex space that some autistic children struggle to express, Houzel offers the imaginative conjecture of what *movement* in such a complex space, represented here by a three-dimensional torus, would be like:

> Look at the back wall and the line of sight passes through that wall and returns from the opposite point on the front wall. What you see is a copy of yourself from behind. Look to the right and you see a copy of yourself from the left; look down at the floor and you see the top of your head. [Thurston & Weeks, 1984, p. 108]

Meltzer used the concept of confusional anxiety in relationship to the capacity for thinking. Here, Houzel offers another crucial point of view: the necessity to consider the function of "orientability" and "non-orientability" as part of the challenge of the autistic child's subjective experience.

This idea has large implications for themes like the "presence" of the object and the absence of the object. In what kind of space does the child meet the object? What kind of space is created by the awareness of the object's presence and its absence? What kind of experience of cause and effect is created when space (and time) are distorted and disoriented? And, how is the child's perception of an object influenced by the nature of its space? These ideas offer practical help in following the phenomenological experience of a patient's material.

I would like to describe an experience with a post-autistic patient, Steven, I have seen in analysis for ten years. The vignette I present comes from the first session after a three-week Christmas break. My purpose here is not to demonstrate the analytic process between us, but, rather, to show the representation in Steven's material of the complexity of the space that I think was triggered by the separation over the holiday.

> Steven, aged 17 at this time, enters the session and greets me cheerfully. Then he says, "Long time since I've seen you, Jeff." "Yes," I say, "it's been a long time." He then asks me if I have heard about the Charlie Hebdo shootings in Paris. Steven considers himself a cartoonist and graphic artist. Over the years he has produced many clever drawings and cartoons both inside and outside his sessions. Several have been published in his school newspapers. Now he tells me that he is starting to create a graphic novel, a project begun over the break.
>
> He takes several minutes to draw a stylized image. We are both silent as he draws, though sometimes he looks up at me and makes eye contact. He is sitting on the couch drawing on a small table I provide. I sit next to him in my chair. When he has finished he gives me a detailed explanation of the image. I will summarize what he says about his drawing:
>
> *Test subject A wakes up in a windowless chamber. He does not know what time of day it is, or what day of the week it is. There is no colour in the room. The floor, the walls, the ceiling are all white and look the same. There is one tiny grate in the wall, and in the grate is a strange-looking wrench, on which is written one instruction: "this is the tool you need to make your escape". There is a door hidden in the room somewhere but A doesn't know where. If he can find the door, he can open it with the tool and it will lead to another room just like this room, and there will be a different tool to use to find a different door, which will lead to yet another room. There is no way to tell how many times he must go through this procedure until he finds a way to "the outside". There are dozens of other rooms if not hundreds or even thousands. There may also be other test subjects and you do not know where or when they might appear.*

This story seems to evoke, in all its details, something powerful about Steven's feelings when he is separated from me. Our sessions provide him with a kind of orientation that can be suddenly lost over the long holiday break, but now, rather than concretely living out this disorientation and withdrawing into autistic and omnipotent defences, Steven can begin to symbolize his experience and present it creatively as a graphic novel.

Now I want to return to Maiello's discussion of "the Theatre of the Mouth". She writes:

> Let us just evoke the emotional intensity of a newborn baby's first encounter with the breast, his search for the nipple, his mouth's passionate latching to it, pulling it inside, and his vigorous sucking which calls for the milk that he never had before. What happens in the Theatre of the Mouth (Meltzer, 1986b), long before the baby starts lalling and babbling? The milk enters the oral space on one side and is swallowed on the other. A *sphincter* function is implicitly present. A primary rhythm develops. The lips organize themselves around the nipple to form a tight circle, but then there is the dynamic inward pull. The act of sucking itself can be described as a realization of a preconception of three-dimensional functioning. Incorporation is the physical precursor and counterpart of introjection. Esther Bick describes the experience of the "nipple in the mouth as the optimal object" capable of "holding the parts of the personality together" (1968/1987, p. 115), a kind of forerunner, we might say, of an internalized psychic backbone

Bick also linked introjection with the discovery of inner space. In her well-known paper, "The Experience of the Skin in Early Object Relations", she wrote:

> Until the containing functions have been introjected, the concept of space within the self cannot arise. Introjection, i.e. construction of an object in an internal space, is therefore impaired. [1968/1987, p. 114]

Can we imagine that, in Steven's drawing, the wrench that opens a secret door to a new room represents a fugitive nipple, experienced as disembodied, not reliably linked to the part-object breast, to the mother's body, to her mind and reverie? Do these complex, disorienting spaces express the attempt to construct a world despite the loss of the primary cooperation formed by relying on an analytic nipple-mouth partnership?

To the degree that this fragile couple has slowly been constructed over many years in analysis, does the experience of the holiday break revivify the unconscious memory of a primal separation as catastrophe? My sense is that when analyst and patient achieve the status of a symbolizing couple, they can begin to work through such early catastrophe in repeatedly more nuanced variations until the child has a new relationship to time, space, cause and effect, and, most importantly, to self, other, and relationship.

CHAPTER FIVE

Dimensionality, identity, and security: finding a home through psychoanalysis

Louise Allnutt

> "Adoption is outside. You act out what it feels like to be the one who doesn't belong. And you act it out by trying to do to others what has been done to you. It is impossible to believe that anyone loves you for yourself."
>
> Jeanette Winterson, *Why Be Happy When You Could Be Normal?* (2011)

Being at home

Dimensionality, identity, and security are concepts that I would like to draw together and house descriptively as the experience of "being at home". In my view, one needs to have developed a clear sense of the dimensions of space and your own place in it alongside a strong and secure-enough relationship to oneself and others to have the opportunity to feel at home, either in terms of "joining the human family", as Maria Rhode has described it (2008), or in terms of being capable of making transitions and crossing thresholds into different spaces without a sense of losing one's own coherence. My experience of working with one particular patient has highlighted these issues at both a developmental and emotional level, but the absence or presence of "at-home-ness" is something that I find lies at the heart of many clinical relationships, sometimes in relation to oneself, sometimes in relating to others, at times due to concrete displacement and at other times through difficulties related to misrecognition and misperception. My clinical experience with a 2-year-old boy, who came for intensive psychotherapy for three years, brought the experience of being "outside" and the developmental problems of "homelessness" sharply into focus. It is some of this clinical material alongside the theoretical ideas that one can draw from Donald Meltzer, among others, that I would like to discuss here as an example of some of the processes one might traverse in finding a home through psychoanalysis.

In essence, this chapter is an attempt to understand the relationship between inside and outside. It considers how we develop a sense of orientation in relation to our internal and external worlds and how they take shape and link up. The brief examples taken from the first few sessions of a psychoanalytic treatment of 2-year-old Joseph illustrate the predicament of a child who was struggling, both emotionally and developmentally, to make sense of his place in the world and his relationship to others. His early traumatic history was punctuated with loss, separation, and maltreatment. I was particularly struck by the way his emotional security seemed inextricably linked to his capacity to orientate himself physically in the world and establish a place of his own. Being able to establish such a place appeared to be dependent upon a capacity to feel a sense of security inside, facilitated by the way in which the external world had been experienced and taken in from the outside. Not feeling securely emotionally held together, or at a high risk of disintegrating, when faced with relating to the world and its inhabitants is what I mean by security. This is a developmental problem, whether it has been derived through environmental failure or otherwise.

In relation to his description of "two-dimensional" relationships between one's inner and outer worlds, Meltzer (1975b) describes how the circumstances that threaten the inherent changelessness of this state would tend to be experienced as a breakdown of the surfaces. While Meltzer was largely taking the lead in his theoretical formulations of dimensionality from autistic patients, there are similar accounts of phenomena of this kind within the clinical work with children who are fostered and adopted, particularly with those children whose experience of trauma and environmental failure took place in their earliest years. It is striking to note how many papers and books describing psychotherapeutic work with looked-after children note the experience of being lost and found, such as *Waiting to Be Found* (Briggs, 2012) and *Psychotherapy with Young Children in Care: Lost and Found* (Hunter, 2001).

Joseph left a strong impression of being a lost little boy at the start of treatment. It was extremely hard to feel one had him in one place and in one piece. His experiences of relationships were highly unregulated and extreme. One minute, he seemed to be buoyant, in control and ahead of the game; the next, he was in a state of collapse and appeared terrified and emotionally broken. The experience of being with Joseph was a challenge both physically as well as emotionally and, of course, this was also true for Joseph himself. What slowly seemed to develop, however, was a sense that the relationship between us could hold him and give him a greater sense of gravity and orientation which, in turn, seemed to facilitate a greater capacity for related communication and the security and solidity that followed.

Finding Joseph seemed to be a central task in bringing him into a relationship where experience could be thought about. There were times when he clearly did not want to be found, and he would let me know that he did have a place, albeit not the one I had in mind but one called the "corridor". He once exclaimed, "I am going home to the corridor!" The corridor seems similar to what Meltzer (1975b) described as the "fifth compartment"—"the 'nowhere' of the delusional system outside the gravitational pull of good objects" (p. 223). For Joseph, the corridor had, in the absence of inner cohesion or an external reliable structure, become home. But in this outside place, development was stymied and contact was severed. In the assessment at the family assessment service at age 18 months, Joseph was observed to spend extended periods of time walking up and down the corridor. During this highly obsessional activity, Joseph would disregard any attempt by parents or staff to make contact. There is no doubt that his status as a child in transition contributed to this experience and challenged any belief that home could be somewhere he could arrive at and feel safe, held, and rooted.

In Jeanette Winterson's autobiographical account of her scarring childhood adoption (2011), she considers its impact upon her capacity to feel at "home" and all of its ramifications. She quotes the Romanian philosopher, Mircea Eliade, who refers to "home" both geographically and ontologically speaking, as "the heart of the real":

> Home, he tells us, is the intersection of two lines—the vertical and horizontal. The vertical plane has heaven, or the upper world at one end, and the world of the dead at the other end. The horizontal plane is the traffic of this world, moving to and fro—our own traffic and that of teeming others.
>
> Home was a place of order. A place where the order of things come together—the living and the dead—the spirits of the ancestors and the present inhabitants, and the gathering up and stilling of all the to and fro.
>
> Leaving home can only happen because there is a home to leave. And the leaving is never just a geographical or spatial separation; it is an emotional separation—wanted or unwanted. Steady or ambivalent.
>
> For the refugee, for the homeless, the lack of this crucial coordinate in the placing of the self has severe consequences. At best, it must be managed, made up for in some way. At worst, a displaced person, literally, does not know which way is up, because there is no true north. No çompass point. Home is much more than shelter; home is our centre of gravity. [2011, p. 58]

The gathering together that Eliade identifies at the meeting point called "home" is close to what I believe to be involved in psychoanalytic treatment. For me, his powerful claim that home forms the centre of gravity, combined with Winnicott's (1952) description of the way that disturbing kinds of anxiety promote a move in which "the centre of gravity of consciousness transfers from the kernel to the shell", create a helpful description of the territory Joseph appeared to inhabit during the early phase of the clinical work. The sense of disorientation was, at times, immense: Joseph lacked a true sense of north—an absence of what Tustin would describe as "rootedness" (1981)—and he experienced the pathways between different spaces as filled with obstacles and terrifying pitfalls. Home was not a place Joseph could trust. Coupled with his spatial confusion and disorientation was his experience and expectation of those he met in transit. How he related to his therapy and also his foster carer seemed to reflect quite a complex and emotionally unsettling picture of his early experience and the struggles to relate and orientate himself it had left him with.

Joseph was referred for psychotherapy due to serious concerns about his development and emotional health during the family specialist assessment when he was 18 months old. As mentioned above, he was observed to wander aimlessly up and down corridors, with little sense of purpose. He made eye contact with neither parent nor staff at the centre and had little language. He did not cry but was heard to grunt and moan. He did not play and sought neither comfort nor the company of either of his parents or any other adult. The initial assessment concluded that parental neglect and emotional abuse were having a profound impact on Joseph's development.

Following this assessment and his foster placement, Joseph returned to the assessment centre for some therapeutic sessions with his new carer. My first contact with Joseph was during these six sessions with a social work colleague, aimed at supporting him and his carer with his transition into care in order to prepare him for adoption as well as serving as an assessment for further therapeutic work.

Joseph did not speak during these sessions. Rather than play, he tended to wander around the room aimlessly, locating objects in a blank way. Initially these objects appeared to have little communicative meaning. As in the assessment, Joseph was observed, during the first couple of sessions with his foster carer, to take a small toy kitchen pan and a wooden spoon and beat the two together repeatedly, the spoon stabbing the inside of the pan with a thud. There was no modulation in this activity, nor did Joseph seek the interest of the adults present in what he was doing. This "mindless" and "one-dimensional" activity (Meltzer, 1975b) continued throughout the first two sessions despite our attempts to make contact with him.

As the sessions developed, so did Joseph's curiosity, and during the third session he turned his attention to the dressing-up box, where there were a few small plastic clothes hangers. Joseph appeared quite enlivened by these hangers, gathering up a few and handing one to each person in the room. His foster carer and the clinicians were surprised and equally enlivened by this process, and our discussion in the room then centred upon how this was his first use of play as communication. Despite Joseph's high level of need and wide range of difficulties, it was encouraging to see him engaged and beginning to make contact with us.

Joseph's foster carer was getting to know him, and this was also having a positive influence upon his development. The hangers became a regular feature in the sessions, accompanied by increased enjoyment and contact with each person to whom he handed one. It was almost as if he were deliberately giving us something from which to hang him in our minds. It certainly had the desired effect, as Joseph was a child whom you remembered and thought about between each session. The hangers were, perhaps, also a communication about his increasing awareness that everyone had their place. From these sessions we decided, with his foster carer's support, to move Joseph into intensive psychotherapy.

Despite his outward appearance, which could seem vacant and unmoving, there was nevertheless a nugget or spark of life in Joseph from the outset of treatment. When he was collected for his very first session with me, he bounded down the corridor with giant steps and excitedly leapt into the consulting room without apparent fear. I was left wondering if this was confidence, faith, or just manic omnipotence. Whatever it was that imbued him with such confidence at this first moment of his therapy, it quickly collapsed as the encounter unfolded. This state of collapse became a regular and distinctive feature of our sessions, but despite this, his initial confidence became something that he and I unconsciously relied upon to keep going with an often extremely difficult treatment.

Transitions: falling and dropping

Soon into his first session, Joseph became preoccupied with falling and dropping.

> Joseph took a car to the sink and rolled the wheels along its edge. He then let it fall from the edge into the sink. He said, "Fall over." Joseph looked down into the sink at the car.
>
> Joseph removed it from the sink and took it to the table, where he placed it on the edge. He rolled it back and forth along the edge a couple of times. He then abandoned the car and returned to the box. [*Following this, Joseph struggled to focus; he located a couple of objects—a rocker stack and then a teapot—which he ended up throwing away; he then returned to the car.*] The car on the table caught Joseph's eye. He wandered back to the table and with his head down to one side he rolled the car back and forth. . . . He returned with the car to the sink and again placed it on the edge. He again let it drop and stated, "Fall over." He repeated this several times. At one point he then turned, leaving the car in the sink and said, "One, two, three!" at the same time jumping with both feet in the air. I remarked Joseph was counting and he shouted, "Three, four, five!" He then turned and banged on the door.

The anxiety of being dropped emerged in this session in connection with a sense that nothing could be sustained. Joseph seemed to manage his fear of falling by trying to take hold of some order or sequence, such as his jumping and counting, a defensive response to the anxiety caused by deep feelings of insecurity. There were brief moments of apparent interest and optimism, expressed through Joseph's interest in the toys, but these were quickly disconnected and his focus either ran adrift or toys were discarded. There was a flurry of activity in this first session that showed me the painful experience of an almost buoyant beginning that quickly disintegrated; the therapy quickly became a place where nothing worked and nothing could be sustained.

Soon after this sequence, Joseph collapsed following a disturbing encounter with the mirror he found in his box. Looking into it closely, he encountered his own reflection, which was, possibly, unrecognizable to him and which frightened him. Joseph threw the mirror and then fell to the floor as if the loss of the reflection meant the loss of his own physical form—an instance of Meltzer's "breakdown of the surfaces" discussed above. From the floor, Joseph stared into the open cupboard beneath the sink, an empty space he had referred to, earlier in the session, as the fridge. It is striking that, following his collapse, Joseph left the relationship with his therapist and fixed his eyes onto the empty cupboard. This space, which to Joseph appeared empty and cold (he seemed, at this point in his development, to have little expectation that spaces can have potential) represented his lack of inner space in which, according to Meltzer (1975b), "experimental thought can take place" (p. 225).

One might say that Joseph loses his more object-related internal capacity at the point when he seeks the stability of the empty "fridge" cupboard, apparently in response to his misperception and terror at his own reflection. Joseph fixes upon this empty shell almost as if he fears he would lose his own fragile coherence without it. Winnicott (1952) describes the response to anxiety caused by insecurity unmitigated by a good-enough environment, as a "lack of relationship of psyche to soma, becoming a sense of depersonalization" (p. 99). Developmentally, then, the implication of being overwhelmed by this level of anxiety is that one loses, or never perhaps even gains, a core sense of self and a reliable sense of one's own coherence in the face of a relationship to the external world and its spaces.

In the second and third sessions, Joseph again collapsed to the floor on crossing the threshold of the room and proceeded to bang his head. These early sessions appeared indicative of the way his experience of being dropped had permeated his experience in the here and now of his relationship to, and coordination in, space. Moving from one place to another appeared impossible without giant leaps, jumping, or being held, without which Joseph would otherwise collapse. The thresholds that separated inside and out, self and other, room and corridor, were junctions that caused Joseph distress and confusion.

Boundaries: holding and rhythm

In the fourth session, Joseph was carried to the room by his foster carer, who then stayed for a couple of minutes to help to settle him. On her departure, Joseph sat with his back to the door and rocked with a blank and vacant expression. This was a development from the first three sessions as he was clearly using the rocking to comfort himself in the face of the separation that, for him, felt like a catastrophe (Tustin, 1981).

> During this moment at the door, I held Joseph's head and spoke to him echoing the rhythm of his rocking. As Joseph calmed down, he looked around the room—for the first time—and I identified that he was showing interest in the inside of the room. At this point, he placed his fingers inside his mouth. Both physical holding during the transition and rhythmical attunement during the emotional transition from distress to calm provided the conditions for Joseph to look into the physical space of the room and immediately equate this interior with the inside of his own mouth. He was, at this moment, held together by the relationship between inside and outside.

This material shows marked developments in Joseph's capacity to make the transition into the consulting room. Joseph sought the support of his foster carer before even attempting to walk along the corridor. He then collapsed when left by his foster carer at the threshold of the consulting room, and following this he was held and rhythmically spoken to about his experience and fear of being dropped. The physical holding in addition to the rhythm of vocalization brought about a moment of calm, and Joseph then looked *into* the room for the first time. Looking into the room implies an evolved capacity for noticing, as distinct from the first session in which Joseph appeared to move from one activity to the next without leaving much space for noticing. There is little reference to the therapist in the first session, whereas the additional support sought out for the transition from his foster carer and then experienced in relation to his therapist appears to create a bit more space for Joseph to take in the environment. This seems to be an example of what Rey (1979) described as the experience of "marsupial space". The shift between collapsing to looking into the room seems to be facilitated by the experience of being held rhythmically. This is very different from Joseph's experience of the "fridge" which followed the perception of a frightening occupant in the mirror.

This experience in infancy is explored by Sorensen in "Observations of Transition Facilitating Behaviour" (2000). Through her observations of nursing care provided to premature infants on a Neonatal Intensive Care Unit (NICU), Sorensen identified that the function of such behaviour is to "create a bridge from one state to another or one experience to another" (p. 49). In this sense, the discontinuity expressed by Joseph's collapse is subsequently bridged by the support offered by me as I physically held him and talked to him. His need for a concrete experience of holding was significant and reflected the infantile level of his anxiety, what Winnicott (1960) describes as the level of "absolute dependency" (p. 113). The rhythmical quality of my vocalizations are in this respect more important than the content and are reminiscent of Tustin's "rhythm of safety" (1986a) and what Canham (1999) identifies as often lacking in fostered and adopted children. Canham noted:

> Many of these children come from backgrounds where their lives have not been characterised by rhythm, but rather by its opposite. Many children who end up being taken into care have been neglected for very long periods of time—left unfed, unwashed and forgotten. [1999/2012, p. 62]

With the development of more language and our increasingly communicative relationship, Joseph began to communicate verbally and to use the toys to show and express his experience. In his twentieth session, he communicated his experience of not finding a place in the world, and his consequent falling out, through play and words. The sequence began when he was filling a cup with crayons but found that one of them would not fit in the cup with the others:

> Joseph persevered and made several attempts at putting the last crayon inside. He got down off his chair and brought the crayon to me and said, "Do it." I looked at the crayons in the cup and said, "There's not enough space for all those crayons in there." Joseph was frustrated and huffed and puffed. He asked again, "Do it," before taking them away and trying to fit them himself. I said, "One of them doesn't fit, oh dear." Joseph then became extremely animated and took the crayon in his hand and held the crayon above his head before then bringing it down to the ground and saying, "Fall down." I said, "Joseph is worried that the crayon that doesn't fit will just fall down." Joseph agreed and went to the sink and put it inside the sink. I said, "Joseph needs to find somewhere else to keep the crayon safe." I then said, "Joseph needs to know that there is enough space for him here with Ms A so that he doesn't fall down." Joseph walked back over to the table and then crouched down towards the floor and looked up at the ceiling. He had removed the crayon from the sink and had it in his hand and now tapped it on the floor. I said, "It feels dropped when it doesn't have a place." Joseph looked up at the ceiling and then down to the floor and I said, "How does it all fit together? There's up there and down there and all this in the middle." Joseph looked interested and then looked over to the window and said, "Window." Joseph then stood and went to the window. I said, "And there's inside the window and outside the window." Joseph climbed up on the chair and I went to hold the back of the chair to stop it falling over, and Joseph noticed and said, "Help me." Joseph climbed up onto the table next to the window.

Joseph's awareness of spatial dimensions and the place objects have within space was increasing, and he was exploring how objects fit inside other objects and how stability can be negotiated. The dialogue between Joseph and me was closely woven and reciprocal, allowing the emotional experience to be somewhat contained and enabling him to communicate the experience rather than act it out physically and emotionally as he does in the earlier examples. The reference to the window suggests something important about the kinds of boundaries he is beginning to internalize. The "helping" therapist also seems to offer a window through her benign observation and attention, offering him a way in, without feeling he needs to bang through, to find a secure place.

As the therapy progressed, Joseph's experience of boundaries seemed to relate more to the environment created by our relationship than the experience of boundaries as obstacles in the physical world. In the twenty-fifth session, Joseph responded negatively to the time boundary that I mentioned five minutes before the end of the session. Having placed his shoes on my lap, he then threw them across the room when I identified the time boundary. He proceeded to the door and, rather than bang his head against the door, as he used to previously, Joseph called out "Open!" while pulling on the door handle. There is clearly quite a shift here. Here, Joseph uses language in place of action, expecting that our relationship is the environment through which negotiation of the boundary can take place.

Separation

With these new realizations came an increased awareness and exploration of the experience of separateness. In Session 26 Joseph explored what he described as the "snap snap scissors"; he drew a line down the centre of a piece of paper and proceeded to use the blades of the scissors to mark along the line, saying, "snap snap scissors," as he did so. I felt Joseph was seeking to identify how the scissors could be used effectively to define separateness.

Interestingly, in the next sequence Joseph used a black crayon to draw two separate circles:

> Joseph drew two circles side by side on a sheet of paper. I noted there were two shapes. Joseph pointed at each circle and said, "One–two." I agreed, saying "Yes there are two: one, two." Joseph repeated this, pointing towards the shapes. I then suggested, pointing between us, "Ms A–Joseph, one–two." Joseph agreed, "Yeah." He continued pointing, and I said, "Two hands: one–two", pointing to Joseph's hands. Joseph shouted, "Hands!" We repeated this with eyes, ears, etc.

This was the first time Joseph had drawn two separate objects, in contrast with a "cut" or "split" singular object. The developments in the material emerged alongside my interest in Joseph's preoccupations and, as he identified "one–two" in response to my enquiry about his drawing, we engaged in a game of identifying different pairs.

This developmental surge, however, becomes overwhelming for Joseph:

> After a short period, he looked a little lost and stared at me in a way that made me feel quite overwhelmed. I was anxious about what might happen between us. He leaned back in his chair and looked up at the ceiling. He then paused silently and looked at me out of the corner of his eye.

With the identification of two-ness and separate but together pairings, Joseph seemed to be thrown back into a more cut-off, but suspicious, state of mind. His challenging look towards me suggests an air of disbelief. When taken all together, the sequences that emerge in this session show a striking development in Joseph's capacity both to use the relationship with me to express and explore his preoccupations and developmental dilemmas as well as to communicate his anxieties about such dilemmas. In this session, Joseph is showing how complex separation feels for him. He questions whether separation causes harm, to himself and to others. He is trying to understand the nature of cutting and separating and the experience of two-ness, which bring him into contact with historic anxieties associated with not having a place, falling out, and being left as well as the presence of a more powerful party whom he fears and from whom he retreats. As Joseph developed a greater sense of cohesion, and could therefore be more in touch with his experience as an individual, his relationship to separation changed. Later sessions suggested that Joseph's anxiety about separation was more rooted in feelings of exclusion, and there was greater working through of oedipal material.

Final remarks

With these brief vignettes of the first few weeks of Joseph's treatment, I hope I have illustrated how psychoanalytic work with very young children can attend to difficulties in spatial organization and orientation and further contribute to stability and security in object relations and identity. My sense is that, similar to what Meltzer described in terms of the developmental process of spatial organization, the experience of "being at home" in both an internal sense as well as an external one is developmentally driven.

Psychoanalytic psychotherapist June Campbell (2006) highlighted these issues in relation to the adult homeless population in Edinburgh.

In an audit conducted by the psychotherapy department at the Royal Edinburgh Hospital, 66.7% of homeless people were shown to have personality disorders, the highest prevalence of which were in the categories of borderline and impulsive:

> Unsurprisingly, the sample also showed high levels of physical and sexual abuse, significant loss or absence of fathers, recurring contact with the police and extensive psychiatric histories, amongst other significant data. [Campbell, 2006, p. 158]

Following this audit, a psychotherapy pilot was developed to offer support to both the homeless people and the workers, who were identified as having a high risk of burnout and high levels of staff turnover. The main cause for concern was the inability of homeless people to make good use of the provision of accommodation. Using a psychoanalytically informed theoretical model, largely drawn from Rey (1994) and Winnicott (1951), Campbell describes how the homeless people were unable to maintain socially expected relationships to their dwellings. Following the work that she undertook with the population and their workers, she was able to highlight that it was the internal relationship that the homeless people had to their sense of place that fundamentally impacted on their capacity to make use of a new home. I think this is a striking piece of research in relation to the case that I have presented here, as Campbell's formulation both resonates with and adds substance to the kind of formulation one might draw from Joseph's response to therapeutic space. It substantiates his need to have a place in someone's mind as opposed to being given a home.

Feeling one has been placed outside the family unit, or that one has been somehow cast adrift, seems to lead to confusion about both the nature and the function of the boundaries and thresholds between inside and outside, as well as the question of how, and if, one is able to make a relational and, therefore, secure transition between the two (Houzel, 1996). It also calls into question the nature of the objects whose presence and absence further disturb the development of security and powerfully influence what then is imagined as necessary to establish one's rightful place. These are as much about the development of internal reality as they are about the nature and importance of external reality. In Joseph's case, the use of primitive defences to manage overwhelming anxiety in the face of his experience of space demanded a developmental approach to psychotherapeutic work. When he first attended his therapy, he depended upon a variety of "second-skin" functioning physical defences (Bick, 1968), including jumping, banging, and covering his head to manage his anxiety. This anxiety broke through at times, and it was clear then that the collapse was both externally and internally experienced. Joseph was seen to lose the connection to his own mind and its functioning at times. The kinds of defences he needed to employ to keep such fragmentation at bay were restrictive and inflexible. The use of rhythmical, physical holding appeared to bring about a softening of these defences at the beginning of psychotherapy, which equally demonstrated the infantile level of Joseph's developmental needs. As Sorensen (2000) stated, the vulnerable infant needs the experience of "holding" that can bridge the otherwise overwhelming nature of spatial and transitional experience.

Note

This chapter is based on a version previously published in the *Journal of Child Psychotherapy, Vol. 42* (No. 1, 2016), pp. 18–29.

CHAPTER SIX

The isolated adolescent

Carlos Tabbia

At all ages, involuntary and persistent isolation is a matter for concern. At the end of infancy, it may be worrying, but the isolation that appears in adolescence is frequently a symptom of emotional disturbance and can feel deeply alarming for the family. This conflicting developmental period can be better understood psychoanalytically but remains a common topic in the media, which often focus particularly on the influence of electronic games in causing adolescent isolation.

After infancy and latency, puberty emerges with a vigour that can surprise the young person, the family, and his or her friends. Particularly unsettling is the imbalance created by the unintegrated movement of the personality, prone to splitting while sustained by obsessional defences. Puberty also seems to destabilize the physical "centre of gravity". This is reminiscent of the physical experience that takes place with ice skaters. The Olympic ice skater Yulia Lipnitskaia won a gold medal when she was 15 years old, at the Olympic Games in Sochi, Russia, in 2014. One year later, she had to modify her skating technique because her bodily changes had shifted the centre of gravity she had established over many years of training. While her coaches refer to her physical loss of equilibrium, we might also imagine a loss of emotional balance in the face of the changing states of internal objects.

The centre of gravity of the personality starts and develops in the highly complex relation between the baby and its mother; with the nipple in its mouth, the baby gazes into its mother's responsive eyes (Meltzer, 1989, p. 133) while its hearing is alert to the mother's voice and words. The baby introjects this experience of the early relationship, gradually internalizing a good object which becomes a cornerstone of the budding personality. Hence the baby's dependence on such an internal object forms the core of its emotional stability. Destabilizing factors, such as the increment of intrusive identification, interfere with the potential to promote further introjective identification with live whole objects.

Shift from latency to adolescence

The pathogenic consequences for a child who reaches the end of infancy with an unstable centre in his or her personality, while going through pathological splittings, are described by Meltzer (1999) in "Clinical Dialogues with DM: Graciela":

> In general we think that puberty takes place as a result of physiological and hormonal changes, but we have found evidence that in anorexia the hormonal system is strongly linked to states of mind and is capable of setting back the physiological developments of puberty: children remain in latency for years and, among other things, do not have menstrual periods and do not develop breasts and pubic hair.
>
> It is also possible to encounter premature puberty when these children were the target of sexual stimulation and abuse, which prematurely awakened their sexuality and interfered with the onset of latency. In this case we may come across early menstruation at 9 or 10 years of age, precocious development of the breasts, and becoming young women at the age of 12. [p. 145]

The adolescent and the group: the nature of isolation

Puberty and adolescence are states of mind. In addition to having a physiological component, the pubertal state of mind is reached when the obsessionality of latency is relinquished. As a result, there will be a dispersal—a splitting of the self—that requires a group structure to hold together the parts of the self to prevent its fragmentation. Progression towards normal adolescence in the face of this fragmentation will necessarily be conducted under the influence of the core of the personality that was operative in earlier life. At this point, the child may throw him/herself into the experience of puberty or take refuge in, for instance, isolation.

The experience of puberty often involves multiple dissociations, which are projected into a group. Each group member becomes a provisional container for an aspect of the personality. Fluctuations within the group are common, and it can often feel like an anguished strategy to eliminate psychic pain. While some adolescents can tolerate oscillations, others become terrorized and prefer to withdraw from the group, remaining on its periphery. The group needs constantly to expel pain, and it does this by projection into the weaker members, friends, and family.

It is important to recognize that the paranoid anxiety triggered by disintegration in the genital period luckily finds some containment in the paranoid group, leading Meltzer to believe that puberty was the "maddest" period in human development. It would seem paradoxical that the road to health should include the experience of a paranoid group, but Meltzer thought it was essential for development to have the experience of "belonging" to a group and that shortcuts were not the best way to prepare for the adult world. Shortcuts are alternative defences, often stimulated by the social intolerance of juvenile conflicts.

Some shortcuts can result in young people remaining as latency members of the family group or—in identification with the parental model—creating an idealized and infantile couple. Alternatively, they might flee from adolescent turbulence by becoming hard-working students, only to become brilliant but emotionally fragile executives or, lastly, joining the worrisome community of those who choose isolation.

In pubertal same-sex groups, individuality is a grave threat to the group mentality and is not tolerated. The same hostility towards powerful people can be found in institutional groups, where expression of individuality, leadership, or creativity is not tolerated. Anyone entering the group with a weak "centre of gravity" will have to either submit to the group tyranny or emotionally isolate him/herself and remain on the periphery.

Within these groups there are roles and functions. Focusing on the pubertal (Meltzer, 1967, p. 67) and adolescent group, Rios (1985) has considered the significance of the leader, the best friend, and the marginal member.[1] A healthy adolescent can perform different functions and roles at different times, whereas a disturbed adolescent cannot. In order to gain access to the adolescent community, it is extremely important to have a "best friend". According to Mantykow de Sola (1991), the best friend's function is to promote sufficient tolerance to bear oedipal turbulence. It is a maturational link that takes place, first with the same sex and then with the opposite sex. The absence of a best friend may indicate a perpetuation of latency and difficulty in moving freely into puberty and adolescence. The best friend may function as a transitional object that allows entry into and exit from adolescence. Having a best friend indicates a capacity to give up isolation, and the adolescent without a best friend suffers terribly.

Within the group, the isolated young person can become a pariah or marginal. He or she will become a receptacle for the psychotic part of the group and will, in this way, contribute painfully to the creation of the gang. This is the price of belonging to a group into which he or she can project the healthier and potent parts of him/herself, in particular into the group leader.

When an individual becomes stuck on the margins, he or she cannot swap roles freely with other group members; the individual loses the benefit of the group experience and can no longer reduce his or her dissociations, omnipotence, and paranoid anxieties, nor distance him/herself from the lure of megalomania. We here have the ingredients of a more disturbed psychopathology. Isolation becomes a dangerous and painful refuge where the benefits to be gained from the adolescent community become unreachable.

What prevents this young person from being part of a group and from being able to socialize his conflicts, as Meltzer (1973a) framed it? One adolescent, 16-year-old Esteban, said, "If I don't hang out with drug addicts and drop-outs, I would have no company and would be all alone". Terror of loneliness may prompt the adolescent to "create" an unconditional friend, as in the case of Hector (discussed below), who adopted a dog, whom he named Samson. Hector turned to Samson for companionship and comfort when he became trapped in a narcissistic gang with his parents. Hector was like a God and, in his splendid isolation, turned to Samson for fidelity and comfort.

From what does the adolescent isolate him/herself? Isolation makes the "socialization of conflicts" impossible. As isolation expresses itself in many ways and responds to different states of mind, it may be useful to make some differentiations, without aiming to cover the whole psychopathological range of isolated adolescents.

First, we must differentiate two types of isolation from the vertex of loss and mourning; an adolescent may suffer from the collapse of his or her same sex group, becoming unable to benefit from its group dynamics; he or she may develop a depressive illness when his or her best friend becomes part of a couple and may end up isolating him/herself.

Then there are adolescents who, after the loss of infantile idealizations, withdraw into a narcissistic organization that may lead to megalomania. These adolescents are unable to recognize their dependence upon parental objects and may believe that they have conceived themselves and that they have a mission in life. The manic basis of their personality may express itself in the conviction that they have to educate their parents to become better parents and to change the state and its institutions. Such arrogance does not disappear when feeling lonely and nor does the sense of isolation (Meltzer, 1971),[2] but increases with their resentment. This becomes worse when delusional jealousy leads to the kind of extreme vandalism involving the murder of children or youngsters.

Beyond the paranoid-depressive and the megalomaniac isolated adolescents, there are other manifestations that deserve scrutiny because of their frequency in psychoanalytic sessions. These are friendless young people who do not belong to a group and who usually lock themselves in at home. They leave home only to go to school but have no relationships with other students, making contact only in the atmosphere of social media where there is no physical contact. I believe that this could be due to the massive use of narcissistic identifications and the fear of having to forego their narcissistic defences through the loss of their obsessional control. This loss of control at the time when they are immersing themselves in an adolescent community creates the conviction that they will not be able to regroup and reorganize themselves. The ambition to join the group can create the secret urge to run it and become the leader. Alternatively, they might join the group but remain slightly apart, like a fly on the wall, spying and judging the other group members. None of these strategies help such adolescents to participate in the group experience. Indeed, this false link enables them to feel grandiose and even to occupy a prestigious place, despite not feeling included, as the group recognizes their partial contact and ends up distrusting them.

This dynamic can alter when the group becomes more depressive and less paranoid-schizoid, and at that point the isolated adolescent may be able to obtain more understanding and containment for his or her suffering.

The ubiquity of projective identification

I would now like to focus on three omnipotent phantasies that impede joining the adolescent community and experiencing its transforming influence.

First, I want to refer to those who live in a retracted state, followed by those who live in intrusive identification, and, finally, those who become sucked into an object. According to Meltzer (1992b):

> At the beginning of psychoanalysis there was a lot of talk about returning to the womb. But all this was discarded when the concept of projective identification was formulated. I do think there is a difference. There are the phantasies that exist before birth and the intrusive phantasies related to states of projective identification. They have a different meaning and also different consequences. In effect we can identify the returning to the womb through which patients retreat inside, isolate themselves and remain in a cocoon. This is where we see states that appear frozen, some with narcolepsia in which the patient sleeps a lot, some in catatonic states and they all have a connection with the phantasy of going back in time, to that marvellous situation of being inside the mother before the father turns up.

The conflict created by the appearance of the father as well as other unavoidable frustrations may lead to the joke: "What do we come to the world for? To suffer? In that case we go back!"

Even when the idealization of intrauterine life is debatable, we have to take on board the belief that in the womb, in the face of unpleasant experiences, "the foetus gets rid of [these experiences] as soon as it can" (Bion, 1997, p. 50). This phantasy of paradise is always possible when facing a conflict and finds expression in a dialogue between Somite Thirty and Term, in the third volume of Bion's *A Memoir of the Future*:

> SOMITE THIRTY: Get back into the Amniotic Fluid.
>
> TERM: Get out into the sun! Glory! The fields are bathed in light. Moonlight! Don't lie snoozing in bed.

> SOMITE THIRTY: Keep warm in bed. Your King and Country want you—you stay in bed. [1991, p. 443]

This staying in bed, locked in a world without stimulation, is the consequence of relinquishing the external world, because it feels too dangerous and frustrating. Meltzer suggests that possessive jealousy is a motivation for projective identification, observing how it is seen "in the autistic children and in children whose drive to maturity is very low, so that they wish either to remain infantile or to die. This means in their unconscious to return-to-sleep-inside-mother" (1967, p. 15). This omnipotent phantasy is at the core of states of retraction and somnolence.

We can differentiate between a wish to sleep inside the mother and a state in which some "parts may be left behind in the womb, producing states of withdrawal quite different in phenomena from those of projective identification" (1992a, p. 127). I think that when there is a predominance of intrusiveness—as in the head/breast compartment of the internal mother—we find states of Oblomovian lassitude, where the subject has no desire to leave the object because he enjoys indolence. In the case of isolation due to unborn parts of the personality, however, the baby shows an absence of stimulation or incentive to come out into the world and appears drowsy. According to Meltzer, some parts have not been born due to a failure in the aesthetic conflict between baby and mother. He relates this to the possibility that puerperal depression may be more common than is reported; if a baby does not find a passionate containing object, it is likely that it will fail to be born complete.

Whether it is returning to the womb or not wanting to abandon it, there is a universal phantasy that there is no experience of need in the womb because a constant provision makes the notion of lack or desire impossible. Nevertheless it is possible:

> to experience unpleasantness, sometimes violence linked to sudden alterations of the biochemistry of the environment as it is also possible to feel comfortable in a stable environment protected from external interference. These differences in intrauterine life will surely have an influence on growth, strength and vitality, on the capacity to take an interest in the objects that are present in the womb and in the last instance on the way in which he can be prepared for the delivery and life. [Caccia, 2007, p. 60]

The phantasy of lost paradise, together with the fear of conflicts in the external world, can attract and sustain mental states characterized by isolation and somnolence. This fear can be observed in adolescents who spend most of their day locked in their room, only emerging in an explosive way, as if in a panic, charging against everything that stands in their way.

Gerard

Sixteen-year-old Gerard had been a "good boy", adapting well to school and belonging to a latency group. Once he reached puberty, he isolated himself after getting into trouble with the police: he had been caught stealing from supermarkets and touching-up girls while stealing their mobile telephones. For Gerard, the external world was full of dangers, and he experienced his sessions as approaching the horizon and being about to fall into hell. His parents were confused professionals with a problematic relationship and were very annoyed with their frustrating adolescent. It seemed that his entry into adolescence was not supported by objects capable of containing him; his parents found it unbearable to see him too isolated to sustain a therapeutic process, and they decided to interrupt his therapy and give him medication. The "case or sheath as an exo-skeleton" (Bion, 1991, p. 431) that Gerard chose for himself was a caricature of a Wild West bandit: his thin arms always looked ready to draw his pistols. He was so terrorized that he could find refuge only within the four walls of his room.

Certain ways of locking oneself in a room can be as serious as those found in the psychotic states linked to addictions and video games (Rosenfeld, 2001). Some isolated adolescents with a borderline psychotic psychopathology manage to go through life appearing to be well-adjusted, enjoying successful academic or sporting lives but enduring great difficulties in establishing intimate relationships. Their painful isolation surprises those who know them. Gerard was an educated, studious, and well-adjusted child, and we can assume that he left latency in a pseudo-mature state; while his brothers played football, he studied philosophy and discussed politics. This enabled him to avoid juvenile emotional turbulence and allowed him to look at the world with arrogance and judge his friends, relatives, and neighbours. In some sense, this arrogance is characteristic of adolescents, because it is the consequence of confusional states. In the same way, however, just as all adolescents go through confusional states, this can become chronic when one tries to escape the limitations of the self and an attempt is made to "seize an object's identity by intrusion into it" (Meltzer, 1973a, p. 53).

To live in intrusive identification, the part that lives in an internal compartment remains alienated from the external world. Meltzer doubted if it was useful to speak "in terms of external world or internal world, because the patient who lives in projective identification loses a sense of differentiation between inside or outside", as he is dealing with compartments rather than inside and outside (Meltzer, 2002, p. 18). These compartments form the barrier that prevents a true emotional contact with the world.

Elitism and arrogance that stem from intrusive identification with qualities of the object stimulate in these adolescents feelings of superiority and self-sufficiency, but these do not anaesthetize completely the state of isolation that overwhelms and persecutes them. Nor does it mitigate feelings of fraudulence, and they feel persecuted by the fear of being found out and denigrated. They do not arouse interest in their colleagues, their telephone seldom rings, and their diary is only filled if they take the initiative. They are efficient and appreciated as cooperative with adults, but their private life is confined to masturbation, pornography, and despair. In relation to people of their own age or younger, they can adopt a protective attitude that can be understood as a desire to look after healthy aspects of themselves projected into them, while at the same time they can jealously control the younger ones to abuse and exploit them.

Alexander

Another young man, Alexander, has been living an isolated life for many years. At first, he was the idealized object of his parents' hopes, but this changed when his brothers were born. Each new baby became their idealized love object while, at the same time, they kept bundling the older siblings together as if to confirm the infantile phantasy that, "Adults are fascinated when they have babies, but later they drop them, and it all boils down to the fact that what they really like is making babies, simply the product" (Meltzer, 2002, p. 30). Jealousy and resentment stimulated a wish in Alexander not to become excluded, and he split his world in such a way that, in relation to his mother, he developed a narcissistic identification and became her counsellor and support. With his father, on the other hand, he became a dutiful son, and, while he tolerated his father's contempt by placating his brutality, he managed to stay near him and become the manager of the family business, without feeling that he had earned it because of his intellect or his managerial skills. He was unable to have a relationship with his sisters and had a sadomasochistic relation with his older brother. His life took place in the greatest solitude.

During adolescence he tried to establish friendly relations, but these, somehow, wore off. Internet pornography became his refuge from isolation in which women would get undressed and praise his penis. But, terrified by the prospect of a physical encounter, he never went beyond the internet. Only intrusive identification allowed him to overcome his isolation, but these invaded objects, far from improving his feelings of safety, undermined his personality and made him increasingly distrustful and fearful of meeting other people. Through his therapy, he has been able, partially, to restore his internal objects, in which he has come to trust. This has allowed him to give up his masturbatory activity and his use of marijuana, diminish his total isolation, and become increasingly dedicated to other children. He has, laboriously, managed to create a group of friends from whom he still feels the pain of being excluded, from time to time. All this does not mean that he has become able to tolerate emotional pain; when this increases, he flees, preferring to placate his persecuting paternal object rather than rebelling: being left alone is more persecuting than being hurt or going out into the external world. As long as the pleasure from the different compartments of the internal mother protect and gratify him, he will continue to avoid the external world in which his parental objects are not very interested in discovering their son's individuality.

In the same way that Alexander forced his way into his objects through masturbatory intrusiveness and, in doing so, acquired a pseudo-identity, there are situations in which adolescents become vulnerable to the intrusiveness of other people. This is the equivalent of being swallowed up by an "aspired projective identification", as occurs with the psychopathology of the *folie à deux*, where mixed projective identifications make it difficult to create an emotional link with one member of the collusive couple.[3] For the adolescent girl, this might entail an inseparable, twin-like alliance with her mother, almost sharing an identity. This might revolve around their beauty, expressed by their referring to themselves in terms of "we, we, we" (Meltzer & Harris, 1998). These perverse[4] alliances can have different objectives, such as exploiting others with the bait of their beauty or intelligence or delinquent plotting. In these cases, the family group has become the adolescent gang, for whom transgression offers shared excitement. It becomes very difficult for an adolescent immersed in this delinquent culture to abandon the group and join the real adolescent community;

the adolescent may feel that he or she is betraying his or her family by rejecting the erotization of orgiastic family life.

Hector

This is what Hector believed when he struggled to prevent his bipolar mother walking around the house wearing only her knickers and feeling free to touch his body, something that his father did nothing to prevent. He was frequently sandwiched naked between his promiscuous parents—three polymorphous "adolescents"—in a state of shared excitement. This did not prevent Hector from feeling isolated; with his excessive greed and jealousy, he struggled to make friends. Hector's imprisonment in his family gang only offered temporary relief that could not protect him from urgently seeking any object that would fill the vacuum. It seemed as if Hector would not have to worry about his future because he would inherit the small business, as well as the various family properties. The family pact was "us against the world", but this did not soothe his sense of isolation and helplessness. His compulsive eating, drinking, promiscuity, and cocaine abuse was not enough to fill his emptiness. For Hector, other children were not so much rivals but objects for consumption. As the geographical confusions and the symbiosis in the family were dissolved, his anxiety increased, and he expressed a great desire to possess the analyst as a transference object. He said in a session: "I get annoyed about having to pay €2 for parking even when I have a nice car, I get annoyed about paying €2.5 for a beer in a nice place. I hate mankind, it is desperate. I would like to eat you up whole so that you become only mine and nobody else's."

Once he recovered from his anaesthetized state, born out of the confusion with his family gang, his needs increased as well as his understanding of his mental states, and he could recognize his wish that everything should be his for free. There was no hunger attached to the erotized family sandwich, but the moment he separated and had to pay for himself, he became furious. Not so long ago, Hector dreamed that he *was robbing a bank. When he reached the safe, he noticed it was open and that other thieves were already present. At this point, he lost interest and left because he wanted the loot just for himself, he wanted to monopolize the object*. After a lot of work, Hector is recognizing that he cannot relate or love in that state of mind. "I feel as if I am in a big continent, in the shape of a bowl or a cone, and that everything that falls into it is for me, but I cannot feel love, I feel I have no love for others, or for you."

Hector is slowly leaving behind the borderline/psychotic gang that isolated him and made him feel that his only friend was his dog, Samson. He is also leaving behind the sad feelings that made him chase people, pay for meals, or offer them lifts, only to receive in exchange their contemptuous and demolishing comments, like being told that he is always running after people.

Conclusion

Adolescence is a time when maturational processes are synthesized and when the gates open towards adult life. If the adolescent arrives at this point with a faulty centre of gravity, the passage towards adulthood will require a restructuring that is likely to have an uncertain outcome.

I believe that many of the disturbances suffered by isolated adolescents fall into the category of borderline psychotic states that are always linked to geographical confusions. In my opinion, overcoming these states of isolation requires going through stages that have been avoided out of fear of emotional turbulence. The itinerary that leads to maturity was clearly described by Meltzer when he wrote:

> the resolution of this configuration of object relations stands as the border between mental illness (psychosis) and mental health, just as the resolution of the obstacles to the dependent introjective relation to the breast traverses the border between mental instability and mental stability, and as the passing of the oedipus complex leads from immaturity to maturity. [1967, p. 22]

In order for the isolated adolescent to resolve conflicts at every stage, he or she must rely on the containing capacity of the analyst, because "if an analyst can bear to persevere when geographical confusions are in the forefront of the transference he will certainly be rewarded with progress" (p. 22).

Notes

1. "Introjections that are linked to the figure of an unconditional friend are of great importance as the basis that is used for the choice of a loved object, and we could almost say that it is the most important identificatory substratum" (Rios, 1985, p. 508).
2. "When a particular infantile part, or organization of them, seizes upon consciousness and dominates a person's behaviour, temporarily, say, the sense-of-identity is bound to be oppressed by the loneliness, however defiant, of the child-in-the-adult-world" (Meltzer, 1971, p. 202).

3. Meltzer (1967) explains how difficult it is to establish the transference situation when the mother involves the child in her anxieties: "I have had [the] experience where it was not the mother who was 'bringing' but was the mother who was involved in the '*folie*' which prevented the 'gathering' from sufficiently taking shape to set the process of analysis in motion" (p. 3).

4. These alliances can be intergenerational or intragenerational, as between children and parents or between siblings: see Meltzer & Harris (1998b).

CHAPTER SEVEN

Supervision as a space for the co-creation of imaginative conjectures

Clara Nemas

"So these are my ideas on supervision. You can see [it] is not like a master class in music. It is more of a participation—more like playing in the orchestra; just contributing . . ."

Donald Meltzer, "On the Nature of Supervision" (in Oelsner & Oelsner, 2005)

Contact with the work and the person of Donald Meltzer has produced in all who met him not only a strong conviction in the value of the psychoanalytic method and a most vivid approach to our clinical work with children, adolescents, and adults, but also changes to our view of the world, of life, and of the human being. All this made of each contact with Meltzer an emotional learning experience: a K-link, to use Bion's term. But it was in his supervisions—"eye openers", as Francis Tustin once called them—that one could feel the passion, the capacity for observation, and the "real proof of his experience" and creativity full at work. I must say that none of this would have been possible without the generosity of Benito López, our teacher for so many years, who first introduced us, in Buenos Aires, to the work of Meltzer and, later, to his dear friend, the man himself in person.

Meltzer was preoccupied with the development and transmission of psychoanalysis. He proposed the need for more experienced analysts to "pause, and teach, and help the others to catch up" (Meltzer, 1986b, p. 203), in order to contribute to developing the next generation and to help them to realize their nascent creativity. He also advised young colleagues to listen to each other, however, to develop their own ideas and not depend only on the "knowledge" of the older generation.

At other times, he stressed the need to develop tools in order to discover the model of the mind the individual analyst is in fact using, in the hope that through such discovery the analyst will be enabled to extend and develop his or her own model further. The discovery of new phenomena is completely dependent on the explicit and conscious use of a model; without that, the emergence of new phenomena, not explicable by previous models, cannot be recognized. For this reason he invited analysts to examine their personal definition of psychoanalysis. Given an agreement over the method—the close examination and the description of the transference by means of an internal examination of the countertransference—each analyst should scrutinize the type of psychoanalytic process he or she is working with. But how experienced should we be in order to be able to follow this proposal? At what stage of our development do we have a stable enough conception of the process we engender?

In our becoming psychoanalysts, a terminable/interminable process, we travel a complex territory, following what appear to be diverging roads: the development of a "mind of one's own" together with the need to acknowledge our dependence on the internal objects as parental figures that provide new ideas which the self, eventually, will be able to receive.

At this point, we may recall Freud's quotation from Goethe's *Faust*: "What thou hast inherited from thy fathers, acquire it to make it thine" (1940a [1938], p. 207) How can we understand this message more than 50 years on? I think that Freud urges us to develop his teachings in the pursuit of what we are focusing on here: a mind of one's own. Certainly, however, this remains a paradox: the fact that the best part of our mind evolves in its relation to its internal objects until it ripens to *inspired independence* under the sway of admiration for the qualities that we appreciate (and this is important) *according to our own potentialities.*

To supervise and also to participate in supervisions with Meltzer was a powerful emotional experience. I remember a senior child analyst, moved by Meltzer's comments on the presentation of a child who had been diagnosed as autistic, told him after the supervision: "You are a poet analyst." I think that this was a good description of his communications. He thought that what we have to do is make the most of the language that is available and to be as poetic and precise as we can.

At this point, I would like to share with you something he said back in 1989, which has remained quite present and alive in my mind since then. I think it relates not only to the way Meltzer conceived the analytic situation, but also to the way he transmitted his clinical experience. I recall it more or less as follows: "At this time in my work, I am more concerned with nurturing and assisting the buds of the mind that are capable of thinking than with clearing out the weeds; that is, more interested in what the mind does well than in what it does badly or, in other words, less inclined to place the accent on the functioning of the paranoid-schizoid position than on the depressive." In my work, I gradually began to apprehend the meaning of this thought, although, as often happens with learning, this started in a way that was somewhat painful for me.

During Meltzer's second visit to the Asociación Psicoanalítica de Buenos Aires, I presented the clinical material of a very disturbed 15-year-old girl who presented with a psychotic breakdown with an erotomanic delusion. Meltzer suggested that she had felt—and probably had been—seduced into talking about her delusion. He felt that the analytic work should focus upon helping her to modify the centre of her preoccupations and to consider the contents of her delusion as "flotsam from the shipwreck", to be allowed to float. He even proposed that I tell her to leave the delusion until later, when she would be able to think and speak about it. My interpretations had been aimed at the patient's fears of feeling overwhelmed by ideas that could not be contained in her mind (on one occasion, she had lost control of her sphincter while waiting for me to open the door of the consulting room). Meltzer proposed that I help her to develop a container for the most disturbed aspects of herself and to discriminate the symbolic thoughts from the *flotsam from the shipwreck*—in this case, the contents of her erotomanic delusion.

"Nurturing and assisting the buds of the mind that are capable of thinking." This is the way Meltzer understood psychoanalysis, and I think that this extends to the understanding of supervision as a facilitation of learning, acknowledging the contribution of both members of the couple to the analytic work.

This conception of analysis seems to consider the reverie function as a factor of what we call countertransference. Reverie function refers, as an extension of the maternal reverie described by Bion, to the capacity of the analyst to be open to all the projections of the patient, whether they are felt to be good or bad, being aware of the masochistic aspect that may be present in this receptivity. Each one of us knows or at least tries to deal with our limits to this receptivity, with our blind spots, and also what I once called our hallucinated spots: our own projections, what we need to find in our patients. Our profession has been described as solitary, which is true up to a point; supervision responds to the need to be contained, to be followed in our oscillations, and to feel our raw material transformed by our contact with other colleagues. Reverie function has been extended to include analytic work with patients. The analyst and supervisor perform alpha-function and what Meltzer has called counter-dreaming. The aesthetic dimension of the mind, proposed by Bion and developed by Meltzer, is expressed in the attitudes, the styles, the language, and also the music of the interpretation, which makes of the session something so ineffable.

The supervisory situation deals with experiences that are intimately provoking emotionally, as does analysis itself, and we need to have this in mind. As supervisors, however, we do not carry the weight of the anxieties that are communicated directly to the analyst. As Meltzer has humorously described it: "You get a second integral or derivative of the clinical situation" (in Oelsner & Oelsner, 2005, p. 455). It has been argued that the core function of psychoanalytic supervision is to help contain the emotional turbulence and the unconscious anxieties arising and evolving in the two interacting domains of the analytic and the supervisory sessions. According to Meltzer, in his re-creating of Bion's concept, the model of container-contained places a new value on receptiveness and the holding of the dynamic situation of transference-countertransference in the mind. The container is formed by the fitting together of the analyst's attention and attitudes to the cooperation of the patient, lending it the degree of flexibility and resilience required from moment to moment.

We need words as tools for thinking, yet we also need imagery: the imagery of the senses that is formed before words as well as afterwards. Symbols are the container of emotional meaning: musicians also think, but not in words. The conjunction of these two areas in the supervision—symbol formation and imagery—is what I would like to explore here.[1]

Vignette 1

A young colleague brings to the supervision her difficulties with a patient who has a history of abandoning analytic treatments in the past. The patient received psychotherapy at the age of 4 years after her mother's death, but all she could recall was not liking the therapist. At the age of 17 years, she was referred to a group for eating disorders, but she stopped going because she found it too invasive and not containing. More recently, she started another treatment which soon ended when she felt insulted by the therapist; she did not feel understood, attributing this to the fact that she came from a small provincial town whereas the therapist came from *the big city*.

The supervisee is not Argentinian; she has recently come from another country and has a distinctive Central American accent. When the patient contacting the analyst by phone and heard her accent, she expressed doubt whether the analyst, being from another country, would be able to understand her. The analyst suggested they have an initial meeting and see how she felt, which the patient accepted.

In the first interview, the patient was very hostile. She would not allow the analyst to finish her phrases, interrupted her whenever she tried to say something, and, on the occasions when she did listen to her, denigrated her comments. Nevertheless—and not surprisingly—she agreed to start therapy. When the analyst tried to describe the hostile atmosphere present in the sessions, the patient would reply, "I don't know what are you talking about! This does not happen to me! This is your problem!"

In supervision, the analyst commented: "In my countertransference I felt uncomfortable with the way she was treating me; I tried to get close to her, but each time I felt that my interpretations were rebuffed and even attacked. I felt doomed to join the list of her failed therapists, and I realized that this had become like a challenge I had to overcome, which complicated my analytic attitude and neutrality." We were aware that, despite her good reputation, the analyst had struggled to get referrals; unfairly, people may have wondered whether she might one day have to interrupt treatment and return to her own country. This had caused her pain, as she was a committed and responsible analyst. As her supervisor, I felt that this situation was weighing heavily in the countertransference, creating feelings of annoyance and exhaustion while, at the same time, the analyst was becoming preoccupied with keeping the patient in treatment. On the patient's side, we knew that her mother had died when she was little, and the fear of being dependent and abandoned weighed heavily in the transference.

During supervision, an image of this patient emerged as a burnt person, for whom any close contact was threatening, painful, and feared. We started to play with this idea, and the therapist became aware of her own sensitivity about feeling foreign and the need to demonstrate herself to be an established professional: her own burnt skin. "This image of the burnt skin", says the analyst, "became a container for her reactions, and also mine, when I tried to approach her. I could receive her rejections without feeling attacked. My voice and the words I used sounded different, and the rhythm of the session became less hurried. We became less defensive on both sides."

We may ask ourselves what changed. Meltzer tells us that the relationship between analyst and patient is contained not just in the words, but in the music as well. For some reason, even if the image of burnt skin was not part of the patient's material, it served as a shorthand between supervisor and supervisee and worked as a leitmotiv in the sessions, a recurring musical phrase associated with this particular patient even if modified on subsequent appearances.

Vignette 2

Ana, an 11 year-old patient, has been in analysis for five years now. The treatment started at the time the parents were in the middle of a turbulent divorce. The school suggested the consultation. The patient was a first-class student who also excelled in sport and art, but her communication was impeded by her persistent thumb-sucking, which had already provoked a degree of malformation in her palate and teeth. From the beginning, her face showed no emotion and she wore a fixed smile. In her sessions, she built elaborate constructions and small-scale models that she kept tidily in her box, together with the strips of paper she had used to make them.

Years passed before Ana showed any emotion in the sessions; she could cry and express feelings of anger and frustration, but her thumb remained in her mouth, despite continued efforts to understand this fixed symptom. In the supervision, I proposed talking to the thumb-in-the-mouth as if it were another character in the session. How did the thumb feel inside the mouth, and how did it think it might feel if it went outside the mouth? Was it scared to leave its sanctuary? Was it curious about what went on outside? Would it be able to get back inside if it felt too scared outside? All of a sudden all these questions started coming up, until we could both empathize with the fear of the thumb getting out of its refuge as a personification of the unborn baby part of the personality, which did not dare to come out into the world.

The analyst started playing this game in the sessions, and it took some time for the girl to engage in it. The therapist would personify the finger, talking in the first person, and Ana would speak for the other characters in the mouth: the teeth, tongue, and lips. Sometimes they changed roles. They started making up stories in the session about the thumb who had been adopted by this mouth family. Mostly, the thumb felt safe but sometimes it felt threatened by foreign things coming in, such as the moving tongue or the biting teeth.

The thumb-in-the-mouth became a subject of shared interest between analyst and patient. It was also an invariant picture of a part of the personality in the way that sometimes happens with dreams, as Melanie Klein points out in her wonderful text "Personification in the Play of Children" (1929), becoming a shorthand not only between analyst and patient but also throughout the supervision.

Vignette 3

Mark, who had been in analysis for six years, was a very disturbed young man who demanded a strong psychoanalytic conviction from the analyst. The latter has been well contained by her supervisor in all the years of this treatment, finding the courage to treat Mark with firmness and commitment. She had one supervision with me when she visited Buenos Aires, after presenting the same patient to me at a clinical seminar some months earlier in New York. I shall focus on one particular aspect of this encounter. This is what she brought:

> In the Spring of 2014 Mark had begun to weigh up whether to continue his undergraduate degree at a college far outside New York or to remain in the city and continue to study from home. One of the attractions of staying in the City was the thought that he could continue his three-times-weekly analysis with me. Knowing I would be relocating to London in the summer of 2015, I felt obliged to disclose the fact that treatment would have to terminate. This impending breach brought about a multitude of shifts in the treatment, most notably impacting on his previous tenacious hold on his omnipotent and idealistic defences.
>
> I have worked with him for six years, three-times a week. Some of his issues have revolved around a "*folie à deux*" with his mother,

> the result of transgenerational trauma, unknown consciously to him. His mother had tried, unconsciously, to keep him a non–gender-differentiated baby because of the trauma of adolescent sexual abuse to which she herself had been subjected. His character structure revealed itself to be extremely narcissistic and omnipotent, always trying to maintain a distance from his objects so as to deny any need for separation. For many months, the nature of the countertransference was the holding of an excruciatingly unbearable deadness. As he began to emerge slowly from the "claustrum" of his own internal world through the ongoing exploration of the space between us—the otherness—I began to be removed from my pedestal and, finally, a negative transference emerged in which he could safely express his considerable repressed aggression. The content of his material became increasingly violent, and I felt, at times, ill at ease. I was trying to work through my feelings of guilt about abandoning him. As the Christmas break approached, he asked me if he could take a risk. He said that he had wanted to tell me something for some time but was scared that I might reject or ridicule him. This is what he said: "I want you to know that I really care about you. I care about you enormously; in fact I think I really love you. Do you know that you will be in my mind forever? I will never forget you. Do you know that? Every day for the rest of my life you will be with me in mind. I will remember you forever."

At this point in the supervision, I was impressed by the patient's assertion. Even though he was talking about love, his promise to remember forever brought to my mind, to my surprise, the "remember me" of Hamlet's ghost, as though both an articulation of remembrance and a call for revenge. I felt that the idea of "never forgetting" and "remembering for ever" could be the expression of an unforgiving superego which also demanded that the analyst remember him in this same way. This distinction between recalling and remembering prompted an interesting exchange of ideas that continued, via email, beyond the hour of supervision.

When people having a conversation do not share the same mother tongue, extra work is needed to make sure they understand each other. What do we mean by the words we use? This also applies, of course, to people who speak the same language, to some degree. The difference between remembering and recalling did not strike the same chords in supervisor and supervisee at the time. For the supervisor, recalling was closer to an evocative memory related to the depressive position and the presence of the good lost object as the nucleus of the self. Remembering had an active quality that, in this patient, seemed to be closer to a superego demand in response to the fear of losing the object. The supervisee shared thoughts that our conversation had evoked in her about the Christian faith (which were new to me), and she brought in a new perspective from which to understand the patient and his violent defences.

Vignette 4

This vignette describes a situation in which a disruption in the atmosphere of the supervision created a new way to understand clinical material. The work between supervisor and this intuitive and experienced supervisee was usually characterized by good communication and receptivity on both sides.

The analyst brought a session of a patient who was having difficulties becoming pregnant. She had consulted doctors at a fertility clinic, who could find no organic cause, but the patient insisted on the idea of being ill. The analyst was caught between a description of the medical procedures involved in the consultation and the problems the patient had relating to the doctors. The analyst felt that it had been difficult to keep the analytic focus in the session, but she did not realize the enactment that was taking place. Each time I tried to draw her attention to this fact, I felt that she, uncharacteristically, seemed to defend herself and her approach to the material. I found myself feeling that I was facing an aspect of the analyst I had not encountered before, wondering if I had neglected to realize that there had been some mutual idealization going on.

I remained silent until it occurred to me that we were having a fertility problem in our supervision. I told the analyst that it was as if there was a condom that was preventing the sperm from penetrating the ovum in the session with her patient and that, somehow, the same situation was repeating itself in the supervision. The atmosphere in the supervision changed, and the analyst became aware of the weight this situation had in her countertransference.

Conclusion

In "Constructions in Analysis" (1937d), Freud introduces the notion of constructions, as distinct from interpretation, wherein the analyst may need, in certain situations, to reconstruct a part of the patient's infantile history. It is important to consider the limits of this particular intervention of the analyst—and of the supervisor—in order to avoid proposing something far removed from the patient's discourse. In Freud's words: "we do not pretend that an individual construction is anything more than a conjecture which awaits examination, confirmation or rejection" (Freud, 1937d, p. 265). It would not, I think, be far-fetched to relate the use of models to Freud's constructions in psychoanalysis in so far as the model construed in the session (and in the supervision) promotes a sense of truth that has the effect of the encounter with a selected fact. By this I refer to the emotional capacity to link imaginatively what seem to be unrelated elements in one's free associations.

In his 1970 paper, "The Problems of Supervision in Psychoanalytic Education", León Grinberg mentions something I have come across quite often and which I consider significant: the supervisee occasionally starts with a trivial remark about the weather, some traffic trouble, or something that has occurred during the seminar or has happened to his or her children. In my experience, these incidental comments are often a kind of free association indirectly connected with the main theme of the material the supervisee brings. In this way, latent aspects of the analytic situation which were still at an unconscious level are brought into the supervision. Grinberg contends that "If the supervisor discusses this situation every time it happens, he will help the candidate to be more confident and to be bolder in handling more directly the discovered content" (p. 376).

The use of models helps develop a more flexible container capable of containing not only the projections of a complex inner life but also the inner life which is deployed in the relationship between two people in a consulting room, both in the analytic relationship and in the supervision. The imaginative conjecture was described by Meltzer in his developments on the aesthetic conflict. The imaginative conjecture owes its provenance to the poignant presence of the object. This object—the other—both inspires the imaginative conjecture and becomes the object of the conjecture. This is what Meltzer called "aesthetic reciprocity" (Meltzer & Harris Williams, 1988, p. 42), and it forms the basis of every meaningful relationship. To grow in an experience means to be able to learn from experience in a process of transformation.

This is far from mutual idealization or mutual fear; we are concerned to generate a space and an atmosphere that will allow for the working through of the crisis that any development has in the search for a mind of one's own, an identity, and a style of life. Only by taking into account the anxieties elicited by a three-dimensional creative growing—as opposed to socializing or fakeness of projective identification or pseudo-maturity—we may develop the true capacity to bear uncertainties and difficult questions.

The challenge we meet in supervision is to generate a space in the thin line where imagination may develop at the same time that our work takes anchor in the basic analytic technique and theory.

Bion, in *Taming Wild Thoughts* (1997), talks about this apparent paradox:

> Unless the analyst allows himself the exercise of his speculative imagination he will not be able to produce conditions in which a germ of scientific ideas can flourish. . . . So while I say that it is extremely important to exercise your imagination, to let it go, to give it a chance to flourish, at the same time keep it under some sort of discipline. [pp. 46, 48]

Working in other contexts where psychoanalysis is still developing, we are more overtly confronted with the problem of colonization: how to help somebody to develop a mind of his or her own and, at the same time, understand what is truly analytic beyond more cultural and historical facts. It is important to be able to understand how much of our identifications, how much of our more conscious elections, enter into the process of developing a mind of one's own. Perhaps it is the work of a lifetime.

Note

1. I am very grateful to Nancy Moreno Dueñas, Adela Vinocur, and Alison Bruce for allowing me to use material from their supervision for this presentation.

CHAPTER EIGHT

Keeping tension close to the limit: from latency towards development

Monica Vorchheimer

"The dream that invents me has its eyes wide open
And I close my eyes to look at the world."

Claude Roy, quoted by Pontalis (2011, p. 16)

A memory

It was during Donald Meltzer's last visit to Buenos Aires that I had the privilege of being supervised by him on a very complicated clinical case that I was treating at that time. A young homosexual woman had been coming for treatment and had developed a very open and intense transference love: "A very complicated woman; very sensual, very erotic, and very homosexual. What is going to happen with her rude demand of and erotic and sensual gratification towards her analyst? We will see. But she seems armed to the teeth against parental care from her analyst." In this way Meltzer opened his comment and shared with us his usual very interesting ideas; but there was one in particular that I kept in mind, echoing down time. He said: "This could be thought of as resistance, but it is not. I guess that she has opened the door to her pornographic concern and to her masochism and she wants you to feel guilty for having profited from the opened door which allowed you to investigate what has been revealed. . . . Everything is opened here, there is no resistance." And later he added, "All the material is now present for Monica to explore as slowly or as fast as she would wish . . .".

This was going to be a challenge, a real test of the courage to analyse—the courage that one can find over and over again throughout his work. I always considered that the image described in *The Psychoanalytical Process* (1967) regarding the analytic attitude as a tension close to the limit would acquire new shades in the "Routine and Inspired Interpretations" paper (1973c). I have tended to go back to the latter more than once, whenever I feel the need to shake off the drowsiness that sometimes hampers my interest or my creativity, in order to recover an awakened state that allowed me to return to the analytic listening "close to the limit".

Exploring as slowly or as fast as I would wish—is it merely a matter of wishing? This question becomes especially crucial with certain patients, such as the so-called protracted latents who get settled in analysis with a phantasy of an endless process, in a kind of mother–baby secret love affair "until death do us part".

Protracted latency in the analytic situation

These patients make us face up to a paradoxical situation: how to remain a patient while allowing development to progress at its own tempo and, at the same time, keeping tension close to the limit. Although we know that the transference situation will unavoidably be the scenario for the actualization of this latent potential, since development seems to have been slowed down or even stopped, we need to avoid colluding in a de-vitalizing process so that the analytic exploration neither comes to a halt nor lasts forever. We must continue to search for passion, even when it seems to be absent, and to pursue the integration of L, H, and K (Bion, 1963, p. 34).

The lack of passion—which, at best, appears dampened, intellectualized, obsessive, or dissociated—is what characterizes latency-age functioning, regardless of the patient's age. In these cases, we usually find that the adolescent crisis has been avoided in order for the child to remain in the family. Such patients inhabit a kind of doll's-house marriage, and social inhibitions are concealed in the continuity of childhood friendships. The calm and obsessiveness of latency can be disrupted by external events that provoke some curiosity about sexual life, quite different from the scant and lack-lustre genital encounters of their marriages. The incapacity to feel excitement, awaken desire in the sexual partner, or the fear of exploring the body or masturbating characterize a diffuse and mainly imitative identity, with orgasmic anaesthesia.

This was the case with a young woman in her forties whom I had been seeing for a long time and who brought me face-to-face with this dilemma. She had married her only boyfriend, and her two daughters were developing well. A sense of fragility coloured her way of being in the world, however, as if she were still the small, sick girl she had been since her brother was born and her psychosomatic symptoms appeared. Her memories from puberty were filled with shame and shyness, mainly related to body changes. Even before these had appeared, she invented a story for her classmates, claiming that her breasts had grown but she had preferred to reduce their size because she did not like to show off.

The lethargy and obsessiveness of latency were shaken after several years when she learned that her best friend was having an extramarital love affair. She was shocked, mainly out of curiosity about her friend's interest in sexual life. This was almost completely absent between herself and her husband or, when present, was dull and passionless. What did this woman have that might awake desire in a man? Why did she not get excited? Why was she so afraid of touching herself or being touched? She had never masturbated, nor had she felt the desire to do so. The turbulence of this period soon died down to some extent, however, in order to avoid conflicts of jealousy, rivalry, and envy. She embarked on new postgraduate studies and reinforced her obsessionality.

A kind of intellectualized contact in the sessions, far from passionate experiences, colours the analytic situation of patients who seem to be comfortably settled on the analyst's lap. These patients provide material that can be symbolically rich, evocative for the analyst's activity, even passionate in its contents, tempting the analyst strongly to go "fast". However, the patients lacks the passion to make use of what we offer; they may find it interesting, but it does not touch them. Their abundance of dreams seems complacent, and they receive our interpretations as if they are spoken by the Oracle. Transference can be spoken about, but experiencing it is completely another matter. It is not only about regulating temperature and distance, but, as Liberman (1976) would say, a complementary style in communication has to be sought. As for the obsessive, a counter-interpretative style is required, close to action, where the risk lies in inducing action or introducing personal values or being prescriptive and losing self-restraint. The process feels static, suspended in a timeless dimension, and the end is nowhere to be seen; stillness and immobility seem to be a hallmark. As Meltzer suggested, if the role of the analyst is to strike fire into the mind of his patient, it is something that we would all find ourselves fundamentally incapable of doing, if it were not due to the transference. But what is it that happens when the transference itself unfolds as a small, pale flame that is not enough to light the fire?

A good pupil/patient relationship, even when there is an interest in dreams, can stimulate a tendency to routine interpretations and psychoanalytic clichés. The negative transference is difficult to find. The analyst wavers between intervening in an unsaturated manner, in order to avoid becoming "the teacher teaching his pupil", and using a more narrative style. Countertransference fluctuates between a feeling of being sharp or aggressive or explaining too much, dealing with a sense that it is difficult to keep "tension close to the limit", as Meltzer (1967, p. 93) would have put it, and the analyst's conscious and unconscious desire to speed up the process can involve countertransferential acting-out.

The question of whether or not an impasse is taking place is always at stake. At this point, it is interesting to remember Etchegoyen's remarks about the forces opposed to the analytic process, which he organizes under three main rubrics (1991, p. 692):

1. acting out: the substitution of action for memory and insight;
2. the negative therapeutic reaction (NTR): the undermining or wiping out of achieved insight;
3. the reversible perspective, as Bion (1962a) and Money-Kyrle (1968) described the subversion of the analytic rules.

Etchegoyen suggests that all phenomena that fall under these headings might coalesce into a psychoanalytic impasse, which must be differentiated from the non-coercible resistance of the patient and the technical mistakes of the analyst. The true impasse is described as neither of these two but, rather, as a total halt of the analytic process achieved by the converging forces of acting out, reversible perspective, and NTR. As we know, destructive emotions are the basis of these anti-process manoeuvres, which I view as quite distinct from the kind of features I am trying to convey with the patients I am describing.

It is clinically important to distinguish the stasis of an impasse from the motionlessness of protracted latency within the analytic situation. The cause for the latter can be found in a detention in the threshold of adolescence which is actualized in the transference situation. Further developments in meta-psychological understanding are needed to answer the question about whether there exists an isomorphism between the developmental infant latency and the psychopathology of protracted latency in *adult* patients.

Dream-life as experimentation

After a long time, however, movement begins to find representation in dream-life, in spite of what appears to be immobilized in daily life. Dreams flourish during the night and can be expanded in the sessions during the exploratory phase, opening the door to the roots of infantile sexuality. At first, the analyst's enthusiasm cannot be satisfactorily transformed into clear interpretations; although conjectures might be plausible, it is not yet clear to whom they can be communicated. A sense of artificiality permeates the consulting room, while the therapist can be suspected of nymphomania or promiscuity, insofar as his or her curiosity is excited by these dreams. Paraphrasing Meltzer, it could be said that "all the material is there", but due to projective identification—with powerful effects on the countertransference—it is difficult to find a way of approaching the material without falling into interpretative stereotypes or formulations inducing the patient to action. There is a strong feeling of sterility despite the richness of the oneiric production, as the material only confirms what has been examined on numerous occasions.

With the patient mentioned above, in the transference, I was either the mother who would teach her how to be a woman and please her husband or the laboratory medical-father who would fecundate her without sex. I remember fighting against my own lethargy, trying to stay awake and alert, and always being grateful when she brought dreams that could enliven the dull atmosphere in the consulting room. Once, she dreamt that

> *she was in a little town in the countryside with her daughter who was learning how to ride on horseback; they passed by a church; people were going inside for Mass, and the girl wanted to go inside with the horse but they passed by. There was a woman standing on the pavement, and the patient shouted at her daughter that she should be careful.*

A memory from her childhood reappeared in this context, when she fell off a horse during a riding lesson. She was wounded and bled profusely and still had a scar on her belly. She traced her fear of riding, airplanes, and speed back to this incident.

As we can see, from time to time, the problem of learning and experiencing novelty and voluptuousness came up in her dreams, and the transference scenario moved to the outside—the countryside—where it is possible to achieve speed in development, although experimentation and exploration could still be dangerous and castration or a cut could be discovered. The temptation to go back to religious–ascetic–church life remained present.

In these patients, the question about how passions are aroused seems to be a central enigma, mirroring the analyst's search for a way to reach the self while modulating temperature, distance, rhythm, and speed. Fortunately, however, difficulties in analytic communication can be also recollected in the oneiric scenario: the search for the penis can be suspicious, introjection might be cheating, and something may elude the analyst; corruption of the analytic method can be reported in dream features like feeding the children rotten food, telephones that don't work, not being able to bring together the feminine, the masculine, the feeding-creative function, keeping the objects apart, and maintaining bisexuality split off. If infantile polymorphism cannot be integrated, neither can bisexuality, and the mystery of how passions are aroused cannot be accessed either.

In the transference and countertransference situation, this has been created by the diminished creativity of interpretative activity, as a result of the dissociation of the combined object in the analyst's mind. Instead, the analyst provided corrupted interpretations—out-of-date food—desexualized and devitalized, in which the fertile and potent penis (and testicles with good "milk") was kept at a distance, unable to communicate with the bitch-sensual-woman. In this way, the desexualization of the parental figures of latency was reproduced, and no passionate quality could emerge in the transference. But in dreams, this problem finds expression.

As time passes, and dreams help to clarify the transference–countertransference field, there are indications that something new is being mobilized in the oneiric scenario; new experiences (rejected while awake) come to life while sleeping. Surprisingly, in dream-life, a new capacity to experience excitement and attraction towards the other sex becomes more vivid, in contrast to what seems to be a small, pale flame during waking life or in the transference relationship. "It looks as if, in dreams, I dare to live what I cannot while awake", a patient vividly commented, as if quoting the epigraph: "The dream that invents me has its eyes wide open. / And I close my eyes to look at the world" (Pontalis, 2011, p. 16). In the same session, he had realized that he had come through an operation quite well, although he was nervous; he realized that it was foolish to reproach himself about his earlier fears. Instead, he felt that he had been courageous, since he had undergone surgery in spite of his nerves and had not postponed it as he would have done in the past. The sessions became more colourful; new childhood memories were recovered spontaneously and surprisingly. At the same time, plasticity, language games, musicality, and poetry can create a flow of associations between patient and analyst as if in a harmonic dance. Almost by chance, the analyst is informed that external life has become more intense, new characters appear in the external scene, language becomes more sophisticated, curiosity about trying new food or new experiences do not seem to be as rejected or feared as they were before. Time begins to be registered, first tinted with claustrophobic anxieties, while the idea of termination shows its face for the first time as a desire and real possibility. The process seems, suddenly, to have gained momentum, and the infantile objects are characterized as courageous and strong.

Discussion

During a conference of the Asociación Psicoanalítica de Buenos Aires in 1995, Meltzer suggested that emotions are first experienced as body states and it is only gradually that those states find their way to expression through symbols that can be dreamed. However, sometimes things seem to follow an inverse direction. Body states and sensations appear initially in dreams, allowing the experimentation that had been avoided in development to unfold, as found in clinical cases such as the ones described above (Meltzer, 1997).

The oneiric space, the "real and vital" dream experience, is the space where confusions can be sorted out and knowledge can be accessed. Although for many years patients, like children, had drawn upon rather conventional symbols in dreams, it is unclear whether those symbols could transmit more than "the shade of emotions" or uncoloured metaphors, as Meltzer suggested on that occasion. However, after years of repetition with weak and subtle transformations, something starts to move. It is reminiscent of how children enjoy listening to the same stories thousands of times over; perhaps patients provide dream material for the analyst to tell them their stories over and over again, never quite sure whether the value is in the lyrics or the music. As children begin to prefer writing their own stories, there comes a time when patients appropriate their own dreams as a way of preparing themselves to move forward; they begin to invent themselves—inspired by the combined objects/gods—although this process is more intense when sleeping, allowing new sensations to take shape in the body and enabling new symbol formation.

Returning to my initial question concerning the difficulty of talking with passion when passion is absent in the patient, I have pointed out the effect of the dissociation of the combined object in the patient's internal world which drags the countertransference towards routine interpretations or into a style that might seem harsh or action-inducing. Both a timeless analysis and spurious behavioural changes, out of identification with the analyst's desire, are a risk when passion is weak or absent.

I will now go back to Meltzer through a beautiful paper by Clara Nemas (2016) referring to courage and reverie as the basis for sincerity and interpretation. Nemas alerts us to the question of keeping the fight for our passions awake, as a source of authenticity and sincerity in the contact with our patients. This becomes particularly crucial when the patient is systematically devoted to fighting against the intensity of passionate life, as happens with latency patients of all ages.

In her paper, Nemas suggests that courage is a function of the maternal quality of the combined object; the opposite, as she says, is not cowardice but giving up on the child's upbringing. How much courage is needed, when raising a child, to trust that the reverie function is food for development yet to unfold! Together with this maternal quality, the paternal function must offer the mother support and reparative penetrability so that she can do her job courageously without giving up. Talking through the analyst's interpretation, the Gods—the combined object, the integrated parental functions—provide passionate inspiration.

Courage is needed to support patience with hope over time, relying on development and trusting the analytic method, so that despair can be contained without having to resort to inauthenticity by promoting a pseudo-development in our analysands. The latter should not be confused with the reparative penetrability of the father's function.

Ultimately, we need maternal courage, supported by the father's reparative function, in order to keep our eyes open to look at the worlds of our patients and ourselves, while, at the same time, needing to close our eyes in order to invent our own analytic dreams and stories and to help them to invent their own.

CHAPTER NINE

Donald Meltzer's supervision of psychotherapy with a psychotic child

Jeanne Magagna

The structure of time is inextricably linked with the concept of hope. In the beginning of a baby's life there is hope, hope for a communion with the mother and father as loving, protective, caring figures. Alongside this hope is a preconception that the breast will meet the baby's requirements to be nourished. As the baby grows and matures, holding on to this hope is both difficult and dangerous; hope can be filled with too much greed to possess all of a mother's and father's life. Hope can involve a constitutional incapacity to tolerate the frustration of waiting for mother's reappearance, filled with rage at mother for not being attuned to the baby's rhythm of communicating needs. Hope is then submerged beneath rage and disappointment with mother. Hope, which promised a future of contentment, then becomes despair. Without hope, there is no sense of the future, just the disappointing present or the yearning for a moment in the past that was experienced as good.

In meeting a child for the first time with his or her parents, I am acutely attuned to the sense of the child's expectation in meeting me. In that first look, I see hope, curiosity, and anticipation that, perhaps, with this new person, some different experience may occur. Alternatively, I see fear or even terror that something dreadful will certainly happen in my presence. I, too, have a sense of suspenseful anticipation as I get to know the child. In this first meeting I am the recipient of the child's unconscious phantasies, developed through internalized past interactions with mother, father, and siblings and suffused with the child's own feelings. I am also myself, with my personality, my inner world, flaws, and capacities in the present, all of which invites a particular configuration of the child's phantasies. What the future holds is uncertain. As a therapist, I arrive with a hope that, together, we might repair some of the damage that has occurred internally, possibly in conjunction with external conflictual events.

A child's sense of time is apparent in the first session and changes considerably during the course of therapy. In presenting my work with a 6-year-old psychotic child in four-times-a-week psychotherapy for three and a half years, I shall contrast the experience of time in a manic state of mind to that in depression and in depressive states of mind. The understanding and repair offered to this child was substantially influenced by Donald Meltzer, whose weekly supervisory reflections on her psychological development are brought alive here. Herein are also contained clinical examples of his work described in his favourite published work, *The Psychoanalytical Process* (1967).

Mia, a child with many psychotic features, made me acutely aware of distortions of time and space from her first session. Aged 6 years, Mia was brought to the clinic by her parents because her teacher was worried that she was "living in a world of her own". Everyone knew when Mia had arrived in the clinic as she darted through the corridors, shrieking. She was a lively, robust little girl with brown curly hair and a hard, muscular body that gave an impression of toughness.

Complaining that there was a large frightening man in the corner of the interview room, Mia constantly moved from one place to another. In the first family interview, when no one responded to her complaints about the man invisible to them, she screamed at the hallucinated figure, "Bugger", "sod", "bastard"! These remarks provoked distaste and alarm in the psychiatric meeting with the family, as did Mia's teasing and hitting of her 12-year-old brother Rick, who seemed to be the focus of both her and her mother's attention. (Her mother whispered to him as a close confidant.) Meanwhile, Mia's father was assertive and flamboyantly hypomanic, in contrast with his withdrawn, subservient, and depressed wife.

According to the family, Mia was conceived so that her brother "would not be left on his own with no one to care for him". Breast-fed until the fourth week, when mother's milk dried up, Mia did not cry much as a baby. For this reason, her mother said, she rarely felt the need to pick her up and cuddle her. At 10 months, Mia was walking.

Her mother encouraged her to draw, as she showed little interest in toys. Sometimes she waved around a hard, sexy fashion model doll, but she never played with it.

The psychologist attempted on two occasions to give Mia intelligence and achievement tests, but found it impossible to get anything but nonsense from her. Certainly her teachers felt that she was not functioning within the normal range of intelligence: she could not concentrate and learned little in her year and a half at school. Teachers said that Mia rarely responded to her own name and would, instead, demand that the teachers call her by different names. Once, at a school bazaar, Mia managed to leave the adults and put on some clothes that were on sale, and her own clothes were inadvertently purchased.

Family life was chaotic, and her father had frequent affairs. There was a history of violent rows between the older three family members, which resulted in doors being broken and the mother needing to have her face stitched while trying to protect the children from the father's frightening shouts. Mia's parents clearly needed assistance in handling their marital conflicts as well as parenting. Much of the time, her mother was too depressed and lonely to be actively concerned with Mia. At times, Mia's father was absent from home, preoccupied with his other sexual partners and work, which he used to relieve the "deadness" he complained about experiencing at home.

Here is an excerpt from Mia's first session:

> As I approach Mia, I see sores around her mouth and under her nose. Her face seems unattractive, particularly because of her dulled expression and her avoidance of eye contact. Mia's movements are extremely swift. Catching sight of me, Mia rushes towards me saying, "soft, good lady". A complete stranger to her, I am startled as she immediately strokes my grey, lambswool jumper and eagerly demands, "Can I go with you now?" Hurriedly she grabs my hand, repeats "soft, good lady" and leaves her mother without even a parting glance to say goodbye.
>
> Upon entering the therapy room, I give Mia a box of play materials and explain that the materials are for her to use during her time with me. Mia ignores the toys and hastily grabs the sellotape and all the crayons. Immediately she begins a detailed drawing of the room and all its contents (Figure 9.1). She draws the chairs, the tables, the sellotape and then a detailed picture of me. I occupy the same space as the desk and the chair.

FIGURE 9.1. The therapy room.

With mounting excitement, Mia names the objects in the room: blonde hair, grey eyes, knickers, table. Drawing and naming the objects suggested Mia's attempt to understand and control them as well as her need to make the place with me less frightening. Mia seriously observes, "You don't have pink skin." She then completes her list: "Knickers, brown knickers filled with smellies and wees." Darting her eyes at me, Mia demands, "Pig, make grunting noises. I'm a lady."

Swiftly she removes every toy from the box while correctly naming the sheep, cow, lion, and other animals she is dropping on the table. While doing so she proclaims, "I'm afraid of the man in the pink shirt!" Subsequently, at lightning speed, she races out of the room into a tent in the waiting room. Shocked, it takes me a second to reach her. As I go near, Mia shouts at me, "Pig! Frightened of you!"

Mia hastily grabs my hand and begs me to take her to the loo. We go to the loo, and as she returns to the therapy room she remarks, "Man in the pink shirt. He's after me." She points at me and repeatedly tries to dash out of the room. Now being more alert, I firmly encourage her to remain inside the room until the end of the session. As the session is ending, with a look of pleasure, Mia notices Turner's water landscape, *Sunrise,* hanging on the wall. Then she exclaims, "It's filled with smellies!" At this point the session ends, and I return Mia to her mother. A few minutes later, the door bursts open. Mia is there shouting "pig" once again. She subsequently races to the exit where her mother is standing.

Contemplating Mia's manic state, I ask myself, "What has happened to make everything go so fast, creating Mia's manic state? Why are her emotions of love, fear, and hate reversible in seconds?" It feels as though a hurricane has enveloped me in a swirl of confusing feelings. Finding a time to think about my own emotional responses was essential before beginning another session with Mia.

Henri Rey's (1994) structure for thinking lends a depth to the process of examining Mia's manic relation to time and space. Like Meltzer in *The Psychoanalytic Process* (1967), Rey in *Universals of Psychoanalysis* (1994) recognizes the essentially spatial structure of the mind and its representation of objects. Rey's developing consciousness of the spatial structure of states of mind can be summed up in his model of thinking:

> What part of the subject
> in what state
> situated where in space and time,
> does what
> with what motivation
> to what part of the object,
> in what state,
> situated where in space and time,
> with what consequences for
> the object and the subject? [Rey, 1994, p. 7]

I used this model as a base for my review of the session with Mia, a baby who "didn't cry". Her depressed mother's milk dried up after four weeks. Mia exists in a sensorimotor stage of thinking. Her mind has easily permeable pores through which all sensual qualities of external objects beckon her, like the tune of the Pied Piper. As she touches my soft, wool jumper, she is dragged into a static sensuousness that obliterates her emotions and thoughts. My hair, eyes, and jumper seem virtually equivalent to the toys, table, and sellotape which she also names.

Mia attempts to "hold on to" a person immediately. All those laborious steps of taking time to get to know someone are skipped over as she grabs my hand and hastily claims me as her "soft, good lady". She doesn't know my inner qualities, but since I am "soft" she assumes that I must be "good". Present is an omniscient certainty about who

I am and she exerts a primitive omnipotent control through naming objects and pinning them down in a drawing. What becomes impossible is waiting for the future with ordinary curiosity and anxiety regarding what might happen in the session.

The unheld, terrified "baby-Mia", finding herself in a new space, grabs the sensuous aspects of the "mother-therapist". Through sensuous looking and touching, she attempts to hold on for dear life. Being overwhelmed with the sensuous qualities of the maternal object, she quickly intrudes beyond the space that the baby shares with its mother and enters into the primitive oedipal phantasies of the mother in an exciting intercourse with the father. Only when I attempt to understand Mia's anxieties about being with a stranger in a new place is she able to say, "You're not pink." However, this quality of "not-pinkness," meaning "not too exciting", is quickly lost in her wish to possess immediately all that the mother has, including the sensuous, sexual relationship with the father: she cannot permit mother to have time with father. Rapidly the hallucinated "pink man" returns to the room and is located within me. In other words, the "soft, good lady" is spoiled by the exciting, hated, and terrifying "pink man" and becomes a "pig".

There is no separation in time of the "nurturing, feeding mother" from the phantasies, which quickly become sensual, sexual, and anal in quality. In her unintegrated state, Mia flits rapidly between different states of mind. This form of splitting exists, but only for a second: mother is good, father is bad. Then good and bad become confused, leading to a monstrous "pig" containing Mia's projections. Mia's greed is stimulated by her lack of inner containment; sensuous erotization is Mia's defence against the pain of dependence and the loss of the nurturing, understanding object. The manic race involving non-stop touching of objects, and flitting through different activities, is a flight from the primitive persecutory anxieties and terrors of the hallucinated monster, "the pink man". Any potential emotional rather than sensuous relationship with me is superficial and quickly loses value. This is the world of two-dimensional time and two-dimensional adherence to the surface of objects as described by Meltzer (1975a), Tustin (1990), and Rhode (1997) in their essays on autism.

In ordinary human experience, over time, there is a continuity of emotional experience rather than the roller-coaster of excited and terrifying states of mind in which Mia exists. The continuity of emotional experience in time is provided through the containing presence of the external mother and father. This becomes internalized to form the child's internal psychic structure. Manic racing through time is thus replaced by an ordinary use of time once there is an internal psychic structure holding Mia's feelings sufficiently long to be perceived and given consideration.

Blistering of the skin

By the third week of therapy, Mia experiences separation from me as being dropped from a state of "at one-ness" into a state of being torn off, bruised and blistered. My heart cries out as I see her futile attempts to interrupt the passage of time leading to the end of the session. Initially, Mia starts wearing lipstick and carrying a small bag containing her mother's eye shadow, lipstick, rouge, mascara, perfume, and nail varnish; she spends time, before leaving the session, making up her "beautiful face". At other times, she puts glue on her feet, tries to stick them to the floor, and continually checks to see if they have stuck. There is to be no "baby" experiencing the passage of time away from the "mother-therapist".

The following excerpts illustrate Mia's search to get into and adhere to the protective skin of the "mother-therapist". In her search, she also covered herself with plasticine, an activity that represented a form of "adhesive identification", described by Meltzer (1975a) and Bick (1968), which involves "sticking" to an object rather than projecting into it. Without an internal space, there is a tendency to relate to objects in a two-dimensional way as though they, too, have no depth. In Mia's play (described below), there is a feeling that one can "stick to the skin of the mother":

Third week of therapy

> Mia pours water all over the room and throws and scatters her toys. She then begins rocking back and forth. She seems very sad, not knowing what to do. Mia then collects plasticine pieces from among the debris and stands near me, saying, "I'm putting plasticine all over myself." She labels a piece of the plasticine "the desk bit" and tries to stick it onto the bottom of her feet. When she is unsuccessful, she tries using glue to make the "desk bit" adhere to her feet. Shortly afterwards Mia collects more plasticine and begins sticking it all over her body, saying, "I'm putting Jeanne all over me." Mia is serious, slow-moving, and quiet. I feel that she is

slightly desperate. She repeats this in subsequent sessions, adding felt tip to cover her navel and arms.

The plasticine cover, the felt-tip colour, and the "make-up mummy beautiful face" are part of Mia's attempt to retreat from any experience of being a kind of stick figure without much inner substance, flesh, or even human shape. These covers are attempts to "hold herself together" in the face of some terrible sense of fragmentation and potential sense of loss of the mother-therapist (Rhode, 1997). Mia's unconscious aim is to obliterate time, a sense of waiting and the psychic terror and pain she feels when she experiences herself as a separate person.

The experience of rage and hurt is emerging, however. The skin as a concrete locus of Mia's separation soreness is particularly evident at the end of many sessions. Frequently she does not want to leave the sessions. When I firmly insist that it is time to go, Mia tries to scratch me, rip my tights, kick me, and pull my hair. In this way I am to concretely experience the flayed-skin sensation, the blistering skin, the hurt that Mia experiences when I say, after a warning five minutes previously, "It's time to go."

Around the third and fourth week, it is clear that Mia is more vehemently using me as a kind of "dump" into which she evacuates parts of her blistered self (Tustin, 1990). For example:

Fourth week

At the beginning of one session she immediately rushes to the jug of water. Pouring water on the couch, she declares, "Pouring water on your bed." She then takes off her shoes and socks. Racing to the desk, she grabs her box and dumps all its contents on the floor saying, "I'm messing up your room again." She pours glue all over and attempts to kick me. When I restrain her, she bites me.

But then she steps on a pieces of fence and cries, complaining, "It pricked me." When I describe her feeling that she has messed the inside of the mummy and now she feels she is being pricked and made to cry, Mia responds, "Yes, it hurts me." This is a sobering moment, for she has put her pain into words.

In the next session, Mia puts the fence pieces in a bucket and places them under the couch along with other hard toys. She explains, "It is so they won't hurt." Emerging for the first time is a concept of a space where the bad bits can be stored. The session is also marked by Mia's uncharacteristic crying and verbal communication about feeling hurt. Now there is a "mother as a dumping place" into which Mia can expel some unbearable destructive and hurt feelings. [After the painful and bad parts of experience can be stored in the room, representing my mind, it becomes possible to see the development of a space to protect "good parts" (Meltzer, 1975a). A splitting of good and bad parts is beginning to emerge. Such splitting is necessary so that not only can there be some "good parts", but also there is a beginning of possibility of establishing and preserving a good object.]

Fifth week

During the fifth week, Mia spends some of the sessions curled up under the blanket on the couch. I feel she is beginning to become painfully aware as we part of her sense of loss, her feeling of bodily damage. She feels helpless without a sturdy internal psychic structure enabling her to consider that there will be another session and another. This internal rhythm of safety could hold her flood of despair and terror arising through fragmentation of the self in the time apart. I talk about Mia wanting a "blanket-mummy" to hold her together and make her feel safe. At the end, Mia cries, pleading that she does not want to go. Later in the corridor, as she meets her mother, she becomes very subdued and begins sobbing. Mia complains that her mother has not brought her scarf. This is the very first day I have seen Mia crying. As she cries in front of her mother, I feel that "Now there is a crying baby, a baby crying for 'a mummy' to hold her pain and protect her."

I remember mother saying in the first interview that Mia didn't cry much as a baby. Now Mia is having a different experience with her mother, who is supported by a therapist and me. For a moment, the obliteration of time through sensuousness ceases. There is an acute experience of an emotional point that is held still. There is a tie and some internal space in which Mia feels sadness and fear of being without a protective cover. Emerging in Mia is a new concept of "mother", the concept of a mother who can experience and understand her sadness and fear of loss of a protective mother.

Mia's new concept of mother transforms her basic structure of time. There is now the possibility of a sense of time followed by a reunion, a sense of loss with a limit. Timelessness, the sense of infinite loss, can be gradually replaced by waiting for a reunion with the "lost good mother" (Meltzer, 1975a; O'Shaughnessy, 2015). A sense of hope for the future gradually emerges as Mia starts to perceive a future reunion as being the end to the present painful sense of loss.

At this stage, feelings and thoughts are still fragmentary and dominated by an emphasis on sensory concretization of her experience. This is apparent in the sixth week of therapy:

Sixth week

> Mia arrives for the first time with a watch on. She requests that I take care of her "ticker" in my drawer. Shortly afterwards she asks me to keep her large red button earrings safe in my drawer during the session. I feel that I am to be a kind of "special secure place" for those saner parts of herself that she wishes to protect from the chaos created by her confusion and continual messing of the room. There is just a hint of Mia's developing internalization of a "talking mummy with a protective space inside her". Mia alternates between messing the entire room and lying completely under the couch cover using my words as an additional blanket to wrap round herself.

Mia has little capacity for symbolic thought; she makes concrete her notion of time passing and a future time—when we will meet again—by asking me to keep safe her watch and her earrings. She cannot keep the notion of our time together safely inside her, and, at the beginning of each session, she recapitulates the internal process that has occurred during the separation from me. Rage at separation and subsequent fragmentation of the introjected experience of feeling understood by me creates internal chaos. Upon entering the room, Mia regularly feels compelled to throw toys and water all over the room, thrusting her furious chaos into me. I must say I feel very confused and disoriented when her mind is in this state, but after I receive this chaos and lend thought to it, Mia can begin to elaborate on other experiences:

Sixth week continued

> The minute that there is a greater sense of my having good containing and protective functions, Mia becomes worried about the time. She greets me, worrying, "What time is it? When will it be time to go?" She curls up under the couch cover and then pops up, rushes

over to me, and explains that she wants to "push the button on my head". I describe how she wants to push the button on my head in order to take control of my speaking and thinking with her. I say she wishes she could turn me on and turn me off as she wished.

This is primitive omnipotent control, showing me that she cannot tolerate the terror of being dependent on a good figure. When she experiences me as someone who is helpful, she feels compelled to hold on to me in this way. This increased dependence on the mother-therapist is heralded by more severe anxieties about feeling helpless outside the sessions. Mia cries plaintively when she leaves this session.

At this time of intensifying dependence on me, Mia also begins to experience sleeping difficulties. She says she likes sleeping in my room and would like to sleep there every night, because my room does not have cracks in it like her room. The external object (the therapist) gives her the feeling of a soothing protective space, a space without cracks. However, with her depressed mother outside the therapy, Mia feels she is left with a faulty, cracked, internal psychic container that does not protect her.

Sixth week continued

In the sixth week of therapy, Mia also inserts a big red dot, called a button, inside a bus she has drawn (Figure 9.2). She indicates that the woman in the bus could "press the button so the bus would stop". She adds that "the button is to make sure that nobody falls out". I describe her desire for the mummy as a kind of "bus-mummy protector" who holds her in mind and does not

FIGURE 9.2. The button to stop the bus and the "bus conductor/daddy-figure".

let her drop out of my mind. Also present, however, is a very monstrous looking "bus driver". She now has a sense of a daddy infringing on her relation to the mother.

In subsequent sessions, the drawings indicate that the "daddy" threatens to leave her feeling dropped out from the cocoon of the "bus-mummy covering". What is meant by the emergence of this figure who can put a time limit on experience, either good or bad? In a very primitive way, this limit on time with mother is felt to be the "role of the father". The structure of time, with the limiting role of the father, is depicted through the button to press to get out of the bus and away from the bus conductor.

Mia now ascribes different meanings to her notion of a "time limit". At the end of sessions, she experiences terror of being dropped into an abyss. She also feels rage towards an already violent external father who assists in the creation of "the internal monster father" who enforces cruel limits and drops people out of mind, thoughtlessly. This contrasts with Mia's other concept, the button that the mother presses in a more kindly role of enabling people to get out safely from "inside the mummy" and making sure that they do not ride inside the "protective bus-mummy" forever. Of course, in the unconscious, there exist many varieties of the protective or cruel father imposing time-limits or limits between the baby and mother.

In psychotherapy, asymmetrical and symmetrical logic challenge one another; the presence of an internal containing mother who permits thinking to take place allows Mia to feel that I am not a monster-father who cruelly pushes her out simply because our sessions have a time limit. When feelings become too intense and violent, however, the deeper symmetrical logic takes precedence: "There is a time limit. People who put time limits are monsters. The therapist is a monster."

Mia drew the pictures shown in Figures 9.3 and 9.4 when she experienced the monstrous time-limiting figure. Before she drew the witch figure, she said she hated me because I said, "No".

The question that follows is what happens to this experience of the cruelty of time limits, once a sense of dependence on a protective mother figure has emerged?

How does a substantial transformation of Mia's personality structure take place so that the "hallucinated monster man" or the "frightening witch-mother" of her drawings do not reappear each time her wish to live non-stop "inside the protective mother cover" is thwarted?

As Mia develops, her singing becomes a bridge between concrete

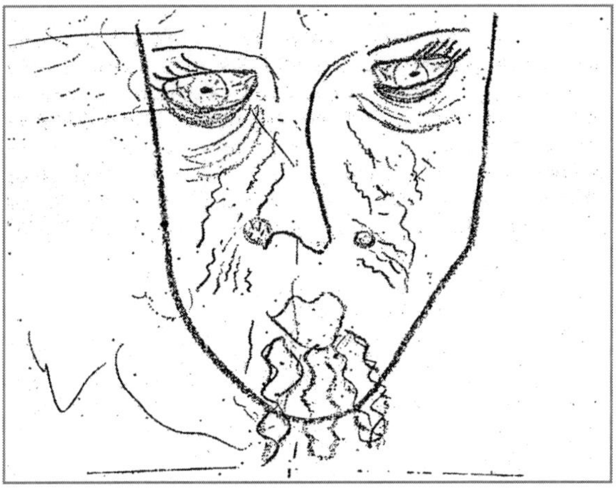

FIGURE 9.3. Mother-therapist hated for saying "No".

sensation-dominated experiences and symbolic thought. At times her singing blots me out, but at other times it indicates her acknowledgement of absence and an attempt to make an internal mother come more vividly alive inside her. Her made-up song about a needy beggar

FIGURE 9.4. The witch-breast mother.

suggests a complexity of thought and feeling that "love makes her a beggar". After singing this song, she asks about the number of minutes remaining and measures the time by singing the scale, "do, re, mi".

Time has become quantifiable through music. Mia is also beginning to quantify time with an awareness of rhythm and pace: going fast, going slow, and having musical notes linked with the sounds of my voice. Accompanying this quantification of time is the sense of intervals, like the breaks in therapy. This is illustrated in a series of drawings made over two weeks preceding the Christmas holidays. The Christmas holiday calendar that I make is linked by her to the musical scale (Figure 9.5).

Another drawing (Figure 9.6) suggests Mia's awareness of the "father-conductor" who directs the flow of the mother's milk-voice understanding and the tempo of the session. Still present at times in the face of the termination of therapy is Mia's wish to replace the father as the conductor of the music of the mother's voice: the different rhythmic movements of the lines on a series of drawings seem to represent Mia's recreation of the rhythm and flow of her therapy music, the intervals and days of the sessions, and her wish for an endless flow of sessions (Figure 9.7). Present, though, is an acknowledgement of the father's role as the creator, along with the mother, of the mother's internal music (Figure 9.8).

In reviewing the sessions, I begin to ask myself, "When does Mia's

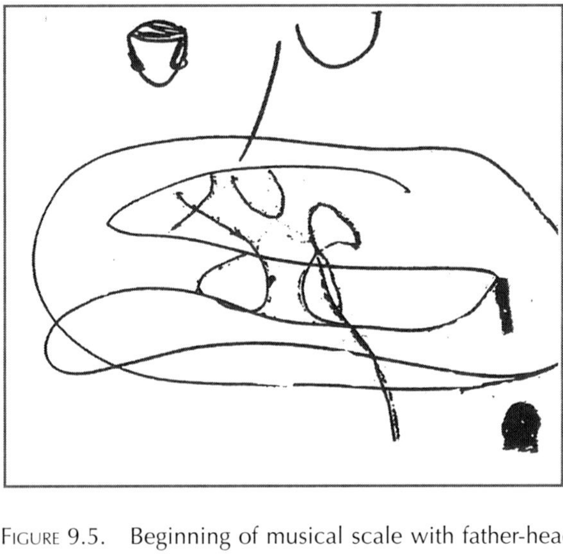

FIGURE 9.5. Beginning of musical scale with father-head.

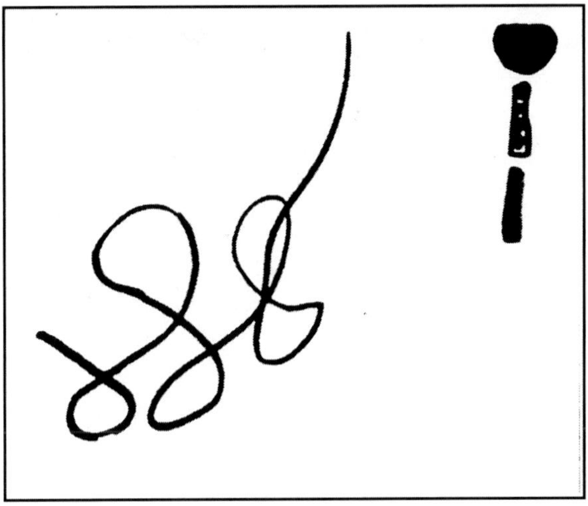

FIGURE 9.6. The father-conductor of music.

copying of concrete sensory details move towards creative symbolic representation?" My tentative thought is that when there is the threat of "time apart" and Mia's destructive self is in a rage against the "conductor-father" who puts an end to the therapy music, several different possibilities emerge. The first possibility is that, in a regressive step, the "conductor-father" becomes hallucinated as the "terrible man" in the room, in an attempt to prevent his introjection and spoiling

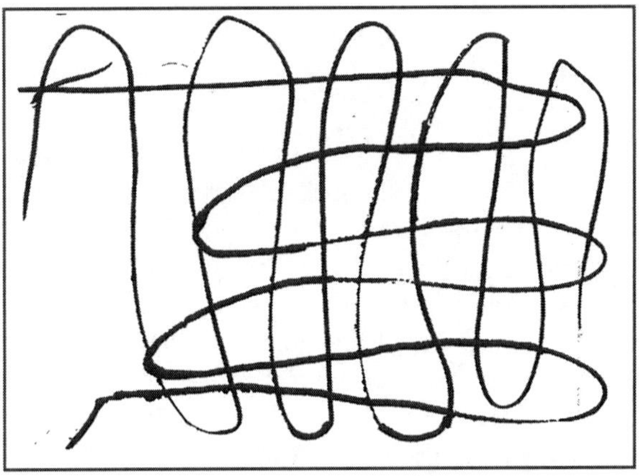

FIGURE 9.7. The wish for "endless flow of music".

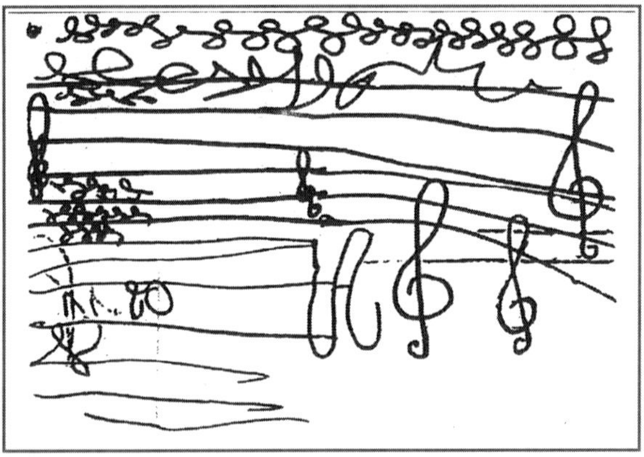

FIGURE 9.8. Father creating the mother's internal music.

the good but idealized mother in a good internal space. The second possibility is that Mia slips into being projectively identified with a mother looking after a baby whom she is wheeling in a pram rather than a mother preoccupied with her appearance, as at the beginning of therapy. The third possibility is that, following a destructive attack on the disappearing "mother-therapist", there is an upsurge of loving, reparative wishes mitigating Mia's hate. When this predominance of Mia's love for a good internalized mother-therapist mitigates her jealous attack, she produces these more symbolic drawings. The flow of the lines suggests that her thoughts and feelings are becoming integrated in a more spontaneous and creative manner (Jackson, 2015).

Thus it is possible to envisage separation from a loved mother-therapist as a crucial moment for Mia to regress or to develop.

Transformations in time

Assessment of a child's therapeutic progress involves examining the changing nature of the time-limiting role of the father, which permits the mother-therapist to have a creative space to join the father and other babies. The role of the father also ensures a regular rhythm of therapy sessions, at a particular time, for a particular period. Near the end of treatment, there may be a resurgence of love and a capacity to appreciate the notion of time; the child may begin to feel supported by the father's protective role in setting and maintaining limits. There is also, often, a resurgence of hate and the potent, perilous feelings aroused by the time limit proposed by the end of therapy.

For this reason, I shall now describe the end of our psychotherapy to show the fluctuations in Mia's concept of time.

> Knowing therapy is ending in a few months' time, Mia arrives pushing a pram with a baby doll inside. (The previous week she had brought a live kitten from home into the session.) Mia says to me, "You are an old-fashioned cushion", and, when questioned about what she means, she says, "It is smelly and wrinkled." I reply, "You seem to feel a nice, fresh young mummy looking after a new baby. I seem to be the old mummy, a kind of old grandmother." Later I wonder, "Perhaps you are having difficulty letting me remain a good lively mummy-therapist for fear that there will be another child following your time in therapy with me."
>
> About halfway through the session, Mia looks at me with amazement, smiles with a lovely expression on her face, and says, "You have the lovely green silk blouse on. I'd like to touch the collar and sit on your lap." She remains seated across from me, simply gazing at me with a contemplative, serene expression on her face. After a moment or two I respond, "You feel grateful for the experience of being with me, being understood by me. You feel the beauty of the good mummy." She continues looking at me.

At this moment, Mia seems to have stopped attacking the goodness of the mummy-therapist. When she arrived, she was projectively identified with the internalized mother-therapist looking after the baby, and then, after my attempts to understand her, she became filled with awe at the presence of the object and love for the object and its resilience (Meltzer & Harris Williams, 1988). Mia's experience shows a transformation from sensuous appreciation of the object—prompting adherence to silkiness and intrusion into the "mother's skin"—to experiencing the love and passion necessary for any creative endeavour to emerge.

Mia's transition is heralded by her creative expression, taking her beyond the immediately perceived present moment with me. She yells at me, complaining, "You don't really love me, you just love yourself!" Then she enquires, "Why are you looking so worried? Your face is all screwed up!" After anxiously looking at me, she says, "Your eyelashes are like spiders, your teeth are like pointed spears, your eyes are like footballs, your neck is like a tree trunk." She proceeds to draw an image of me (Figure 9.9). After she finishes this drawing, Mia contradicts herself, saying, "No, you are not really like that." Then she

FIGURE 9.9. The therapist, containing spider eyelashes and pointed spear teeth.

does another drawing, transforming "tree trunk neck" into a tree with flowing branches (Figure 9.10).

In a subsequent session, Mia says, "You have a child already lined up to be with you when I leave . . . and you will see this child forever and take her go home with you." A series of sessions then occur in which Mia tries to break the window, and she hits me. Regression has occurred in the face of the ending.

Mia seems to allow me to have my therapeutic capacities when apart from her, but she wants to imprison me in my consulting room

FIGURE 9.10. The therapist's neck transformed into a tree trunk.

so that I will have no future except as a therapist. Here is an excerpt from a session three months prior to ending therapy:

> Mia asks me, "Do you remember yesterday when I put you in a prison with me?" I acknowledge her wish to stay with me. She then wants to imprison me in the corner of the room furthest from the door, saying, "I am going to lock you in. I can get out." I say, "You can put into words now what you feel." She adds, "I am going to leave you all the mess and you can clean up and I am going to have a fantastic feast and you are not invited!" Mia covers me with the couch blanket, declaring, "Your eyes are to see beautiful things with and you can use your mouth to talk, but the rest of your body is old, mouldy, and rotting and your head is covered with old grey hairs."
>
> I respond, describing how Mia sees the future: "Yesterday you talked about the mother with lovely white mummy breasts who took care of babies in a good, loving way. Today you are imprisoning me so that I can have no future with the daddy, no babies, no other patients. I am to be *your* therapist and *only* a therapist. It seems this is the only way you can hold the mummy-therapist forever good inside you."
>
> Mia subsequently recounts two dreams: "First, I had a dream of your *being a prisoner locked up with only bread and water. Only your head was showing in the dream.* Then I had a dream of your *dying and ending up with the devils who burn you up. Afterwards you are only ashes.*"
>
> I describe how it is very hard to keep me good inside her, saying, "The baby's rage is spoiling me leaving nothing good inside." I suggest, "We can keep each other in mind forever, you know."

Intimations of the future when ending therapy

During the last three months of therapy, Mia's thinking is dominated by the sense of our ending and our future lives. For a moment, she contemplates the notion of being a girl who can develop:

> Mia says, "I am growing up. I am going to wear dresses from now on." After exploring this statement a little I suggest, "Now there is a feeling that you can grow up to be a woman like me. You can let go of being the daddy with me." Mia looks calm and very pleased

> as she says, "Do you remember when I was seven? Do you remember when I was eight?" She implies by her calmness that she has outgrown all her wild messing of me and the room. "Yes, now you can think about and talk about your feelings. It feels very different inside. It feels safer now when you hold onto the good-mummy-therapist who thinks with you."

The emphasis on growing up and being able to separate from the mother-therapist immediately brings into play notions of the "new baby", the magician oedipal father who takes the little girl from her mother and leaves a little girl left out in the cold, running for safety to her mother. As Mia draws this picture, she says, "You are not allowed to say 'why', 'mummy', 'daddy', 'baby' or 'think'." In other words, it is difficult to contemplate these issues of separateness from the mother, allowing the mother-therapist the possibility of more patient-babies in the future. Yet Mia's future feminine identity is based upon her identification with the mother and her procreative capacities. A brief glimpse of this is in the drawing made just before the end of therapy. In this image (Figure 9.11), the "mummy" is allowed to be pregnant and to have a baby.

As the ending looms, Mia struggles to consider the future, in much the same way as the baby does when mother puts it to bed for the night: how can the baby-Mia allow the mother-therapist her freedom to have a life with the father and with other children? At this point,

FIGURE 9.11. Pregnant mother figure.

she imprisons the mother and burns her mother with her rage; then there is no sense of the future, only the death of the object. Hate and possessiveness are feelings easier to experience than the vulnerability and pain of losing the therapist.

In retrospect, I would say that a much longer time in therapy is needed for such a very ill child in such an uncontaining family setting to consolidate any internal developments made in the course of therapy. The question of how the patient will live in the future is always uncertain, although I do know that, by the end of her psychotherapy, Mia had gained an appreciation of her responsibility for trying to protect her good internal parents from her possessiveness and rage.

Mia wrote a note suggesting that I had given three and a half years of my life to help her to grow up. She also acknowledged that in some ways she had grown to be nice and in some ways she was still nasty. The future is determined by how Mia will be nurtured and understood and how she will allow me to have my freedom away from her. Most important is the question of how she can forgive me for what we were not able to do together to foster her psychological development.

Hope for the future is really based upon recognizing and protecting the goodness of the internal mother. This comes through having sufficient love to forgive the internal mother and father and allow them the possibility of being a procreative couple.

Time for the ending of therapy should arise in the therapist's mind when he or she senses that the possibility of preserving the good internal parents has arisen within the child's mind. As in the ending of Mia's therapy, however, when such total internal destruction of the good object occurs and there is no possibility of going through the mourning process, the therapist needs to reconsider the notion of "time for the ending of therapy". Whatever external crises arise, hope for the future can exist only through the taming of destructive feelings so that the internal parents can be restored to goodness and remain understanding and protective throughout life.

Final hypothesis

Until there is a perception of a good object, separate from the external good object, life is emotionally hazardous with unpredictable out-of-control feelings. The introjection of the good object, and the maintaining of its goodness while allowing the primary object to be absent, produces three profoundly important transformations in the child's experience of time (Colarusso, 1979).

First, the child's sense of time becomes more self-contained and internalized, becoming less dependent upon the presence or absence of the mother. Although the child's sense of time appears more autonomous, it is still largely related to the goodness or badness of the internalized mother. If, for example, the child's rage against the absent object is too intense, the absent good object becomes a damaged and dying internal object. The damaged internal object may then take the form of concerns about the reality of the external object. For example, there may be accompanying fears that the mother has died in a crash or drowned when she is away from the child. In this situation, the child experiences the waiting period as infinitely long until mother returns intact.

When the inner object is destroyed, there can be no personal development, only depression. In depression, the inner feeling of time stops and there is no sense of the future. This sense of no future is often linked with the child's sadistic desire to perpetuate the suffering of others. Of course, the child's sadism may, in part, be connected with a destructive and extremely disappointing external environment, but the sense of time is always connected with one's inner emotional life.

If the child does not attack the external mother for being absent and allows her the possibility of being with the father, other children, and her work, the child is able to hold onto a good internal object. Time away from mother does not seem so long, for the "good mother inside" can be depended upon in the mother's absence.

Second, with the endurance of the good internal object, past, present, and future begin to have some continuity as a psychic experience. The presence of the good internal object allows the child to use the experience of the past to think about the present situation and contemplate the future. In this way, past, present, and future are all of interest and present in the child's conversation and thinking.

Third, the child's identification with the internalized good object allows it an independent existence in the common time–space continuum. In this way, the frustrations associated with time can be endured and mastered. Also, it is the presence of the internalized good object that maintains the child's hope for the future.

The sense of time is reflected in the language of a young child (Ames, 1946). "Soon", suggesting a sense of future by connoting waiting or delay, is usually first spoken by a child at around 18 months of age. "Soon" is used knowingly when the child is around 24 months. "Tomorrow" is not verbalized spontaneously until the child is around 30 months, and then it is expressed only after "today" has been

Figure 9.12. Images of persecution.

expressed. "Yesterday" appears when a child is around 36 months. "Now" and "when" also appear when a child is between 18 and 36 months.

In her therapy, Mia seems to follow a similar sequence of relating to time, but first she goes through a severe depression in which she feels that the torture to which she is exposed will last an eternity. Her sense of destruction and consequent despair is implied by the initial non-stop messing of my room, her persecutory experiences (Figure 9. 12), and her images of death (Figure 9.13).

If hope is directed solely towards an external event changing, rather than the development of the capacities of the good internal

Figure 9.13. Images of death.

object, the adult is left in danger of facing devastating despair. A young child, however, is emotionally dependent upon external figures to develop internally and, hence, is at greater risk of hatred and despair when these are not sufficiently containing, protective, and loving. As a therapist, I try to alleviate the child's despair and provide hope for his or her future by providing parental work as an essential accompaniment to individual psychotherapy. Hope for the child's future is based upon the security provided by the capacities of the good internal object to look after the self. When good internal objects are present, appreciation of the present moment, as well as hope for the future, are noticeable.

Meltzer's supervision accompanying this therapy

Mia was one of my first three psychotherapy patients when I was training as a psychotherapist. Naturally, I was filled with ignorance, lacking both clinical experience and conceptual knowledge. Meltzer focused neither on Mia's history nor on my inexact interpretations. Rather, he aimed to illustrate, as precisely as possible, Mia's intense transference in the current moment-to-moment interaction between us. He delineated the nature of her internal mother, father, and siblings. We also looked at what supported, inhibited, and obstructed her capacity to think about her emotional experiences. We also took careful note of her response to my interpretations, considering how she evaded, evacuated, or contained some of the emotional sense of what I was saying and how I was being with her.

My supervisory experience with Meltzer was not very different from an analytic encounter and is well captured in Clara Nemas's description of psychoanalysis:

> . . . shared responsibility for the analytic task transforms the relationship . . . into a work group of two, operating in a non-authoritarian atmosphere in which each does his or her job according to his or her capabilities. The function of understanding, divested of the expectation of knowing, allows for greater freedom to speculate and to make imaginative conjectures. [2000, p. 41]

Meltzer created an atmosphere of exploring, getting to know, and counter-dreaming. The supervision, like analysis, involved the formation of a symbolizing couple with the willingness to discover together the nature of the linking between Mia and myself (Eaton, personal communication, 2015). I sometimes described in detail my intensely disturbed feelings in the countertransference. Meltzer responded that unless I deeply felt Mia's emotional turbulence, it would be difficult for her to develop emotionally. I needed to receive the projections of her very confused and confusing inner-object relationships and lend meaning to them for her to introject an emotionally receptive and thoughtful therapist.

More precisely, as Mia's drawings illustrate, the state of her inner objects determined how she saw me, how she approached me, and how she felt about me. I moved from being "a sensuous object" with whom she merged, to an object into whom she could project "bad stuff", and, finally, into an object who created a sense of safety for both her loving and her hating feelings. She moved from hallucinating to dreaming and drawing, from "being in my shoes" to identifying with a "mother with a baby who needed care".

Meltzer was particularly interested in the way in which free-flowing creativity occurred in the spontaneous rhythmic lines and musical sequences (Figure 9.14).

In looking at the aesthetic experience of being deeply understood in the analysis, he often alluded to art and sometimes to music. Meltzer at times quoted Keats's poem "La Belle Dame sans Merci" (1884) to describe the "analytic baby's" suffering the pain of love and hate in the separations and disappointments of the psychoanalytic encounter.

My supervisory encounter with Meltzer provided psychoanalytic understanding of Mia in a non-judgemental, non-persecutory manner. This suffused my style of talking with Mia in an emotional reflective manner that was felt as a greeting of her internal state and physical

FIGURE 9.14. Free flowing rhythm of feelings.

gestures through a very wide range of varying tones of voice, words, and attitudes. I was not told what to say, nor was I expected to think what Meltzer thought. What predominated was an experience of being on a shared journey towards getting to know the truth of Mia's inner experiences at that moment in her relation to me representing her internal objects. I have internalized Meltzer as a mentor, enabling me to sustain feelings without searching for a thought, but, rather, waiting for a thought to emerge. For this I am eternally grateful to him.

CHAPTER TEN

The second life of dreaming

Jeffrey L. Eaton

> "[W]hat of the fruitful harvest of those dreams which succeed in grasping the nettle of mental pain, resolving a conflict, relinquishing an untenable position? We will surely wish our hypothesis about dream-life to shed some light on this question of growth."
>
> Donald Meltzer, *Dream-Life* (1983)

For Donald Meltzer, dreaming is at the centre of the psychoanalytic experience. He links the exploration of dreams with the efficacy of the psychoanalytic process. Exploring dream-life helps to glimpse the way dreaming contributes to what Meltzer calls "the question of growth". Here, I offer some personal reflections, inspired by Meltzer, on the fruitful harvest of dreams and dreaming.

The second life of dreaming

What is the fate of the dream, the thing-in-itself, upon waking? The situation is simple: the dream has vanished. In fact, we never remember our dreams. Upon waking, we can collect only bits of evidence that the dream was recently alive and wandering inside us. The fragments and details, the emotions, and the unpredictable residue that lingers from the inventiveness of our dream-life are like the skeletal traces of a fabulous lost beast. The dream itself can never be recovered, relived, or represented in any complete way.

Dreaming creates what can be poetically called "a country of the mind", a place where we can go, usually while asleep, to yield full attention to psychic reality. In this new country, we can live a second life while dreaming. This second life may become a laboratory where unconscious experiments in living and feeling are carried out each night. While dreaming, problems are pictured, solutions are sought, alternatives are realized, and emotions and memories are tested in ways that may not be available during waking life.

Dreaming may be seen as a form of unconscious play; watching children play is, perhaps, as close as we can come to observing a dream being made. The child playing makes a scene populated with characters, actions, backgrounds, intentions, conflicts, and rapid transformations of anxieties, ideas, fantasies, and emotions. Something similar takes place in dreaming. The concreteness of the experience of entering a dream scene lends the experience emotional power, while the transience of dreaming makes possible the realization of myriad circumstances.

Even violent impulses can be safely expressed in play and dreaming because there is a mysterious process of symbolization developing—an atmosphere that children call "just pretend" and that adults call "just a dream".

Dreaming, then, like playing, opens up a space of psychic freedom. Somehow, something troubling, or something new, or even something reaching towards us from the future makes its way into the dream scene and, from there, sometimes proceeds on into waking consciousness.

Through dreaming and the production of dream thoughts and events, there is contact with a continuous unfolding unconscious conversation between the self and its own experiences. As one continues to dream, night after night and year after year, autonomous symbols naturally emerge, and the result is what the poet Shelley (1891) calls an "expression of the imagination".

Meltzer emphasizes that we import meaning from one world (the dream laboratory) into another (the world of our waking lives): dreaming leaves the gate to the psyche open every night, and the emotions generated by dreaming wander back through and linger into the day, shaping our perceptions.

The many experiences accumulated in the second life of dreaming influence our choices in waking life. Successful dreaming means that less pain must be hidden in the body, projected into the group, or split off, denied, and located in other objects or dimensions. Through the intimate exploration of the patient's dreams, shared in the analytic encounter, waking and dreaming processes begin to cooperate. Contact with dream-life, paradoxically, helps one to develop a greater tolerance and deeper respect for the facts of external reality.

Grasping the nettle

According to Meltzer, there is always one important question at the beginning of every treatment: *Who shall have the pain?* In the analytic setting we can observe that some people turn towards the analyst, hoping to find someone capable of tolerating the expression of painful emotions. Other people turn away, overtly rejecting the possibility of glimpsing, feeling, facing, and sharing their emotional pain.

There are, of course, many obstacles to sharing emotional pain. Some patients report that they cannot dream, or that they cannot recall their dreams. Some claim that their dreams mean nothing. Still others hate their dreams—or are terrified to go to sleep, hoping at all costs to avoid having a dream. Some patients seem convinced that, at a deep level, revealing the truth of their suffering can only lead to punishment. And, finally, in some situations, people expect awareness of the pain, so vividly made present by certain kinds of dreams, to excite and stimulate cruelty in the minds and actions of others.

The self absorbs the impacts of dreams, for better or worse. Dreams devolve into nightmares and into night terrors. These shocks and insults accumulate over dozens of nights, with no sense of relief or rescue. What happens if, for some, dreaming is more difficult to bear than waking life? People can be haunted by their dreams. Dreams can be traumatic objects; you can feel injured not just in your dreams but by your dreams. No wonder some people hate the experience of dreaming and, even, of having a mind that dreams.

Yet painful dreams can also be important beginnings. When a person is unable to ask or formulate the question "Who shall have the pain?", his or her dream may be capable of giving form to the question instead. Dreams bring psychic reality directly into the foreground and allow this question to emerge and to seek an adequate reply.

Now I want to share an example of such a dream. I am neither presenting a case study nor offering an analysis of the patient's dream. I present the dream simply as a specimen of the emergence of the intensity of mental pain in the early months of an analysis.

> *I am in a crowded street somewhere and there is an evil force coming towards me. I can't see it or hear it but I know it is there, and getting closer. Horrible things are happening all around me. Women and kids are dying in horrible ways. I have a mirror or something and somehow I'm supposed to use it to fend off this "thing". It is getting closer and closer and I know something terrible is going to happen.*

The figures and events, the objects and emotions that emerge in dreams like this one are painful to register and intimidating to behold. The intensity of the dream strains both the analyst and the patient. Yet at the same time such dreams are really gifts if one can find the psychic space necessary to welcome their intensity; if it can become possible to turn towards the dream, it can become a shared object that takes on its own life between the patient and the analyst. The shared dream (and the pain) can then be explored against a new background of gradually expanding spacious awareness generated by a dreaming couple.

To me, this is the heart of the therapeutic action of psychoanalysis: the discovery of a symbolizing couple and its growth in the interaction between analyst and analysand through a process that can become repeatedly internalized and elaborated within the patient's own dream-life.

The background of dreams

I value dream-life. I encourage my patients to pay attention to their dreams, to report on them, and to explore them with me in our sessions. Over many years I have heard many hundreds of dreams narrated by my patients, and often, in an analysis lasting several years, I have the privilege to hear dozens if not hundreds of dreams from a single dreamer. From this richness of this raw material I have abstracted three domains that can, I think, offer meaningful shape to the analyst's listening strategy when approaching the significance of any patient's dream-life.

I have come to believe that we must pay more attention to the background of people's lives and experiences. The context and setting of every experience is important, including—perhaps especially—the background of dreams. The background of the dream offers a different kind of information than the objects of the dream or the actions of the characters in the foreground do. Deliberately slowing down and focusing on the background of the dream can highlight other dimensions of psychic reality for both the patient and the analyst. The background may be an indicator of profound psychic stress, conflict, or the emergence of new psychic functions and has, as I suggested, three general domains or patterns within the larger, more elusive and mysterious process of unconscious symbol-formation. This can be observed through the development of a deepening analytic process.

I want to contextualize this conjecture in relation to Meltzer's description of life in the claustrum. It is possible that the background of dreams may show evidence of life in the claustrum and the corresponding attitudes associated with the compartments of the internal mother. The domains that I am proposing, however, refer more generally to all dreams, not just to dreams in which the subject is living inside an internal object through intrusive identification.

Three more dreams from the same patient will, I hope, illustrate this, although I recognize that these ideas require further elaboration. Nonetheless, I want to open these new avenues for thought, even if they are, thus far, only partially travelled.

Survival

> *I was driving a truck, a real beater, and even though I was not going over the speed limit, everything felt really shaky. Then, all of the sudden, the road collapsed and I and all the others cars plunged into a gigantic hole. I just kept falling, there was no bottom. I woke up and I couldn't go back to sleep.*

Survival is an existential life problem of the organism or individual. The dreams in this domain convey profound psychic distress. They have to do, I think, with the unconscious memory of the problem of the viability of the organism in relationship to the environment.

These are areas described by Winnicott (1974) as "primitive agonies" and by Bion (1962b) as "nameless dreads". I am also impressed by Tustin's (1984) descriptions of the earliest impacts of the premature awareness of separation. I describe all these kinds of agonies as linked by an experience of primal exposure. This is a state of unthinkable vulnerability characterized by the awareness, however rudimentary or intuitive, of the absence of protection from annihilation. In other words, the preconception of not existing has been stimulated much too early for the individual to be able to use it as an inauguration into thinking through and elaborating this particular reality.

One solution to the presence of such primal exposure may be intrusion, through projective identification into an internal object, as

Meltzer has compellingly described. But that is only one possible fate. I believe dreams in this domain convey the beginnings of a process that attempts to make thinkable the unthinkable through picturing experiences of catastrophic background events.

As an individual's dream-life evolves in the analytic process, we may discern plausible patterns that suggest how the person has unconsciously coped with his or her own personal primal catastrophe. Dreams such as this one suggest that the patient feels he or she is missing what I call "a reliable floor" for experience. Without such a floor, the very possibility of survival is called into question.

I believe that identifying this dimension of the dream background can be crucial in giving the patient not only a feeling of being understood, but also belief that it is possible and worthwhile for the analytic couple to face such intimidating pains and go forward together. It is through sharing these disturbing images and the sensations and affects that they carry that a gradual trust in the reality of an emotional floor for experience can be discovered and built.

Adaptation

> *I'm standing on a stage with a group of men with a giant Nazi flag behind us. I'm wearing a Nazi uniform. I'm giving the Heil Hitler salute with everyone else. I'm terrified people will see that my heart's not really in it.*

The theme of adaptation has, of course, a long and complex history. The concept is central in biological and evolutionary sciences as well as in some streams of psychoanalysis, especially in ego psychology. As I am using the term, the dreams in this domain have to do with the struggle to create personal meaning versus complying with (or being dominated by) the family and the group. Obviously, such a theme involves a kaleidoscope of issues: obstacles to intimacy and sincere expression are often pictured, or patients may describe feelings of helplessness and frustration that coexist with thwarted initiative. There is often the feeling that the patient may be selling out, settling for less, cutting his or her losses, being a coward, playing the fool, and running out of time.

Once the issue of survival has been adequately addressed in the analytic process by successfully creating an emotional floor for experience, the next domain often involves entering the profound realm of adaptation to the family, the group, the community, and even to a particular moment in history. The environment can then be explored as a multitude of variables that both constrain and facilitate the development of the self. Within it, emotions are patterned and processed through the challenges of adaptation and through increasingly personal interaction with the environment, which sponsors learning and maturation across the life span. Dreams help show the history of this process as well as its progress.

An important aim of the analytic work is to help the patient differentiate between contractual interactions (dominant in the adaptive domain) from opportunities for real intimacy and the development of sincerity in relationships.

Thriving

> *I'm in a beautiful place in the mountains with a woman I am in love with. I have some kind of arithmetic problem I'm trying to solve. I'm trying to write it out on a large piece of paper on the ground. The woman offers to help me and I let her. I wake up with a feeling of incredible happiness.*

The dreams in this domain have to do with learning to trust one's own internal objects, letting them be free, and establishing a space for creativity where one can harvest the fruits of intuition and welcome thoughts in search of a thinker.

To outline a model of the factors that promote thriving is beyond the scope of this chapter. However, I think we can say that the development of an apparatus for thinking, feeling, and experiencing is crucial, beyond the immediate demands for survival and social and emotional adaptation. Bion emphasized what he called the K-link, a robust curiosity to know about others. This desire to know can widen into an impulse to investigate the vast scope of the mystery of creation, life, and the universe, the domain Bion noted as O. James Grotstein (2004) has taken this yearning to learn about life in the fullest ways possible and emphasized the motive force of a "truth drive" that, I think, is linked to the subjective orientation I am calling "thriving".

What I am offering is an outgrowth of reflections on Bion's *Elements of Psycho-Analysis* (1963) and Meltzer's description of the psychoanalytic process. Dreams give us glimpses and preconceptions of thriving, as well as, over the course of our work—and with careful attention—clues to the structure of the personality that can help it to thrive and learn from experience. I believe that, to some degree, thriving implies going beyond self and emotion and beginning to consider one's relationship to what Bion called O, an unknowable, absolute reality that is the ultimate background for all our dreams and experiences.

The analyst's own dreams as a guide

I want to briefly describe how a dream helped me to symbolize the emotional impact on me of my relationship to a young schizophrenic patient whom I shall call Andy. I shall also describe how this dream guided me in making deeper communicative contact with him.

When I first met Andy, he was thin, dishevelled, and haunted-looking. Andy told me he spent most of his days in bed, "under cover". He said he enjoyed daydreaming. This intense activity seemed to insulate him from powerful feelings of persecution. I vividly recall a session in which Andy felt so persecuted that he threatened to break the window to escape.

His communications sometimes flowered into religious delusions of intense grandiosity. He believed, for example, that he had been secretly placed at the centre of a giant cosmic net and had been chosen to absorb the pain of the entire world. His job was to filter the pain of millions of lives through his own body and mind.

In the early months of our work, Andy often withdrew into wordlessness. He would sit in the corner of the couch, slumped and silent. He would not look at me. In the silence I often noted feelings of helplessness, frustration, and sometimes extreme anxiety in my body. I also had the feeling that I might suddenly fall asleep.

I understood all these experiences as elements of intense projective identifications. I struggled to find words for this experience and to share my understanding with Andy.

One night I dreamed:

> *I am standing outside a tall, round brick tower that looks as if it is part of a castle. I go inside and climb a steep, circular stone staircase. At the top of the stairs is a small, round room with windows. In the middle of the room is a table and on the table is a hunk of clay on a pedestal. Next to it is a computer screen. As I watch, the clay begins to form itself into a human head, with the face of a man. I feel, suddenly, incredible fear. The clay is making itself into something. Then I notice that the process is being represented on the computer screen, which also shows the picture of the clay face. This makes me curious and I'm aware of both fear and curiosity powerfully combined. When the clay is fully formed, I become even more frightened. Now I feel an enormous force coming from inside the empty eyes of the clay face. I feel I am being physically sucked into the clay head and that I will be trapped inside. I wake in terror.*

I was relieved to wake up. But I had a strongly uncanny feeling, a bizarre and disorienting feeling in my body. The atmosphere of the dream lingered for a long time, and I thought, "This is Andy's dream!"

Upon reflection, it seemed that this dream might be about my experience of the conscious and unconscious impact I was ambivalently trying to welcome as I got to know Andy. The dream, I felt, was showing me what it was like unconsciously for me to be with Andy.

Another way of looking at the dream is to say that my contact with Andy introduced me to a split-off psychotic element of my own personality. Spending time with Andy invited this new "character" to enter my dream theatre and to inaugurate an improbably intimate conversation with psychosis. Unconsciously, I was trying very hard to make sense of the emotional experience of schizophrenia.

There came a moment, in a subsequent session, when Andy withdrew again into silence. I waited for several minutes and, during that time, the atmosphere of my dream returned spontaneously. I had not planned to make an interpretation based upon my dream, but, drawing on that experience, I said something like, "I wonder if you're afraid to look at me because you fear that, if you do, something terrible will happen. Looking at my face might feel overwhelming. You're afraid something powerful will take you over and trap you. Maybe there just are no words for such awful things."

Andy now looked directly at me. Suddenly, he found his voice. He told me, in a very lucid way, about a night at the psychiatric hospital. He said he had been given an injection and had terrible cramps that had paralysed him. He remembered feeling that he just wanted to die. He described being taken to a locked ward where he later witnessed a patient assaulted by another patient. He said he did not speak for days after that.

A mother cannot dream her infant's dream. But she can dream her own dream about what it might be like to be her infant. This does not give her access to her infant's subjectivity in the sense of knowing it directly, completely, or transparently, but she can imagine it in a meaningful and embodied way. When she shares that meaning, made from the inside out, the song and dance of her voice and her actions carry intuitions that awaken her infant's preconceptions about what contact with the mind of another might ultimately make possible. In its own way, this is the genuine and fruitful harvest that the psychoanalytic setting seeks to make possible: an intimate contact with psychic reality that can be shared with another, like the experience of a dream.

Opening a window into psychic reality

Dreaming, according to Meltzer, is a process that creates the possibility of transforming emotional experiences into meaning. One of the most important problems, which every analysis will face, involves the patient's capacity to recognize and develop the organ of consciousness—the capacity to tolerate and explore psychic quality. For this to take place, a dream space (which, I have emphasized, has various evolving background qualities) must gradually be helped to develop. Meltzer (1983) calls this space "the theatre of meaning" and, by collecting, exploring, and discussing the patient's dreams, the analyst can observe, over time, the transformations of many different psychic functions through the evolution of this theatre of meaning which is made visible by looking into the window of dream-life.

Meltzer paid close attention to several different aspects within the theatre of meaning. One important question was whether or not the patient could turn towards his dream-life or whether he repeatedly turned away from it. Turning towards dream life involves growing the capacity for tolerating contact with psychic reality, and this, in turn, is related to the "organ of consciousness", which, according to Freud (1911b), is defined as a "sense organ for psychical qualities". Meltzer wonders which characters in any particular dream represent this function and its fate, and, additionally, he asks what happens to this function upon waking.

In chapter 6 of *Dream-Life*, Meltzer writes:

> If we remember that we are not dismissing the distinction between consciousness as an "organ for the perception of psychic qualities", we can ask the question, "Which character in our theatre is, at the moment of dreaming, in possession of this organ?" But also, "Is it the same as the recaller and narrator of the dream during the analytical session?" We must allow for the possibility that they may not be—in fact probably usually are not—the same. [1983, p. 93]

Meltzer seems to have paid particular attention to the development of this capacity to perceive psychic qualities and, additionally, to investigate which part of the personality either sponsors or captures (or even exploits) this function. Indeed, if one of the goals of analysis is to successfully establish the possibility of self-analysis, then attention to the growth of the organ of consciousness must take a central place in the analyst's ongoing observation of the process. In thinking about the complexity and importance of internal object relations, the question of which (or what kind of) internal object controls the organ of consciousness opens a new window through which one can observe the evolution of the self and its circumstances within a psychoanalytic process.

In Meltzer's view, a dream is a construction that reveals an evolving continuity, not necessarily within one dream, but over the course of many dreams strung together in time. This crucial time dimension can be measured over a span of nights, weeks, months, years, or even decades. In particular, Meltzer speaks of dreams being able to depict a problem that the patient is unconsciously trying to work out. If this can be noticed, he suggests, then a problem can be investigated more clearly, and with greater depth and nuance. If this psychic complexity can be tolerated, rather than evaded, then it can be thought about and reflected upon. This opens another dimension of experience, which brings with it not only different forms of anxiety, but also, over time, evidence of transformation and even, in the best instances, novel solutions proposed through the unconscious creativity of the dreamer's inner work.

What I think should be highlighted is the way that the background of the dream evolves into an inner workspace for the organ of consciousness. Dream exploration starts with the analyst getting to know the patient's dream-life but may soon become a shared task. The psychoanalytic setting is a workspace for exploring dream-life, and, if it is successfully elaborated, a kind of apprenticeship in exploring psychic reality can unfold. Gradually, dream-life reveals the construction of an inner workspace, a space capable of welcoming, tolerating, investigating, and learning from dream events. The patient's capacity to recognize this transforming inner workspace is one factor that makes the creativity of analysis an aesthetic experience for both participants.

One obstacle to this kind of process would seem to be the discomfort that patients, as well as many analysts, feel in handling dream material. There is a mistaken conviction that one must be able to decode the dream, rather than simply getting to know it and exploring its details. If an analyst can assume a humble role of curiosity about the dream and all its particulars, a spontaneous force field of emergent meaning may be detected. Over time, patterns with linking power become clearer. Meltzer felt he had a gift for opening dreams as a generative process, not as a source of fixed meaning.

The process of exploring dreams promotes a deep sense of intimate cooperation and can inspire an evolving appreciation for the process of expanding self-awareness. Gradually the patient begins to take an interest in and develops a desire to actively explore, learn from, sustain, and protect the analytic project because she realizes that the analyst is not trying to do something to her, but, instead, is present to help her discover herself as a complex subject in process.

I met Meltzer only briefly towards the end of his life. He seemed both vibrantly intelligent as well as irascible. His physical presence and communicative intensity made a strong impression that still lingers many years later. Meltzer, not unlike some Buddhist teachers, transmitted something simply through his way of being. I remember him rather like an old Alaskan miner somewhat hardened by life in the deep backwoods. I like to picture him in the Alaskan wild, standing hip deep in the stream of the unconscious, panning for gold. As an experienced dream explorer, Meltzer would patiently sift the contents of each dream, taking in all the details before deciding which specific elements to examine more deeply. He did not seem to be looking for a single golden nugget (of meaning) but, rather, allowed himself to become fascinated by all that the dream stream produced and left in his tin pan (the clinical hour).

In his gruff but often humorous way, Meltzer showed a remarkable freedom to lend his agile attention to patterns that spontaneously emerged to him. Once he had described them, the patterns seemed somehow obvious. He was patient, relaxed and receptive as he repeatedly dipped his attention and sifted the material he gathered from the river of the unconscious (including the natural history of the transference). He gave me conviction that it was necessary (not grandiose) to seek to contact the heart of the matter in any given moment.

For Meltzer, the dream is neither debris nor pure gold but is the raw material for important inner work. One sensed that Meltzer relished getting dirty, bending close to the muddy river, and that he was inspired by its changing conditions across the seasons of life. His intimacy with the energy and the landscape of the unconscious showed him the continuity of the dream process, the unity of the dream itself, and revealed what he called "the grammar of the dream". I admired his profoundly disciplined imagination, and he offered a model of clinical intuition that remains inspiring.

Psychoanalysis sponsors an improbable conversation, not just between the analyst and the analysand, but also between the patient's discovery of psychic reality and the many complex links to daily life and the external world. Of immediate interest is the dream's linking function in the interaction between the external world and the internal world, between the body and symbolization, between relationships with others and how our fantasies unfold, between thinking and feeling, and between getting to know and the illusion of always already knowing.

There is no such thing as a dream, only a dreaming process. Dreaming is a kind of river. You cannot show someone only a part of the river, except as an abstraction. You can only really speak about moments in the flow of the river, just as you can only really speak about moments in the process of dreaming. This is why the focus on process is so important in understanding the sensibility that Meltzer brought to understanding dream-life. The habits of language create a distortion of this larger truth. The better we can describe the actuality of dreaming, the more we may be open to question the mystery of the experience of becoming a self. Is there a self that creates a dream and then narrates it? Or, is dreaming a process that creates a feeling of self which, later, becomes aware of living moments in the river of dreaming?

In a deepening analytic process the patient will also learn how to wade out into the river of dreaming. The patient will not idealize the analyst and wait for him to deliver his knowledge, but will join alongside him, increasingly able to share the task of gathering and sifting the dream material for fragments of emotional gold. Meltzer left me with a visceral sense of the task shared between patient and analyst, both at work together, waist deep in the river of dreaming, opening to whatever arrives, surrounded by the wilderness of O.

Notes

This chapter is dedicated to Franco Scabbiolo with gratitude for the many conversations we have shared regarding dreaming and dream-life.

Much of the text in this essay appeared as a chapter in my book *A Fruitful Harvest: Essays after Bion* published by The Alliance Press, Seattle, WA, in 2011 and used by permission.

CHAPTER ELEVEN

On having ideas: the aesthetic object and O

Meg Harris Williams

> "The new idea presents itself as an emotional experience of the world and the beauty of its wondrous organisation."
>
> Donald Meltzer (in Meltzer & Harris Williams, 1988, p. 20)

I should like to talk about what we mean by "having ideas", using, as reference points, Donald Meltzer and three of the Kleinian thinkers who had an influential bearing on his own ideas—Wilfred Bion, Adrian Stokes, and Roger Money-Kyrle—to sketch a composite picture of their idea of how we have ideas. This is equivalent to asking how we learn from our internal objects without being overawed or inhibited by them. These objects are those advanced aspects of the mind that are formed progressively from a complex mixture of external influences, intimate relationships, and innate internal qualities.

Psychoanalysis, Meltzer said, works through holding "conversations between internal objects" (see Williams, 2003, p. 219)—those of analyst and analysand working together to form a symbol for the idea of the current emotional experience. As the definition of mental health shifted to one of self-knowledge, the goal of psychoanalysis changed from one of cure to one of facilitating the formation of ideas, through the creation of symbols. This endeavour is not unique to psychoanalysis: it runs through all artistic disciplines, as it does through life.

Meltzer, especially in his later talks and writing, tried to convey the "simplicity" of this process, by which he meant its complexity. But the message itself is a simple one. To quote Martha Harris:

> Introjection remains a mysterious process: how do involvement and reliance upon objects in the external world which are apprehended by the senses (and, as Wilfred Bion has pointed out, described in language which has been evolved to deal with external reality) become assimilated and transformed in the mind into what he calls "psychoanalytic objects" which can contribute to the growth of the personality? This is a process about which we have almost everything to learn. [Harris, 1978b, p. 176]

The great psychoanalytic thinkers are well aware that psychoanalysis has, to date, added only a little to our knowledge about the mind. This is not surprising when we consider the awesome global cultural heritage. Meltzer saw the cultural significance of psychoanalysis as contributing a new aesthetic object—the psychoanalytic method—a way of using the transference that is a fundamental feature of human nature and that already exists and operates in other human relationships. Meltzer, Bion, Money-Kyrle, all repeat that the "new idea" we are considering is really an old idea in a new context. It is the new link, the new context, that brings it to life, so that it begins to mean something, either to a particular person or to a whole school of thinking or an artistic–scientific methodology such as psychoanalysis. "Meaning something" means it becomes "known", not just "known about".

At the end of his final paper, "Making the Best of a Bad Job" (1979), Bion cites Plato's *Theaetetus* on the difficulty of ensuring that a young man's education fill his head, not with "phantoms", but with "live thoughts". Bion made it clear that we don't invent our ideas: we discover them, after they have somehow made their way into our mind—what the poets call inspiration, or psychoanalysts introjective identification. In response to Roland's question in *A Memoir of the Future*—"Why can't you make up your mind?"—Bion's heroine Rosemary replies that she doesn't make up her mind: "I let my mind make *me* up" (Bion, 1991, p. 407), or, as Meltzer has said, "I haven't done psychoanalysis my way—I've been done its way" (quoted in Cassese, 2002, p. 104). Ideas "make up" the mind. Having ideas is a "passive" if strenuous process (with its connotations of turbulence and suffering), accompanied by a sense of dependency—not on external objects or persons but on internal objects.

The Platonic quasi-theological system, adopted by all these thinkers, is the philosophical bedrock for object-relations psychoanalysis, as it has always been for poetry. It supports the view of mediated levels of knowledge, through which truth or reality filters down to the self, via internal objects, finding a symbolic form that is an aspect of truth—even though never the whole truth, but clothed or fictionalized in a digestible way. All cognition is essentially re-cognition. Culturally, psychoanalysis is seen as a pre-existing thing-in-itself, waiting (as Meltzer describes it in *The Kleinian Development*, 1978) to be discovered, digested, and become part of modern society. Bion often speculates on the "non-Mendelian inheritance" of ideas and the mysterious way in which they pass from the global treasury (as it were) into individuals, so it is worth thinking of ideas in the context of their origins or tracking system—for which Bion uses the classical metaphor of the River Alpheus (1979, p. 256). It is a pity that our current academic culture pushes us towards a false presentation of this tracking system: in citing only the first source of a reference, we lose the individualistic colouring of how a particular thought has entered a particular mind and mated with the existing contents.

Perhaps it might be helpful to consider ideas as awaiting us, as individuals, to notice them and integrate them in our mind. The act of noticing entails developing a certain type of perception, a link between internal objects and subject. The part played by the self in "having ideas" is to make these links—or, rather, to notice different vertices so that links can form between them. The essential pre-requisite for this is a capacity for self-scrutiny, for looking inwards, as in Bion's binocular vision or observer–observed. The only ideas that come within our observational orbit will be those that our existing mental structure is ready to incorporate: they are *new to us*. We "notice" them when they impinge via an emotional turbulence—not necessarily a crisis, just a feel-ing. Given the universality of human nature and the logical functioning of the brain, some will have had the same idea hundreds of years before us, while others may never have it (for whatever reason). The alternative to incorporating an idea authentically is to appropriate it (colonization), to ignore it, or to fossilize it.

Ideas are absorbed through internal communication—"symbiotic links" between vertices, as Bion terms them. The original communicative link or "base" for having ideas is the baby's first feeding experience, as Money-Kyrle explains in his 1968 paper, "Cognitive Development". He lists three essential innate preconceptions upon which all subsequent conceptions are based: the good breast (and, we note, this must logically precede the idea of an absent breast, as in the idea of aesthetic conflict); good parental intercourse (based on nipple-in-mouth experience, which must be achieved by the age of six months); and fear of death, which creates awareness of time and the realization that no good thing can last for ever—hence the need to mourn loss and thus to establish the capacity for introjection, which is key to thinking and mental evolution. Without the innate awareness of death and loss, symbols can have no structure, no three-dimensionality, and the new idea can have no container.

When Meltzer came to formulate the "aesthetic conflict" for psychoanalysis (Meltzer & Harris Williams, 1988), it became clear that all three of Money-Kyrle's preconceptions needed to be engaged for the "baby" in the human personality to experience the aesthetic conflict of a new idea entering the mind: the baby link, the combined-object link, and the end of all links.

So, in having ideas, we put two vertices together and allow them to communicate—that is, to find where they adjoin or complement each other in a way that accrues meaning rather than depletes it. Keats, in his famous formulation of Negative Capability, calls this "dovetailing":

> Several things dovetailed in my mind, and at once it struck me what quality went to form a Man of Achievement especially in Literature and which Shakespeare possessed so enormously—I mean Negative Capability, that is when man is capable of being in uncertainties, Mysteries, doubts, without any irritable reaching after fact & reason [in Gittings, 1970, p. 43]

He doesn't specify what the "several things" are, although we can guess from the context that they may be linked to his preoccupation with learning poetry—both technical skills and poetic inspiration—from the "great poets" such as Shakespeare and Milton. We note that dovetailing is an involuntary act: it is something that happens and strikes the personality, the self, rather than being deliberately pieced together. A congruence suddenly manifests itself, and this results in a new idea.

When Bion adopted Keats' formulation, he was paying homage not just to the idea but to Keats' capacity to think for himself, his demonstration of how to think—by means of thinking about poets who had preceded him. He was incorporating Keats' way of thinking, in order to become introduced to himself—a marriage that will last "for as long as he lives", as he defined the aim of psychoanalysis (Bion, 1980, p. 40). Minds can encounter one another in a teaching–learning experience outside their bodies or earthly lifespans. This encounter generates an "emotional storm" and the chance to form (or deny) a symbol of the emotional experience: either to dovetail in conversation, or to split or cover over with dogma or denial.

Bion called the dovetailing "intersecting with O" (1970, p. 32) the ultimate source of knowledge; it is something that happens throughout life, not only in psychoanalysis, and not only between mother–baby or analyst–analysand, but between any two minds that spark a contact, or any two parts of a mind (such as prenatal and postnatal), any two art forms, or any two fields of knowledge of any sort (amongst these Bion emphasizes the three basic vertices of art, science, religion). Following Socrates, we can know nothing without the knowledge of our ignorance. The formulation "O" (as Bion uses it) has two levels of reference: the unknowable world of absolute reality, and the unknown, underlying idea or meaning of an emotional encounter. The greater O is like the godhead, whose function is to emphasize dimensions beyond time and space that we can never penetrate, hence giving us the concept of infinite possibility, beyond our comprehension. The smaller or lesser O refers to the underlying but abstract idea of a specific conflict or situation at a specific time; we become aware of its existence through an emotional experience; this is Money-Kyrle's (1968) conceptual "base" of the mouth-and-nipple (p. 218).

Hence Bion concludes *Attention and Interpretation* with the declaration that we need both the "restoration of god (the mother)" and "the evolution of god (. . . the ineffable)" (Bion, 1970, p. 129). God the mother is the first object, the conceptual base; god the ineffable is the larger O, the guarantee of the evolutionary quality that will extend that first oneness ("at-one-ment") to othernesses in the future: unbounded, unknowable, infinite in potential. (We note that, to Money-Kyrle's three preconceptions, Bion seems to add another: the infinite, although this may actually be a sub-category of the idea of death.) The object's own capacity to develop depends upon this belief in the infinite source of all qualities, a source that cannot be tapped directly but only mediated. Its existence, though unknowable, is an essential feature of our innate worldview.

The two levels of O are both necessary to picture learning from experience. As Bion says, "the Absolute . . . is not so biting as a toothache" (1991, p. 574); O does not impinge upon human experience or sensation in any direct way. What "bites" is the emotional experience, which becomes fictionalized in the form of a symbol, something that is an incomplete or slanted version of the abstract or absolute truth but is nonetheless truthful and therefore mind-building. According to tradition, Truth enters the world not as a whole or perfect shape but in pieces, as in Milton's description in *Areopagitica* (1644): "The Absolute enters the human world in many pieces, these pieces are perceived by our senses . . ." (p. 143). A symbol is produced by the intersection of O with the life of sense. The mother is knowable on the sensuous level, yet contains the abstract or unknowable god-principle that is infinite and ineffable, hence is the source and guide of vital curiosity (the K-link). In Meltzer's version of the myth, this idea takes the form of the aesthetic conflict and the tension between the mother's beautiful exterior and enigmatic interior. Where the traditional neo-Platonic system envisaged a ladder ascending from sensuous to divine beauty, stepping towards the heart of meaning, the aesthetic conflict describes the interaction of outside and inside, in which the search for the inside is stimulated by the contrast between the sensuously known and the unknown meaning or truth.

Every symbol demonstrates the intersection of the abstract noumenon with a sensuous phenomenon—as described by Coleridge (1816) when he says that a symbol, as distinct from an allegory, always "partakes of the reality which it renders" (p. 30). The abstract or noumenal level allows for the evolution of the internal object as it searches in the world of Platonic forms for the next little piece of truth required by the infant-self in its current phase. This mediated communication with the object via different levels of intersection (towards godhead) thus allows the self to introject not only the object's understanding of its present emotional experience (via the symbol), but the object's capacity to think, which entails its dependence on a greater object or O. For although the object knows more than the self, it must be simultaneously learning from a further O, a fount of truth that has no logical endpoint, since mental development is not circumscribed by bodily growth or decay.

For this reason it does not make sense to talk about "becoming O", any more than "being O". Bion likes to speak of "becoming" but in the context of becoming *oneself*, not becoming one's object or object-source. Instead, to designate what happens when we have ideas, he suggest alignment with O, or "at-one-ment"—"transformations in O" not transformations *into* O. (Milton pictures this as the earth hanging from heaven by a golden chain.) It is more like iron filings in a magnetic field, or "consensuality" as all the senses come together and point in the same direction in an act of recognition. Alignment is not the same as fusion or unity in the primitive oceanic sense but, rather, indicates a sense of direction and proportion. Alignment with truth results in our ingestion of a particular truth about ourselves, a piece of self-knowledge; and every piece of knowledge has an aspect of self-knowledge about it: it is never purely objective (neither in art nor in science). The idea of alignment stresses the aesthetic quality that accompanies having ideas. It fits. It is known not to be the absolute Truth: this nonetheless governs it, since it gives the sense of *evolution* of the object or, rather, its infinite potential for evolution. Alignment means aligning oneself with this evolutionary potential, the O that lies beyond the concept containing the present small experience. O is infinite: there is more to come, if we align ourselves with an evolving internal object.

Aligning with O requires a paradoxical sense of feeling contained and feeling left out, that Adrian Stokes analysed in terms of two modes of aesthetic experience required to either create or to creatively appreciate any work of art (Williams, 2015, p. xiii). One type allows for partiality, closeness, and evolutionary process; the other type allows for inviolability, inscrutability, unknowability, and inviolable otherness of the object. Even though the object (O) can never be known, changed into, or possessed, these very qualities initiate our quest for self-knowledge. In aesthetic conflict, the desire to *imaginatively* know the object establishes the container–contained, reciprocal, symbol-forming dialogue.

Stokes notes the dialectical structure of all philosophical quests (Williams, 2015, p. xiii). Two basic principles or positions are required, which need first to be distinguished, and then integrated. This certainly applied to his own lifelong preoccupation with the way the two fundamental modes of object-relationship operated in aesthetic experience: otherness and fusion, separateness and possession, the whole-object and the part-object viewpoints—for which he adopted the idea of an interplay between "carving" and "modelling" approaches to the object. He came to see that the two modes are both essential to object relations and are, in fact, complementary, each with a necessary function: one ensuring the aesthetic harmony of a particular achievement, the other ensuring a continuing process of development: being and becoming. Both play their part in having ideas and are founded upon the vision of an aesthetic object with an inside and an outside, which invite different modes of contact. This is indeed the basis of the deep grammar in poetry. The function of any form of art is to model this educational process of flux and stability so that the viewer can "appreciate"—that is, imitate and introject—it. Through art and psychoanalysis we become more aware of the internal dialogue that is awoken by the aesthetic object's O, with its intimations of infinity, of eternal development. The psychoanalytic reverie has its antecedents in the artistic or poetic reverie.

There is aesthetic conflict in the coming together of art forms or other disciplines as well as of minds, with the attendant temptation to divide or split these internal objects or their mediators. Yet all thinking relationships have the capacity to be generative—that is, to inspire others who introject the dovetailing in their own way, evolving autonomous symbols. The postnatal group at the end of Bion's *Memoir* conclude: "Fancy? Or fact? Just fancy, if there was something about ideas which might make them 'generative'!" (1991, p. 572). It is not the term "aesthetic conflict" that is the new idea but, rather, its new life in the context of clinical psychoanalysis. And perhaps ideas can only become generative if they are conveyed in their true colours, with their mediators and tracking systems, their progenitors, as felt on the pulses.

The concept of the restoration of the good mother is the foundation for Stokes' declaration that successful art is a representation of "sanity" and that, likewise, sanity is "an aesthetic achievement" (in Williams, 2015, p. xv). Meltzer founded his view of the psychoanalytic process as an aesthetic object (promoting sanity) on this central humanistic vision, writing about its "compositional" and "iconographic" aspects (in his 1981 paper on Money-Kyrle's concept of cognitive development). Then, in *Studies in Extended Metapsychology* (1986b), as a result of reflecting upon his work with autistic children, he describes how the "new idea" of psychoanalysis gradually became clear to him: "In the beginning was the breast and the breast was the world. . . ." (p. 204). Psychoanalysis itself is the O, the idea-generator; individual psychoanalysts and analysands can be mediators in relation to this object, if they have an artistic capacity for self-scrutiny, which is what enables the reception of emanations from the object. Meltzer states that the analytic couple comprise the "container" for the meaning between them (the symbol), by means of the conversation between internal objects. He goes on to relate how the key of alpha-function and the lock of symbol-formation dovetailed in his mind to form his own new picture of the self's three-dimensional relation to the object and how meaning can be flattened out of it, preventing the formation of symbols. In normal development, the container for an emotional experience takes on a certain shape (the symbol) reflecting the world–mother—the partly or fictionally knowable O—which is itself an elaboration of Money-Kyrle's mouth-and-nipple "base" (1968). If the analysis as aesthetic object has its compositional aspects, so do all relationships, seeking to achieve fit or congruence, and to avoid the "paramnesias" that arise through "envy of the growth-promoting objects" (Bion, 1970, p. 128).

The process of symbol-formation is therefore the same thing as having ideas, and it depends upon inspiration or introjection-and-projection. Bion doesn't really delve very much into the nature of symbols; until he starts specifically to evoke aesthetic experience in his late writings, he tends to equate symbol with verbal symbol. Money-Kyrle, too, says that a concept is grasped once it can be named—which is a signing action, not a symbolic one. But Meltzer, steeped in the "origins of language" tradition that flowered in the philosophy of Wittgenstein, Ernst Cassirer, and Susanne Langer, emphasizes the dreamlike quality of the symbol that contains the new idea. This is not a new thought: it was brought into focus by the eighteenth-century philosophers of language and was given its essential modern shape by Coleridge, who said that an idea cannot be had except through a symbol. But it didn't really dovetail with psychoanalytic thinking until Stokes made vivid the connection of the Kleinian drama of part-objects with exploring the inside and outside of the art-object. This could then be connected with the philosophy of poetry, deep grammar, organic form, musical diction, and so forth, as distinct from didactic statements and the manipulation of words in a conventional or superficial manner. Knowing *versus* knowing about; or in literary criticism, "thinking with" rather than "thinking about" a book. New symbols, transformations in O, can only be formed by thinking *with* the aesthetic object, of whatever type—an attitude of dependency, but oriented inwards, not outwards to external or social figures. "Trust in your good objects", as Meltzer said in his "Good luck" speech in Barcelona: "Good luck for the survival that you never could have planned, and which happened in spite of all your cleverness and ingenuity" (Meltzer et al., 2003, p. 318). Inspiration, he believed, must be happening all the time, but "if it weren't for the transference [from internal objects] we would be absolutely helpless to assist our patients . . . [it] enables us to seem to perform functions for the patient that are essential to the development of their thinking" (in Williams, 2010, p. 135).

But the problem of types of knowing starts a conflict of identifications. The mental and the "protomental" now "compete for the soul of the child" (Meltzer, 1986, p. 12). In professional terms it is hard not to let cleverness and ingenuity get the upper hand, to defend against doubts about the enigmatic interior of the psychoanalytic object, to believe that we are "developing" ideas rather than scavenging, as Meltzer called it (Meltzer & Harris Williams, 1988); relabelling or parasitizing, in Bion's (1970) words; or "misconceiving" as Money-Kyrle (1968) kindly yet very precisely put it. (He said he had encountered in patients almost every phantasy of the internal parental intercourse "except the right one".) It is worth remembering that the meaning of an idea is inseparable from a sense of its having arrived in our mind from somewhere else, undoubtedly from someone else, via some type of internal intercourse or combining of objects. It is generative outwards because it has generated inwards. The fact that it will undoubtedly have been had before doesn't matter, because that is not where originality resides: ideas are alive and useful when they are authentic—that is, when we can incorporate them into our existing web of life without needing to claim we have invented them.

Keats said his friend Charles Dilke could never "come at a truth" because he was always "trying at it" (in Gittings, 1970, p. 326). If we can remove the clouds of misconceptions and obfuscations that are created by our own cleverness and ingenuity, we will find that ideas can dovetail or propagate themselves; all we need to do—or can do—is develop our skills of self-observation, which means our awareness of being observed by *internal* objects, not *external* ones. When the idea gets through the smog, a sign of its arrival is our astonished sense that—as my mother said of Bion—it is "blindingly, obviously true" (Harris, 1980, p. 50). We have been put in touch with its ancestors, in the Platonic realms of being and becoming. In conclusion: we do not develop ideas, but if we could stop trying, then ideas would develop us.

CHAPTER TWELVE

Degrees of entrapment: living and dying in the claustrum

Pamela B. Sorensen

In his evocative and difficult book, *The Claustrum* (1992a), Donald Meltzer offers an investigation and description of claustrophobic phenomena. I suggest that these phenomena might be viewed on a continuum from relatively ordinary, with potential to yield to the developmental momentum of object relations both internal and external, to so severely disturbed that the life of the mind hardens into a death of the soul. To illustrate this continuum, I use two films: *Coraline*, directed by Henry Selick (2009) and based on the 2002 novella by Neil Gaiman, and *The Talented Mr. Ripley*, directed by Anthony Minghella (1999) and based on the 1955 novel by Patricia Highsmith. These films characterize the predicament at either end of the continuum; they show how escape from the non-life of the claustrum is made possible at the more benign end and how the possibility of exit is foreclosed in the most extreme form of pathology. Studying the films through a psychoanalytic lens brings into focus the critical factor in determining the degree of entrapment suffered by the self caught in a claustrophobic world, devoid of emotional intimacy and filled with dread.

The concept of the claustrum is an unconscious phantasy of a space inside the body of the internal mother that has been forcibly entered and occupied. With this concept, Meltzer has elaborated Melanie Klein's (1957) idea of projective identification in three ways. First, he emphasizes that this phantasy space is inside the *internal* maternal object and therefore suffuses all aspects of mental experience. Second, he describes this space as characterized by particular qualities specific to the imagined compartments of the space, which he divides into three: head/breast, genital, and rectum. Third, he changes the term used to designate the mode of entry into the object from *excessive* projective identification to *intrusive* projective identification, since he wishes to emphasize not so much the idea of frequency or quantity as that of the force and quality of intrusion—whether by violence, stealth, lies, or trickery.

The function of the claustral phantasy is defensive. Where the containing process has been unable, for whatever reason, to mitigate infantile anxiety the frantic infantile part of the personality pushes in phantasy into the impervious internal maternal object and takes up residence, finding short-term relief from the fear of death and abandonment, but long-term enslavement to lies, cruelty, and fraudulence. Such enslavement or addiction serves the function of temporarily obliterating awareness of helplessness and vulnerability. Lies provide a more desirable version of events and motivation; cruelty displaces fear into the other; and fraudulence provides an entirely alternative version of the self. Thus, the possibility of escape from this claustrophobic world through the growth of genuine intimate connections becomes a most terrible trial, because it rests on the capacity for bearing depressive pain and allowing the beauty and goodness of a creative couple to take shape in the inner world.

What distinguishes Meltzer's description of a claustrophobic retreat from other psychoanalytic writers is that he conceptualizes this as a life space—an internal landscape or world with a particular geography and its own specific qualities and values associated with that geography. Each compartment is suffused by characteristic atmosphere and attitudes, lived through the intruder's unconscious mind. Meltzer's descriptions of these phantasied dwelling places and the feelings they generate are immediately recognizable. This is because Meltzer shows how the qualities found in the external world are internalized and their subjective meaning externalized, so that there is continuous "commerce" (Meltzer's word) between the inner and outer world, resulting in the subjective experience we can all recognize. In this sense, the possibility of claustral life is ubiquitous, albeit relieved much of the time by the vitality of real connections, so that we feel grateful to be alive, notwithstanding the agonies of inevitable loss. But when despair extinguishes the possibility of intimacy and sincerity, the non-life inside the compartments of the claustrum takes hold. The visual metaphors of the films illustrate this, but a brief review of the characteristics of the claustral compartments may be useful.

The head/breast compartment

The primary quality of the head/breast is richness. Viewed from the outside by the infantile part of the personality able to tolerate separateness, the qualities of the breast and mind of the maternal object inspire love and gratitude, as well as hate and envy. But viewed by the intruder from the inside of the object, those qualities observed from outside the object, such as beauty, knowledge, wisdom, and compassion, are distorted so as to evade painful emotions. They become vulgarized as ostentation, arrogance, self-serving indulgence, lavish display of pseudo-generosity, and a know-it-all interest in status and possession. Through the mechanism of intrusive projective identification the attitudes of cynicism and contempt prevail, and elitism disguises the loneliness of superior separation. A sense of fraudulence infects life in the claustrum of the head/breast, where no meaning can grow through authentic struggle. The personality skates on the thin ice of pseudo-maturity, threatened at every turn with the icy plunge into the waters of infantile anxiety.

The genital compartment

The phantasied space of the genital compartment, viewed by the intruder from the inside, is a wild and continuous orgy, where feminine beauty is meant to incite the irresistible erect penis to masturbatory display. There is an obliteration of the generational divide, and sex is entertainment verging on perversity. There is constant fear of treachery and abuse, and a total absence of mystery and creativity. There is no trust or loyalty; rather, frantic erotic transience heightened by the conviction of irresistibility.

The rectal compartment

The rectal compartment is the phantasied space where tyranny reigns. There is only one value—survival—for there is the ever-present dread of being found out to be an impostor and interloper, to be cast out into a bizarre world of absolute loneliness. The rectal claustrum is a world of total degradation, not only of behaviour but of mental function. There is no justice, only rank. There is no truth, only manipulation.

There is no trust, only obedience. Meltzer says that this is the world of the concentration camp, where survival is all. Deviousness and self-idealization serve to postpone the dreaded reckoning with the phantasied sadistic paternal object that rules this world. There is no escaping him, only becoming him.

These descriptions of compartments represent the emotional geography of the claustrum. Inhabiting this world means living not in relationships, but in transactions. These phantasied spaces are like commercials where cliché substitutes for thought, and where there can be no mysterious ambiguity of another because the other is never beheld within the context of separateness— the other has been invaded so as to obliterate separateness and thus obliterate what can never be known, only contemplated. Such states of mind afflict us all from time to time with loneliness and fear. We need the help of other people to overcome them, and sometimes we cannot.

The films

These two films make an unlikely pair. The first, *Coraline*, is an animated film that is as whimsical and funny as it is thought-provoking. The main character is a strong-willed little girl who is quite endearing. The second, *The Talented Mr. Ripley*, is a tale of murder and intrigue with a sumptuous Italian setting. The main character is capable of chilling manipulation, exploitation, and murder. Yet both protagonists suffer forms of entrapment in their respective claustra, skilfully conveyed through plot and visual detail. Coraline escapes her entrapment to find the opportunity for repair and restoration of her good objects, while Ripley sinks deeper into hopelessness and despair. The critical factor that allows for development in the one and death in the other is discussed below.

Coraline

Coraline is the story of a girl aged about 9 or 10 years, who is very angry with her parents. They have moved from a neighbourhood with many friends to a new home that we see through Coraline's eyes as a drab and desolate house, ironically and provocatively called the Pink Palace. This house has other tenants at the top and bottom of the building who will become significant in filling out the picture of Coraline's inner world. Coraline is contemptuous of her mother's lack of home-making skills and resentful of her preoccupation with the work she does with her husband from home, which is creating a seed catalogue business. Although her father takes a bit more notice of her and shows an amused affection, he too, from her point of view, is unwilling to take proper care of her—for instance, offering disgusting, slimy vegetables as the only food. The refrigerator never has anything good in it.

Defiant, Coraline marches out of the house to explore the barren, empty landscape beyond her home. The tilted void of the animated drawing conveys the feeling of being nowhere, just as Meltzer describes the fundamental fear of the claustral dweller. Coraline unknowingly plucks a dousing stick from a poison oak to assist her furious foray into the unknown in search of water, when she is surprised by the noisy arrival of a helmeted boy on a motorcycle named YB (short for Why Born). This name, Why Born, suggests that he too has known the feeling of falling into nothingness—perhaps finding no welcome in the eyes of his mother at birth.

Fellow sufferer or not, Coraline is contemptuous of anything YB might have to say and rejects his overtures of friendship, only to retreat into her lonely house. She has noticed a small door in the downstairs hall, but her mother has shown her that there is only a brick wall behind it and places the key where Coraline cannot find it. Of course, late at night, when dreams conspire to reveal emotional truth, Coraline follows the helpful scuttling of a guiding mouse to discover that the door does, indeed, open into another world—the claustral world of the *other mother*, where Coraline is treated as the special child she longs to be and where she is offered all the wonderful food she could possibly eat, in abundance and without waiting, and all the adoration and comfort she could possibly want. There is only one hitch. In exchange for being the idealized and spoiled daughter of the *other mother and father* she must agree to allow them to replace her eyes with buttons. Why? Button eyes do not see. Thus, there can be no authentic connection between two people, which necessarily includes ambivalence, both love and hate, only the flat acquiescence to the lie of idealization. No let downs, no waiting, no uncertainties. Initially, Coraline declines the invitation and returns to the exigencies of her disappointing daily life with her disappointing, though hard-working, parents.

Meltzer suggests that intrusive projective identification may be accompanied by secret masturbatory phantasies that propel entry into the object in a damaging way. The depiction of the little door as a hidden opening into a spiralling chute leading to the delusional world of the *other mother* shows how such phantasies may rev up the manic conviction of being in possession and in command of every treasure inside the pink palace of the mother's body. There are many images of hands throughout the film, some disembodied, some performing frightening tricks, another sore from a poisonous plant. Even gloves enter the imagery as Coraline's rage with her parents begins to shift, perhaps suggesting that she is trying to restrain her damaging masturbatory phantasies.

But before this turning point, the seductive power of being the special one inside the claustral world increases as Coraline's loneliness and frustration with her quotidian life persists. She crawls through the little door by day, tempted by promises of pampering, and is encouraged by the *other mother* to visit the exotic and exhibitionist neighbours who live at the top and bottom of the Pink Palace. This false maternal object urges her into a greater and greater whirlwind of voyeuristic excitement, enflaming her further with the cruel suggestion that her real parents have become bored with her and left to go to France (the destination of choice for romance).

Coraline finds that her eccentric neighbours have put on shows just for her. Upstairs, Mr Bobinsky, looking like an acrobatic phallus, preening and whirling in his magic show of jumping mice, excites and amuses her. She is dazzled, losing the capacity for moderation or discretion; she eats chicken-poop popcorn and exploding candy-floss. Downstairs, Miss Spink and Miss Forcible compete to display bottom and bosom in a wild circus of erotic acrobatic feats, culminating in Coraline flying through the air to land on top of them. But this excitement is mixed with menace, both upstairs and downstairs, as the jumping mice turn to rats and the circus audience of Scottish terriers, who previously had been a legion of interchangeable turd-like pets, turn into frightening bats.

It is becoming clear that things are not what they seem in the home of the *other mother*. She treats her husband with such scathing contempt that he deteriorates into a flaccid puppet. Her body gradually transforms into the shape of a spider and her coaxing lilt into a piercing staccato. Terror mounts. In a state of bewildered excitement, Coraline backs away from the promise of being special forever and begins to look again for her real, though imperfect parents.

Coraline realizes that she is trapped. Her own projections have become so powerful that they threaten to wipe out her memory of being loved as she is. She misses her parents and needs them. The plot turns and Coraline fights, using her parents' gardening tools as weapons to aid her escape from the web of narcissism in which she has become entangled. Here is the first image that carries the metaphor of the good combined object needed to provide the grounding for emotional growth and development. The process of reclamation and restoration of her good objects now begins with all the pluck and energy with which Coraline marched away from them in her yellow boots in the first place. Coraline's greed for adulation has yielded to an appreciation of the love she has been given, and her struggle has led to a greater capacity to endure depressive pain, allowing it to enrich her mind so that she can tell truth from falsehood in both herself and others.

What is it that allows Coraline to resist the temptations of the claustral world and struggle to find her real parents and her real self? It is a combination of internal and external factors. Coraline has the good fortune to have loyal friends who tell her the truth about herself and, in so doing, strengthen her hold on her good objects. One of these friends is an analyst in the form of a cat who is reliably available at critical moments, disappearing at the end, as analysts do, to leave Coraline to live her life with greater confidence in her own capacity for love. He has assisted her by pointing out her arrogance, helping her recognize what is false, bearing with her in facing the cruelty of her own projections in the form of the *other mother*, and offering the tenderness of friendship—a guide, philosopher, and friend, as Roger Money-Kyrle defined the role of the analyst (personal communication).

Coraline's first friend, YB from the earlier scene, has persisted despite her contempt. He is loyal, protective, and funny, offering Coraline the possibility of being part of a creative couple at the end of the film, when, together, having vanquished the *other mother*, murderous in her jealous rage, they make a garden of their own, using the seeds and tools Coraline's parents have given them. But most important, Coraline has parents who can withstand her jealous rage and hold on to family life. Amidst the destruction wrought by the *other mother's* violent attempt to capture Coraline and prevent her from finding her real parents, Coraline notices an object over the hearth in her home. It is a broken snow globe from a family trip, dripping water like tears onto the floor. Inside it, the distressed faces of her parents peer out. Coraline now knows that she has hurt them through her dismissive contempt and realizes that they love her, nevertheless, and can forgive her. The reliance on an internal couple who can withstand attacks through lies and distortion, yet persist in the task of building something worthwhile, like a garden or a family, allows Coraline to retrieve and restore the good objects in her internal world.

Twice during the film there has been an aerial view of the garden belonging to the Pink Palace, once in its beautiful form and once in its nightmare from. The garden is the shape of a girl's head. This visual metaphor clearly conveys that Coraline's story is the story in her mind, in the world of unconscious phantasy, where objects can be lost and found, destroyed and reclaimed, in all their aesthetic and emotional complexity.

The Talented Mr. Ripley

The situation for Tom Ripley is at the other end of the claustral continuum where the degree of entrapment increases until there is no escape. Tom, a baby-faced young man, slides into a life of fraudulence within the first few minutes of the film. He borrows the jacket of an acquaintance in order to perform the piano accompaniment to a beautiful, classical singer. The jacket bears a Princeton insignia, and in a split second Tom goes along with the misperception of the wealthy Mr Greenleaf that he went to Princeton with Greenleaf's wayward, dissolute son, Dickie. Tom agrees to accept payment for a trip to Italy with the stated purpose of persuading Dickie to return to his family.

The psychological ground of the film is laid in the imagery of the opening scenes. Tom is without the necessary clothing. One might see this as a suggestion that he is without an adequately functioning skin, in the sense that Esther Bick (1968) means when she describes the mental skin, provided by mother's attention, that the infant needs to hold himself together. Tom Ripley's second skin, which is, according to Bick, the defensive means of holding the self together, represented initially by the Princeton jacket, becomes the pretence that he has a status not his own. His actual job is that of a lavatory attendant, where he hands out towels and brushes off the coats of wealthy men.

Having accepted Mr Greenleaf's offer, as Tom is packing his meagre belongings in his dark basement flat, he is disturbed by the angry yelling in the flat above him. It is clear from the expression on his face that he has been witness to the violent quarrelling of the couple living just above his head many times before. This couple's angry yelling appears again in a dream towards the end of the film as Tom is trying to hide the second murder he has committed. Tom emerges from his living quarters in a meat-packing district, where skinless animal carcasses are pushed through the streets, a visual metaphor, perhaps, for Tom's extreme vulnerability to those around him and for how easily he can be swept along by forces outside his awareness. Tom gets into a limousine paid for by Mr Greenleaf, and so begins the long, lethal journey of Tom's fraudulent intrusion into the lavish and exciting idyll of Dickie Greenleaf's Italy.

Part of the tension in this journey of lies, trickery, and fraudulence propelling the complicated plot of the film comes from the persistent glimpses of another side of Tom Ripley conveyed through his responses to music. The film opens with Tom at the piano and later practising alone in a theatre. At different moments throughout the film, when Tom listens to classical music his face loses the shallow cheeriness of his false smile and expresses an authentic vulnerability to beauty. His only genuine love is for another musician whose musical sensibilities Tom shares. But this aspect of Tom's personality is not sufficiently robust to withstand the corrosive effect of the lies, trickery, and fraudulence with which he insinuates himself into the life of Dickie Greenleaf. He is driven to steal all the privileges, qualities, status, and power, real and imagined, that belong to Dickie. Ultimately, he steals his life.

This first murder takes place when Tom and Dickie go boating. For Tom, this outing is a prelude to a longer and more intimate trip. Tom is in love with Dickie and believes that his feelings are returned. But for Dickie, the outing is nothing more than a distraction, just another one among the hundreds of fleeting pleasures with which he crams his life. Dickie is suddenly bored with Tom and tells him so, calling him a leach and saying that it's time he moved on without him. Without warning, the surge of humiliation and rage overwhelms Tom. He had imagined they were like twins, sharing sophisticated tastes and knowing ways. (When they travelled together on trains, Tom would slyly merge their reflections in the window.) Tom smashes Dickie's skull with an oar, and as he lies dead in the bottom of the boat, Tom rests his head on Dickie's chest in a delusional lover's embrace.

Tom tries to cover up the murder by sinking the boat and assuming Dickie's identity. This leads to complicated deceptions with other characters, mainly Dickie's fiancée, Marge. Tom plays himself with those who recognize him as Tom, and plays Dickie with those who do not. Eventually, one of Dickie's dissolute chums suspects foul play and confronts him. Tom commits the second murder to protect his secret and stages a car crash to make it look like an accident.

Once Mr Greenleaf comes to Italy to find out what has happened to his son, Tom thinks the game is up. But to his astonishment and despite the protestations of Marge, who knows Tom is guilty, his guile succeeds in convincing Mr Greenleaf and the authorities that he is innocent. Only at the very last minute, as Tom is leaving Italy with his musician lover, Peter, who knows him as Tom Ripley, is he spotted by another passenger on the ship, a girl he has feigned interest in, who knows him as Dickie. He fobs her off with a kiss. When Tom returns to his cabin, Peter is hurt because he has seen the kiss. Tom, knowing now that his ruse will be exposed, pretends to embrace Peter and strangles him with a necktie.

The life that Tom Ripley steals from Dickie displays all the claustral characteristics Meltzer describes: the elitist and entitled display of material riches in the head/breast compartment, as seen in the luxurious lifestyle of Dickie and his friends; the sexual frenzy of the genital compartment, seen in the heady scene in the jazz club, where Tom jumps in to mimic the louche singing of Dickie's friends; and the ultimate tyranny of the rectal compartment, seen in the three murders Tom commits. Although there are brief moments when Tom views the beauty of the maternal object from the outside, as when he wants to go sightseeing in Rome and when he listens to music, his utter despair and fear of abandonment drive him to force his way into the maternal space, represented by the gorgeous landscape of Italy, and steal the identity of Dickie Greenleaf through violence, trickery, and lies. The fear of being found out as an impostor fills the atmosphere with dread.

Tom's homosexual ardour for Dickie—his longing to merge with him in every way, through dressing in his clothes, singing his songs, joining their reflections in the window glass of trains, sharing his bath—is an expression of his utter loneliness and fear of being nothing and no one, as he tells Peter at the end of the film, "I'm going to be stuck in the basement, alone in the dark. No one will ever find me".

Degrees of entrapment

Both Coraline and Tom Ripley are trapped in inner worlds where greed and self-delusion dominate: Coraline for a while, and Tom forever. In this world, sorrow cannot yield the fruit of remorse. Gratitude cannot soften the pain of separation. Hope cannot allow the unknown to unfold. Coraline develops in her capacity to bear psychic pain and in her capacity to face the truth about herself through struggle with her demons and with the help of a good internal couple and a cat. Tom cannot escape his claustral world, but is driven deeper in with every violation. The fleeting impressions of the internal couple he carries (the angry voices above his head in the early scene and then again in a dream) are damaged and damaging. Even music is murdered when he kills Peter, the one person with whom he might have shared his true nature.

How does a good internal couple protect against the ravages of intrusive projective identification? The respective functions of maternal and paternal objects play their parts, as does the collaboration between them. The good internal maternal object can accept distress without falling apart or retaliating; she can make room and even more room for all the children, so that no one is cast out; she can mitigate the toxic mix of envy, jealousy and fear through her struggle to comprehend their meaning. The good paternal object not only protects the maternal space from infant excess, but also offers a bridge to the baby to find new worlds outside the maternal space. By doing this, he engenders the possibility of a future. Together, the good internal couple can mitigate the sorrow of inevitable loss through their creative interdependence, generating hope in the infant that one day he, too, may become part of a creative couple.

Both films reveal the importance of the role of an internal couple in psychic development through the appearance of phantasies about inside babies. Coraline discovers the ghosts of children that the *other mother* holds hostage. They float in some mysterious, dark, and hidden world that we can understand as the world of unconscious phantasy. They cannot come to life because their eyes have been stolen and hidden. Without them, they are mere dolls, not real babies. In her work of repair, Coraline finds these eyes and returns them to the children, thus restoring their individuality and their ability to seek and find the reciprocal gaze of their own mothers. Here, Coraline shows the capacity to acknowledge that other children, too, need authentic contact with their mothers. She is not the only one.

Emerging from the unconscious in quite a different way, the phantasy of dead inside babies rises from the ocean in *The Talented Mr. Ripley*. While watching a village religious ritual in which a statue of the Madonna is carried through the waves, Tom, Dickie, and his fiancée, Marge, see the drowned body of Dickie's secret paramour rise to the surface. She is pregnant, and even the callous Dickie is overcome by the thought of the dead baby inside her. Tom instantly offers to publicly accept the blame for this doomed conception, and, although Dickie waves him away, this strange idea fits Tom's inner world, where no independent life can thrive.

The "mystery of the nuptial chamber", as Meltzer calls it in his penultimate book, *The Apprehension of Beauty* (Meltzer & Harris Williams, 1988), evokes awe and envy, placing upon the infantile part of the personality the strain and burden of being on the outside, not knowing and not being able to know what happens there. The unconscious phantasy of entering the maternal space through lies, trickery, and violence puts a stop to this, silencing mystery and killing the new life that it may engender.

Coraline and Tom Ripley are not our patients; they are fictional characters. But the defensive unconscious phantasy of a claustrum is not a fiction. Meltzer's description of such a frightening world, one of falsehood without reprieve, conveys a terror we all can recognize, and some cannot escape. His imaginative elaboration of Kleinian theory is compelling in the way it explores the experiences of the infantile part of the personality by delineating the emotional meaning of unconscious phantasies about the inside of the internal maternal object.

This infantile part of the personality, as we have imagined it through *Coraline* and *The Talented Mr. Ripley*, suffers in a particular way as a consequence of intrusive projective identification. As an occupant of the claustrum it is both a refugee and an invader, seeking to get under the skin of the internal maternal object to escape the terror of utter loneliness. But once inside, the world beneath this skin becomes a false container, growing tighter and more constricting as mental pain increases. Seeming to offer relief from suffering through glamour, importance, excitement, or power, the claustral space is like an exclusive hotel, one you are dying to get into, only to find that you are nowhere, after all.

Note

This chapter is based on a version previously published in the *Journal of Child Psychotherapy, Vol. 42* (No. 1, 2016), pp. 45–53. Copyright © Association of Child Psychotherapists, reprinted by permission of Taylor & Francis Ltd, http://www.tandfonline.com on behalf of the Association of Child Psychotherapists.

CHAPTER THIRTEEN

Trapped in a claustrum world: the proleptic imagination and James Joyce's *Ulysses*

Mary Fisher-Adams

"Oh Jamesy let me up out of this pooh."

"Molly": James Joyce, *Ulysses* (1922b)

In this chapter I look at *Ulysses* as a description of a claustrum world and how fear and dread can produce, in the so-called "replacement child", a proleptic imagination that keeps the claustrum dweller imprisoned and paralysed. A link is made with Shakespeare, who is a presence throughout *Ulysses* and was himself a replacement child.

I had been struck by similarities between two of my patients and James Joyce. They had all lost siblings in early childhood and seem to have felt emotionally cut adrift by the mother's grief at her loss—a feeling marginalized that had extended into adulthood. They all showed particular sensitivity as children and were possessed of a highly active imagination and exceptional literary creativity. Above all, they seemed tormented by fear in the extreme. My two patients came into analysis in their forties *still* plagued by nightmares of lions, monsters, and dead babies. Most strikingly, both expressed the fear that they had murdered someone and that they remain lethal and shouldn't be allowed out into the world. James Joyce also suffered great fears and nightmares. He spoke of "that skull" that came to torment him at night (Ellmann, 1982, p. 178). He was highly superstitious, had crippling phobias causing fainting fits—afraid of dogs, rats, and water, for example—and lived in fear of thunder and lightning.[1]

In *Ulysses,* Joyce seems to portray a stuck and confusing world: what he calls a "paralysis of the insane". It is a world packed full of allusion, information, and philosophizing. As Wyndham Lewis put it, "*Ulysses* confines the reader in a circumscribed psychological space into which several encyclopedias have been emptied" (Lewis, 1927, p. 91). *Ulysses* is also a *tour de force* of the imagination.

For my patients and for Joyce, their heightened imagination and creativity seems to have been a mixed blessing. On the one hand, it brought them some glory and allowed a form and expression for their fears, but at the same time their childhood experience produced what James Fisher (2009) termed a proleptic imagination that actually perpetuated those fears. It seems that, as children, murderous wishes they felt towards their mothers' new babies coincided with the actual deaths of their siblings, triggering the belief that they had caused the deaths. This kind of congruence between fantasy and reality feeds into the magical thinking of the proleptic imagination and can paralyse a child emotionally. The child is left with the fear that one's wishes and one's imagination can cause disaster.

Silvio Fano Cassese states that in "Terror, Persecution, and Dread", Meltzer describes an extreme form of paranoid anxiety, terror:

> ". . . The object of terror (being in unconscious phantasy dead objects) cannot even be fled from with success" (Meltzer, 1973d, p. 105). The mother's internal babies are not only damaged . . . but killed by the destructive-possessive jealousy of oedipal rivalry and intolerance to separation, and "what is feared is the retaliatory re-projection of the murderous attacks on the mother's internal babies" (Alberto Hahn, personal communication). [Cassese, 2002, p. 43]

The proleptic imagination

Proleptic means a leaping ahead, and in the proleptic imagination a world of certainty is created in which the patient "knows" what will happen. It is an unconscious attempt to control the imagination, but one that traps one in the deluded state. Fisher describes it as "whatever is pictured—in the moment as well as in the future—is taken concretely as reality" (2009, p. 35).

It differs from Klein's concept of "symbolic equation" (1930, p. 220) in that it focuses on the role of the imagination and describes an overall state of mind. Symbolic equation refers to a difficulty thinking symbolically. I am looking at patients who can think symbolically but who try, unconsciously, to control their thinking out of fear. There is, perhaps, too active an imagination—"a dangerous prevalence of imagination" (Bloom, 1999, p. 535)—that makes it hard to know the reality. As a result, rather than being free, as children, to imagine, play, and fantasize, in their terror at not knowing what else might go terribly wrong they have sought certainty. Rather than allowing things to take their course and finding out, they tell themselves they know what will happen. It is the antithesis of Bion's image of reverie and receptiveness and of being without memory or desire.

Although based on fantasy, this state of mind works, in fact, to block the free use of the imagination. As described by Ogden (2005), this has particular consequences for work in analysis:

> The imaginative capacity in the analytic setting is nothing less than sacred. Imagination holds open multiple possibilities experimenting with them all in the form of thinking, playing, dreaming and in every other sort of creative activity. Imagination stands in contrast to fantasy which has a fixed form that is repeated again and again and goes nowhere. . . . To imagine is not to figure out a solution to an emotional problem; it is to change the very terms of the dilemma. [p. 26]

In *The Claustrum*, Meltzer differentiates between "a conception of the inside of the internal mother derived from imagination and one that is the product of the omnipotent intrusion, and thereby of omniscience" (1992a, p. 62).

One patient refers to this omnipotent state of mind, which perhaps we should call proleptic *fantasy*, as her tendency to "catastrophize", the way she anticipates and "knows" that there will be a disaster of her own causing. So firm was the belief in her murderousness that she quoted a murderer released from prison who asked: "'How can I make a life for myself when I have killed someone?' I know what he means", she said. This is a fearsome state to live in and, tragically, as frightening as living in a state of not knowing. Writing on the claustrum, Meltzer says:

> . . . in response to this hovering sense of immanent catastrophe, the picture of the world becomes compartmentalized and stratified. The compartments . . . resemble . . . the divisions Hell, Purgatory and Heaven: in the rectum, the genital or inside the breast or head of the primal mother. [1992a, p. 119]

"The dead third"

To lose a sibling and the mother's attention at this early stage of development, when there is a delicate back and forth between the use of fantasy and a gradual accommodating of reality, would be traumatic, and it brings us into the sphere of the "dead mother" syndrome (Green, 1986). Samuel Gerson eloquently expands the concept of the "dead mother". He describes the child in this situation as having lost the "containing third" (Britton, 1989) and finding himself in the presence of a "dead third":

> Rather than the potential for growth and security found in the notion of triangular space, the absence of an involved and caring other leaves only a dense and collapsed heap of destroyed internal and external objects for whom no one mourns. Imagine life, when the third is dead, when the container cracks and there is no presence . . . to represent continuity. It is a world constituted by absence, where meaning is ephemeral and cynicism passes for wisdom. [Gerson, 2009, p. 1343]

For both of my patients, in their eyes the mother seemed to become wooden following the sibling's death. One patient's mother told her, "my face cracked when the baby died", and her family took to their beds. The other patient learned the cello, practising for hours trying to bring life and music out of this wooden mother.

Important in Gerson's description is the lack of mourning. Helene Deutsch, in a discussion of mothers mourning their deceased children, observes that the replacement child "has very poor chances of conquering the mother's heart", and that "during the period of mourning even the woman's own children are deprived of love and exposed to the painful silent reproach, 'Why did you not die instead of the other?'" (quoted in Silver, 1983, p. 520). The picture my patients conveyed was of a mother turned away.

Fury at the mother

Along with the fear of impending disaster, there is a profound fury at the mother for abandoning them in her state of grief. James Joyce had good reason to feel aggrieved. Before he was 2 years old, his mother lost a baby son. She then went on to have nine more children and at least three miscarriages.

Furthermore, he was sent away to boarding school age 6, and then his mother died of cancer age 44 when he was only 21. He bitterly attributed her death to the constant pregnancies, and he blamed the Church and his alcoholic father—and also himself. In a letter to his wife, Nora, he said, "My mother was slowly killed, I think, by my father's ill treatment, by years of trouble, and by my cynical frankness of conduct" (Liegner & Motycka, 2003, p. 151).

His novel, *Ulysses*, is filled with betrayal, grief, guilt, and fury at the mother. It begins in the Martello tower—a small, almost windowless fortress on three floors, with narrow stairwell. Stephen Dedalus, lodging there with Buck Mulligan, is feeling usurped by a new arrival (another new baby): the "privileged" Englishman, Haines. As he decides to leave, he is haunted by a dream of his dead mother returning to reproach him. He cries out, "Ghoul! Chewer of corpses!" and then pleads with her, "No, mother. Let me be and let me live."

Joyce speaks of the mother's "hardness of heart", "black basilisk eyes with the power to poison", a "withering mind", her "cold blighted love for him". In *Ulysses,* Stephen says: "But thou has suckled me with a bitter milk; my moon and my sun thou has quenched forever. And thou has left me alone forever in the dark ways of my bitterness; and with a kiss of ashes hast thou kissed my mouth" (1922b, p. 387).

The first woman to appear in *Ulysses* is the old milk woman—"a scary wandering crone, with shrunken paps" (p. 15). And elsewhere Joyce compares the lights and shadows of the mother's falsely smiling face to the hues of rancid food—her body emerges as an odourless flower, her mind a quagmire, the green hue of her dress metamorphoses into lush grass, "the hair of graves" (Joyce, 1984, p. 12).

Ulysses is suffused with Stephen's guilt regarding his mother's death. He refused her dying wish, and Mulligan condemns him for it:

> You could have knelt down, damn it Kinch, when your dying mother asked you. . . . To think of your mother begging you with her last breath to kneel down and pray for her. And you refused. There is something sinister in you. . . .
>
> Ah poor dogsbody, he said in a kind voice. I must vie you a shirt and a few noserags.
>
> I'm the only one that knows what you are. Why don't you trust me more? What have you up your nose against me?
>
> Don't mope over it all day . . . I'm inconsequent. Give up the moody brooding.

Mulligan could be seen as the most real-life person in the book and the only one to challenge Stephen as a father might. There is a sense of homosexual longing between them, with references to Oscar Wilde and "the love that dare not speak its name" (p. 259). But Stephen, full of guilt and ill equipped to engage with him, makes Mulligan the cruel one and walks away. There is talk of fathers throughout *Ulysses*, as though seeking someone to lift Stephen out of himself and his resentments, but, in his wish to deny generational reality, Stephen proclaims himself his own father, "made not begotten" (p. lxix).[2] Joyce's biographer, Richard Ellmann, comments that "paternity is a more powerful motif in the book than sexual love" (1982, p. 371).

Guilt was also a major feature for my two patients. But this was not depressive-position guilt seeking forgiveness. They did not expect or even seek compassion in life, only condemnation. The "guilt" seems more an expression of fear and anger. It is a persecutory anxiety based on a fantasy rather than an actual crime or hurt the person has caused. "I know it is all my fault", we hear patients say, even though intellectually they know that is not the case. It is one of those "end of story!" statements—a state of mind fearful of exploring what might be their fault and what isn't. The "I know" becomes the certainty with which they try to hold themselves together, but it conveys, "I don't really want to know." It is as though the act of imagining has become a dangerous act that might lead to new awareness and pain.

Feelings my patients had were intense and hard to control and often produced behaviour that one might well condemn. It was almost as though they wanted to prove their badness, but any attempt by me to address this seemed to touch on real fragility and fear. One patient described her life as being tirelessly available for all and sundry, but at the same time she was telling me about behaviour that was clearly unethical and hurtful to others.

Ulysses is full of Joyce getting revenge on the many people he felt had wronged him. Leon Edel (1980) called Joyce an "Injustice Collector", and Hugh Kenner points out that Joyce imprisoned himself and had to remain in exile because of all the lawsuits he would have had against him had he returned to Ireland: "Joyce's revenge on Oliver Gogarty [Buck Mulligan in the book] was to shut him into a book for all to see" (Kenner, 1962, p. 49).[3]

In real life, Joyce's sense of entitlement—born of fear and guilt—particularly with his wife and brother, made him notoriously ruthless. It is a curious dynamic: the way some who lost siblings latch onto another sibling in a most intense and controlling way. Van Gogh and Thomas Mann are two examples. It becomes a sadomasochistic *folie à deux*. Julian Barnes refers to Van Gogh as the "flat-sharer from hell, an insistent, overbearing presence, needy, demanding, free with advice and always knowing better" (Barnes, 2015, p. 8). One of my patients tried to control a younger sister to such an extent that she ended up feeling she had ruined the sister's life, and I think she had a point.

A letter from Joyce's brother Stanislaus, on his return to Trieste after having been interned for four years in an Austrian camp, conveys how fed up he was with Joyce's treatment of him.

> I have just emerged from four years of hunger and squalor, and am trying to get on my feet again. Do you think you can give me a rest? [McCourt, 2000, p. 249]

But Joyce couldn't and didn't.

It is as though the fear and anger associated with the survivor guilt of the "replacement child" becomes so unbearable in the circular prison of the proleptic imagination that the only escape is to actually *be* bad—"break all the windows" and enter the world finally in their rightful place, as a criminal, achieving a perverse kind of authenticity. At the same time Joyce, like my patients, could be very good company, and with his brilliant mind and wit he was funny and seductive—especially when drinking. According to his biographer, "no one could laugh more wholeheartedly or more infectiously". With his head back and mouth wide, he resounded throughout the room, and he was always bursting into song. Another image is of him doing his spider dance down the street—his long legs flailing around (Ellmann, 1982, p. 95). And his many admirers went out of their way for him. Meltzer refers to this mysterious charisma that paralyses the opposition—especially loved ones. Joyce's wife, tested to the limit with his late-night drinking and problems with money, while strangely unwilling to read his masterpieces, still stood by him devotedly, tuned in, like a mother, to the tragedy of this genius mind at the mercy of inner fear.[4]

Thirst for knowledge

Joyce dazzled with his encyclopaedic knowledge and verbal pyrotechnics and is described as a latter-day "worldwide web", with a "spider's eye" constantly absorbing information. From early in life he made copious and exhaustive lists and elaborate designs, eliciting from his father the wisecrack: "if that fellow was dropped in the middle of the Sahara, he'd sit, be God, and make a map of it" (Kiberd, 1992, p. xxii).

In *Ulysses* and *Finnegans Wake*, he includes the names of Shakespeare plays, all the books of the Bible, the chapters of the Koran, the rivers of the world, figures of rhetoric. Joyce seemed to rely on the power his brilliance gave him. "I've put in so many enigmas and puzzles", he said, "that it will keep the professors busy for centuries arguing over what I meant and that's the only way of insuring one's immortality" (Ellmann, 1982, p. 521).

Similarly, one of my patients avidly devoured extraordinary amounts of knowledge and information. Within the first few months of her analysis, she had not only noted the books on my shelves but ordered and read the complete works of Melanie Klein, quoting to me from the couch. She was so all-knowing and had such verbal facility and humour that in the analysis I had to withstand feeling both seduced and intimidated by her.

Meltzer talks of a specific aspect of projective identification being bound up closely with the epistemophilic instinct. He describes this thirst for knowledge and the omniscience it seeks as being too impatient to learn from experience.

> Where the thirst for knowledge is still strongly dominated by motives related to envy and jealousy, the thirst for knowledge is [too] impatient to learn from experience, example or demonstration. It seeks [instead] the immediate emotional satisfaction of omniscience and this it accomplishes by intruding inside the sensory apparatus and mental equipment of its internal object. [1976a, p. 142]

But for my patients, and for Joyce, the intensity of feelings from their early experience felt, I believe, barely survivable. They did not have the space and security to let things take their course. They were poised ready for disaster, wishing to "jump the life to come" (*Macbeth*).

The claustrum

One way to control the object is to get inside, and *Ulysses* seems a striking example of an author entering right into his characters in a way that goes beyond mere imaginative identification and becomes the intrusive identification characteristic of the claustrum dweller. Molly's monologue in the final scene could be seen as a particular example of this—a kind of intrusion by Joyce himself. At one point Joyce has Molly say, "Oh Jamesy let me up out of this pooh", as though Joyce is controlling things (18: 1128). There seems to be a subtle difference between conveying what the character is like and thinks and Joyce bringing to it his own fantasies, denying the woman, in this case, her separateness and essential unknowability. Writers talk about their characters as independent selves with minds of their own, but here Joyce seems caught in an unconscious masturbatory fantasy of his own having intruded into the mind of his character.

Lionel Trilling talks about Joyce's attempts to distance himself from the "filth and depravity" of his fantasies, as expressed in his letters to his wife, Nora, by locating them in all his characters except those—such as Stephen Dedalus—more identified with himself (Trilling, 1967, p. 475). Stephen, as artist, is idealized as detaching himself from emotion, being "above desire and loathing".

Lewis (1927) describes *Ulysses* as "telling from the inside", and Joyce himself, in *Finnegans Wake,* describes his character, Shem, as "self exiled in upon his own ego" (1939, p. 184). *Ulysses* has 18 sections, each one linked to a body part, and the three main characters seem located in the compartments of the mother's body: Stephen Dedalus, the poet-artist, is located in the head-breast (Meltzer's "Lotus Eaters" lassitude; 1992a, p. 119); Molly Bloom, fantasizing in bed with "compulsive greed for sexual stimulation", is located in the genital compartment; and Leopold Bloom is in the anal world of the rectum.

I quote from Meltzer's (a) description of life in the maternal rectum:

> . . . [S]een from the inside, intruded into by stealth or violence in anal masturbation or anal assault, it is a region of satanic religion, ruled by the great fecal penis, the world of Orwell's "Big Brother". . . . Truth is transformed into anything that cannot be disproved; justice becomes talion plus an increment; all the acts of intimacy change their meaning into techniques of manipulation or dissimulation; loyalty replaces devotion; obedience substitutes for trust; emotion is simulated by excitement; guilt and the yearning for punishment takes the place of regret. [pp. 91–92]
>
> . . . [U]nlike the other two compartments where comfort and erotic pleasure dominate the value system, in the rectal compartment there is only one value: survival. Although the sadism may vary in intensity as one moves along the spectrum from boarding school to concentration camp, the atmosphere of incipient terror is probably little changed, for one meets evidence that the nameless dread consists in being "thrown away". . . . [T]his nameless dread is exponentially worse even than exile and Cain's lament: it is absolute loneliness in a world of bizarre objects. [p. 91]

At the age of 40, Joyce had a dream that has elements of inevitability of a proleptic and persecuted state of mind in a compartmentalized claustrum world where there is no escape. It is set in a luscious Persian pavilion:

> There were sixteen rooms, four on each floor. Someone had committed a crime, and he entered the lowest floor. The door opened on a flower garden. He hoped to get through but when he arrived at the threshold a drop of blood fell on it. *I could know* how desperate he felt, for he went from the first floor all the way up to the fourth, his hope being that at each threshold his wound was not capable of letting fall another drop. *But always it came,* an official discovered it, and punctually at the sixteen rooms the drop fell. There were two officials in brocaded silk robes, and a man with a scimitar who watched him. [Ellmann, 1982, p. 547]

Joyce, disparaging of psychoanalysis and opting for self-analysis, interpreted the rooms as the twelve signs of the zodiac; the three doors are the Trinity, the man who committed the crime was himself, and the man with the scimitar was his "wife next morning". The pavilion with light-blue lattices was "like a box", he said (Ellmann, 1982, p. 547). We do not know the context for this dream, except that he had seen the Russian ballet the night before and was writing *Finnegans Wake,* but as well as a "criminal" entering the lowest floor trying to evade being discovered, there is a distinct sense of nameless dread and "ineluctability"—Joyce's favourite word—meaning inevitable and inescapable, which has the ring of proleptic certainty: "I could always know" and "always it came". Most poignantly, the man in the dream was wounded and felt desperate with no way of escape.

Perhaps the desperate wish to "escape" from some obscure guilt and getting stuck, instead, in a luscious palace with erotic overtones gives a glimpse of the state of mind in which Joyce wrote *Ulysses.* The dream pales in comparison with the wild nightmarish pantomime "Circe" section in *Ulysses,* in which lonely Bloom is hauled before a court of judges and accused of everything under the sun in front of a baying mob. While full of Joycean hilarity, it is also the extended heartfelt outcry of someone caught in the bogus persecutory world of the claustrum. It is a world replete with all kinds of "sluts and ragamuffins", bishops and ghosts, and a seductive Molly Bloom "in Turkish costume, her opulent curves filling out the scarlet trousers and jacket slashed with gold" (p. 570). Stephen's dead mother also appears, as do Macbeth and the three witches (p. 682).

James Fisher sees *Macbeth* as a moving portrayal of the proleptic imagination in action. He emphasizes the depth of emotion expressed in the play while describing Macbeth's proleptic state of mind as an attempt to control the emotions. He points out that there is no fool or "truthsayer" in *Macbeth*—no Paulina, for example, who, in the

Winter's Tale, could speak the truth to Leontes. Instead, there are a few moments when Macbeth himself briefly reflects on what was happening—moments, Fisher says, that Shakespeare marks "with some of the most unforgettable poetry of the play, indeed of any of his plays":

> Macbeth senses that his conscious action can never match this strange experience where wanting and having appear to be one. Perhaps as a warrior hardened in battle he distrusted the omnipotence of action, although he had never given up his infantile omnipotence of thought, at least not when it seems thrust upon him. It is remarkable that Shakespeare chooses to have Macbeth give eloquent expression to an emotion we can only suppose threatens to overwhelm as he thinks feelingly about the murder of Duncan. Pity, seemingly an emotion as fragile as a "naked new-born babe", is pictured "striding the blast", blowing "the horrid deed in every eye". It is as if Macbeth, for the moment at least, sees a link between pity and an infant, not as helpless but "striding the blast" of the heavens. It is a picture of the power of the emotions, the kind of thing a Fool might say to Macbeth, reminding him of reality, the reality of emotional experience—tears that "drown the wind". [2009, p. 15]

Rather than reflecting on reality, *Ulysses* seems more reality-evading, or reality-trashing. Virginia Woolf described it as the work of a man who "in order to breathe had to break all the windows" (Kiberd, 1992, p. xviii). The "Circe" section in *Ulysses* has the same manic, unintelligible, unstoppable quality as Lucky's outpouring in Beckett's *Waiting for Godot* (2006b) and the character Mouth in his play *Not I* (2006a).

Leopold Bloom as a character seems quite extraordinarily strange. Joyce tries to lift him into a realm of great humanity, saintliness even, as though this "womanly man" might be the ideal. But at the same time he is portraying a grieving, cuckolded, marginalized Jew who distracts himself with endless bits of information, inhabits a world of masturbation, and seems unable to cry out his pain. Joyce, perhaps feeling the absence of a mature combined couple, may want to save this bereaved couple, Molly and Bloom, who lost a child, and bring them to life again. But it doesn't happen. At the end, they remain lying topsy-turvy, with Bloom kissing Molly's buttocks, unable to overcome their grief.

Intrusive identification

Sabbadini describes the replacement child who lost a sibling as "treated more as the embodiment of a memory than as a person in its own right". Being allowed a life of their own was problematic, given their sense that they should not have survived when their siblings had died (1988, p. 530). Desperate to prove their worth, and feeling angry at their situation, can make them very competitive. (See Meltzer, 1992a, p. 66, for a discussion of the *Odyssey* and the "Telemachus part of the infantile personality *vis-à-vis* the bad and naughty brothers and sisters, fraught . . . with savage infantile competitiveness".) However, success immediately brings new fears. Whatever survivors do, they feel that being competitive risks causing the demise of the other. The proleptic imagination pictures only one possible outcome, a devastating one, whatever is wished for.

One of my patients is an accomplished writer, but, afraid of publishing in her own name, she works as a ghost writer instead, disguising her own identity. Anisfeld and Richards give a description of this dynamic in their paper on the "replacement child":

> He could never be certain that he was loved for who he was or for the genuineness of his achievements. When he performed an action from which he reaped a reward at someone else's expense, he was convinced that he had initiated it; if his deeds were in any way altruistic, he doubted their sincerity. *He believed that he should have been able to do the impossible and save the lives of his half-sisters even though he had not yet been born.* This grandiose fantasy paradoxically made him scorn his actual accomplishments as worthless and even led him to be taken advantage of by others for their own glorification. [2000, p. 314; emphasis added)

Here we get a vivid picture of the patient's proleptic belief system—he believed it even though he had not yet been born—and a sense of how imprisoning it can be.

Joyce, whose competitiveness was extreme (Trilling, 1967, p. 463) faces the competition head-on, outsmarts everyone, destroys the way things have been done before, and is credited with the birth of the modernist novel! As T. S. Eliot put it, "His book destroyed the whole of the nineteenth century" (in Trilling, 1967, p. 452).

The lively and seductive qualities in both of my patients seemed partly to be ways of trying to lodge inside and be as one with me rather than engaging as separate people and developing the kind of intercourse in which play and trust could develop. Often they seemed to take over sessions and fill the space, almost as though they were "killing me off", the way they felt killed off, and which perhaps reinforces their belief that they are lethal. Joyce's (half-joking) comment that the demand he makes of his reader is that he should "devote his whole life to reading my works", has a similar feel to it (Ellmann, 1982, p. 703).

The depressive-position capacity to put one's self in the other's shoes, accepting the separateness of the other, is a very different state from intrusive identification, in which the patient gets inside in order to take over the other. In an early dream, one patient was being invited to play a musical instrument:

> *It was a combined instrument, half harpsichord, half viol, at different angles facing away from each other and a deep red colour. One side was alive and like a dragon, and the other inanimate. To play it you had to* get right inside it. *It seemed impossible to play.*

Her difficulties getting inside me and "playing" me frustrated her. She tried from all different angles, and she expressed fury at these mothers who won't let her in. The two sides of the instrument seemed a picture of her only alternatives as either being wild like a dragon or silenced and lying low. Again, one is reminded of Beckett's character, Lucky.

She brought poems *to* me and *about* me, seductive in their skill. I became a *wiry witch* in a difficult-to-enter or -manipulate box. There are images of "portals of entry", getting through the double doors, into my shoes and my eyes. Then she has me "*thrusting*" her out. At the same time there was the wish to make us the same, both mothers, for example, and knowing the same to avoid our separateness and having to imagine herself in my shoes—or even put herself in her own shoes, so to speak, and feel compassion for herself rather than guilt and fury.

Ghosts and witches abound in her poems, reminiscent of Macbeth. And the poems have the "knowing" quality of the proleptic state of mind. She is waiting outside my door, waiting to get in rather than waiting for insight into herself or to imagine things differently. I become as unreal, slippery, and controlled as she is.

Her imagination is given a kind of free rein, but with a purpose to control and express her love and fury. What seems less free about her imagination is the willingness to imagine alternatives and risk having her anger collapse into grief. The poet–critic D. J. Enright said: "Poetry itself is a way of preventing something or other you can't defeat from getting the better of you" (quoted in Wilkinson, 2012). And T. S. Eliot said: "Poetry is not a turning loose of emotion, but an escape from emotion; it is not the expression of personality, but an escape from personality" (quoted in Ricks, 1993, p. 1).

Dreams are themselves the proleptic imagination at work in that we experience images as reality during the dream. Fisher differentiates between a positive proleptic imagination, which allows us to picture our emotional experience through images and stories, and a negative proleptic imagination, which becomes a defensive attack on the capacity to become aware of our emotional experience (Fisher, 2011, p. 6). It is only when we wake from the dream that we can reflect on the images as an expression of our emotional states. My patients, however, found it difficult to create a distance from their dreams—they felt their dreams were more factual evidence of how dangerous or guilty they were. One patient worried about having unconscious murderous wishes: "Does this mean I am guilty having such feelings or not?" she asked. We can see in this question her confusion and a switch to the concrete.

After several years in analysis, she said to me, "You talk about my *picturing* being lethal everywhere I go, whereas I *know* I am lethal." Although this conveyed a growing awareness of a difference between picturing and knowing, between reality and fear, I still had the sense that part of her really believed she is dangerous. Her interest was in finding out what it is about her that is dangerous to others. What was more difficult was to entertain the idea that she is not dangerous. Or to make space to think and imagine differently. She even quoted Lady Macbeth:

> These deeds must not be thought,
> After these ways: so, it will make us mad.

Shakespeare and the "Dark Lady"

Like Joyce, my patients found a resonance in Shakespeare. Shakespeare himself lost siblings as a child, and there was a similarity of tone in one patient's poems to the Shakespeare Sonnets addressed to the "Dark Lady".

Donald Silver (1983) sees the "Dark Lady" Sonnets as Shakespeare's plea to his mother, who, having lost three daughters, turned away from him in her grief. Silver says that in Sonnet 143, "it is not difficult to imagine the boy Shakespeare speaking poignantly from within himself to the mother of his past who mourned to the point of neglecting her eldest son . . . the sonnet could be entitled, 'Ode to a Replacement Child', because it so tellingly depicts the fate of such a child" (Silver, 1983, p. 52):

> . . . So runn'st thou after that which flies from thee,
> Whilst I thy babe chase thee afar behind;
> But if thou catch thy hope, turn back to me,

And play the mother's part, kiss me, be kind;
So will I pray that thou mayst have thy *Will*,
If thou turn back, and my loud crying still.

A poem of Joyce's, *Ecce Puer*, has a similar quality and includes the lines:

Of the dark past
A child is born,
With joy and grief
My heart is torn.

Joyce sees something of himself in Shakespeare but cannot pin it down. He is not sure whether his identification is with Shakespeare or with Hamlet. He tries to sort out who betrayed Shakespeare and pictures it as the wife, Anne Hathaway:

> He chose badly? He was chosen, it seems to me. If others have their will Ann hath a way. By cock, she was to blame. She put the comether on him, sweet and twentysix. The greyeyed goddess who bends over the boy Adonis, stooping to conquer, as prologue to the swelling act, is a boldfaced Stratford wench who tumbles in a cornfield a lover younger than herself. [1922b, p. 244]

He has Stephen reinterpret the entire works of Shakespeare as a developing narrative of exile and loss and adds that:

> . . . the theme of the false or the usurping or the adulterous brother . . . is in Shakespeare always with him. The note of banishment, banishment from the heart, banishment from the home, sounds uninterruptedly from *The Two Gentlemen of Verona* onward till Prospero breaks his staff, buries it certain fathoms in the earth and drowns his book. [Kiberd, 1992, p. lxxii]

However, Shakespeare does not seem trapped in a claustrum world. Located outside his plays, he portrays a complex range of emotions in his characters who move towards maturity and relinquish their resentments, their paranoia, and their certainty. Hamlet, as well as accusing, is also questioning and moves finally to a "let be". Prospero can let go of the omnipotence and magical thinking—something that Joyce seems ultimately to recognize.

Unlike the harsh mockery in *Ulysses,* Shakespeare gave Hamlet all kinds of humour. Similarly, Samuel Beckett's humour conveys not only the humanity of his characters but also "the pity and understanding of the characters for each other" (Rustin & Rustin, 2000, p. 171). About *Ulysses*, Kiberd (1992) says:

> The virtuoso set pieces are less acts of creation than of parody; and parody is the act of a trapped mind which, realizing that it cannot create anew, takes its revenge by defacing the masterpieces of the past. [p. xlviii]

Samuel Beckett, in comparing himself with Joyce, said: "The kind of work I do is one in which I'm not master of my material. The more Joyce knew, the more he could. He's tending toward omniscience and omnipotence as an artist. I'm working with impotence, ignorance" (Beckett, 1987, p. 78). This is a useful distinction, but Beckett, though not himself a replacement child, knew very well the tendency to omniscience that he saw in Joyce.[5] Beckett's own traumas, and all he experienced during the war as a member of the French Resistance, changed him profoundly and "brought him out of himself, distancing him from the arrogant, closed-in young man of the 1930s" (Knowlson, 1996, p. 350).[6] (See O'Toole, 2015, on Beckett's similarities with Joyce.)

Joyce, in a moment of self-deprecation in later life, and with perhaps a painful recognition of the truth, said: "I've not developed. If I had matured I wouldn't be so committed to this *folie* of writing *Finnegans Wake*" (Ellmann, 1982, p. 703).

Conclusion

It has been pointed out by Stephen Greenblatt (2004) that Shakespeare found it difficult to portray or even imagine fully achieved marital intimacy in his plays. Joyce's own experience of a parental couple was marred by the breakdown of his parents' relationship. Perhaps it is no surprise that in *Ulysses* Stephen proclaims that only the imagination can be the source of rebirth and regeneration (Schwarz, 1987, p. 113). James Fisher has shown that if the imagination is a paralysing proleptic one, defending against emotion, there can be no creative intercourse. In discussing the K-state-of-mind that makes possible the experience of the full range of human emotions, he states:

> As Bion emphasized numerous times, it is the hatred of emotion that lies at the heart of psychotic phenomena (Bion, 1959, p. 311). Paradoxically certain emotions, such as anxiety, envy and hatred, attack and make impossible the experiencing of other emotions. Actually, rather than envy, perhaps we should put fear at the head of the list of the –K factors, the fear that emotional experience is not survivable. [Fisher, 2006, p. 1233]

I conclude with Joyce's original ending of *Finnegans Wake*, written two years before his death. The style in this passage is strangely different from the rest of the book, and he abandoned it. It is a dream image that seems like a mother with her little boy and is reminiscent of the Shakespeare sonnet. Perhaps the dream, in this "resurrection" chapter, is of waking the "dead mother".[7]

He said he felt completely exhausted after it and sat for a long while on a street bench, unable to move. One wonders why he abandoned it—whether the emotion, linked with his early experience, seemed not survivable.

> Come. Give me your great big hand for miny tiny. We will take our walk before they ring the bells. Not such big steps. It is hardly seven mile. It is very good for health in the morning. It seems so long since. As if you had been long far away. You will tell me some time if I can believe its all. You know where I am bringing you? You remember? Not a soul but ourselves. We might call on the Old Lord, what do you say? He is a fine sport. Remember to take off your white hat, eh? . . . I will tell you all sorts of stories, strange one. About every place we pass. It is all so often and still the same to me. Look! Your blackbirds! That's for your good luck. How glad you'll be I waked you. My! How well you'll feel. For ever after. First we turn a little here and then it's easy. I only hope the heavens sees us. A bit beside the bush and then a walk along the [Ellmann, 1982, p. 713]

Notes

1. For Joyce, life was all coincidences and superstition. He referred to *Finnegans Wake* as having a "prophetic and magical nature"; he knew the superstitions of most of Europe "and adopted them all" (Ellmann, 1982, pp. 517, 525). For Joyce, reality was "a paradigm . . . the perception of coincidence . . . reality, no matter how much we try to manipulate it, it can only assume certain forms; the roulette wheel brings up the same numbers again and again" (p. 551).

2. "James Joyce once remarked that *Ulysses* was for him essentially a way of capturing the speech of his father and his father's friends: ". . . so much literature stems from a wish to assuage homesickness . . . [T]he modernist is one who is likely to use his intimate life as material for his art, shaping the ordinary into the extraordinary" (Oates, 2015, p. 84).

3. For all his seeming dismissal of Oliver Gogarty, the two books left on his desk when he died were a Greek Lexicon and Gogarty's *I Follow Saint Patrick* (Ellmann, 1982, p. 742).

4. One night in the pub he had drunk one glass of wine when someone pointed out a rat running down the stairs. Joyce said "Where? Where? That's bad luck" and a minute later lost consciousness. They took him home, and "Nora was about

to scold him but became tender when she saw he was suffering from fright rather than alcohol" (Ellmann, 1982, p. 517).

5. In *Molloy* (1955), Beckett recalls his own unwanted birth: "My mother, I don't think too harshly of her. I know she did all she could not to have me, except of course the one thing, and if she never succeeded in getting me unstuck, it was that fate had earmarked me for less compassionate sewers" (p. 15).

6. "The shift to writing in French may have been an important way of escaping the influence of Joyce—greater simplicity and objectivity—could concentrate more on the music of the language, its sounds and its rhythms" (Knowlson, 1996, p. 357).

7. Joyce asked Beckett to read this original ending to *Finnegans Wake,* and Beckett was very moved by it. Interestingly, in one of his own last works, *Company,* some forty years later, Beckett describes walking with his own mother, thinking back to the skies of his childhood: "You make ground in silence hand in hand through the warm still summer air. It is late afternoon and after some hundred paces the sun appears above the crest of the rise. Looking up at the blue sky and then at your mother's face you break the silence asking her if it is not in reality much more distant than it appears. The sky that is. The blue sky" (in Johns, 2010, p. 27).

Gaudete: a response to Mary Fisher-Adams

David Mayers

Let me begin by stressing that I totally agree with Mary Fisher-Adams about the importance of both Meltzer's *claustrum* and Fisher's *proleptic imagination*. My difficulties lie with the way she brings these concepts to her reading of Joyce.

The relation between a writer's work and his life and states of mind is a vast and vexed topic—one that I shall not address here. I want to confine myself to the interpretation of *Ulysses*. I think that one difference between Adams' and my vision relates to the personal attitudes that we bring to understanding Joyce: I have the impression, based on her descriptions of his undoubted and manifold personal faults, that she rather dislikes him; whereas I find his life and work so heroic that I will largely forgive him everything. I recognize that his demand of the reader that he will devote his whole life to studying the work can seem omnipotently self-important; but I, and countless others, are grateful for having been given the chance to do so.

Adams' claim that Stephen, Bloom, and Molly are claustrum-dwellers implies that their lives are tunnel-visioned and lacking in development. I cannot avoid remembering that the Dublin of Bloomsday was in many respects a narrow-minded philistine place in which artists' wings were relentlessly clipped. The atmosphere is poignantly captured in the stories "A Mother" and "The Dead" from *Dubliners* (Joyce, 1914): also in Yeats's poem "September 1913" (in Yeats, 1989). Joyce and Stephen had to escape to be free to think. Similarly, Molly had to fight for her capacity to be a woman who enjoyed orgasmic sex. Adams sees her "Ah Jamesy get me out of this pooh" as Joyce intrusively identifying with his character ("pooh" was not at that time a euphemism for excrement but, rather, a generalized term of disdain or disgust). She does not mention that Molly had just realized she was beginning to menstruate; nor that in demotic Dublin "Ah Jamesy" was a mock-polite version of the ubiquitous "Ah Jaysus!".

To be sure, a psychological reading is, in principle, quite compatible with the one I offer. So let me give examples of why I find the claustrum interpretation a bed of Procrustes that lops off vital parts, whereas I see Joyce mobilizing a variety of points of view reminiscent of Bion.

One feature of *Ulysses* that I cannot square with the claustrum interpretation is that it is constantly side-splittingly funny. Now there can be humour in the claustrum: in Beckett's *Endgame* (1958), as vivid an evocation of the anal claustrum as I could hope to find, Clov says "If I don't kill that rat it'll die." But this is gallows humour. In *Ulysses* (1922a) and *Finnegans Wake* (1939), Joyce offers a spectrum of laughter much more generous and life-enhancing, running from metaphysical wit to slapstick.

Consider the Cyclops scene: a working-class pub; a place of hospitality, bonhomie, meanness, pretentiousness, spite, gossip; a place where life is down-to-earth or heroic, celebrated, ridiculed, reviled, mourned; where food and drink offer the chance to feast with the gods or make a pig of oneself; where singing can be uplifting and beautiful or a social embarrassment; and so on.

Against this background, Bloom is attacked for his Jewishness by the Citizen and counters triumphantly by pointing out that Jesus was a Jew. He then flees the pub, pursued by the Citizen/Cyclops and his barking dog, hurling an empty biscuit tin after him (think of the din on the cobbles). Heroic, mock-heroic, triumphant, a rout, magnificent, ridiculous? The lot.

Or think of the scene where Gertie MacDowell, crippled and isolated, drowns herself in sentimentalized romantic fancy and shows her knickers to a masturbating Bloom while the Host is elevated at Benediction in a neighbouring chapel. Grubby, pornographic, blasphemous, of course: but also heart-warmingly accepting and sympathetic—what else has the poor girl got? The claustrum interpretation doesn't leave any room for Joyce's essential warmth and breadth of vision.

When it comes to *Finnegans Wake* and its altered ending, I'm not sure I understand what Adams thinks Joyce essentially discarded. I think of two passages: the first from Anna Livia Plurabelle: where

Shem (Irish for James) has been renamed Mercius (the grateful, the merciful, the forgiven, the messenger and how many more?).

> With a beck, with a spring, all her ringringlets shaking, rocks drops in her tachie, tramtokens in her hair, all waived to a point and then all inuendation, little old-fashioned mummy, little wonderful mummy, ducking under bridges, bellhopping the weirs, dodging by a bit of bog, rapid-shooting round the bends, by Tallaght's green hills and the pools of the phooka and a place they call it Blessington and slipping sly by Sallynoggin, as happy as the day is wet, babbling, bubbling, chattering to herself, deloothering the fields on their elbows leaning with the sloothering slide of her, giddy-gaddy, grannyma, gossipaceous Anna Livia.
>
> He lifts the lifewand and the dumb speak.
>
> Quoiquoiquoiquoiquoiquoiquoiq! [p. 194]

Hardly claustral: rather, mummy's little duck, full of questions, luxuriating in the beauties of mummy's body. And, some 200 pages later:

> Three quarks for Muster Mark!
> Sure he hasn't got much of a bark
> And sure any he has it's all beside the mark. [p. 383]

King Mark, cuckolded like Bloom; Mr. Mac, the eponymous Irishman, Everyman, to be given three cheers. Because we're all sons of Anna and all loved, despite our manifest failures and shortcomings. This last is a reminder of the judgement passed on Bloom in the Circe scene that Adams mentions:

> You've made your second-best bed, and others must lie in it.

Bloom is a cuckold. He is not a hero with magic weapons, so rather than coming home to kill the suitors, he lives with them. Yet he gets three quarks and a Shakespearean mention. And how many ways do we interpret "lie"?

I once had a patient in work with whom I was much helped by Donald Meltzer's thought. In the beginning he brought a dream where *he was in an underground kitchen with a tribe of cannibal brothers who were cutting their wrists, dropping blood into a cauldron of mother's shit and eating it. He was expected to join in, but was too scared.*

He spent many years dreaming of trying to escape this anal claustrum, but was so afraid of the outside that he went back in. Gradually, he was able to dream of living outside and learning to survive there. In his last session with me he brought this dream: *he was coming to have lunch with me in a college that was mine but not his; when he arrived, the college had many qualities of a mausoleum; we had a pleasant lunch, but he was acutely conscious that we should not meet again; he left and walked sadly to the station; suddenly he saw a little house for sale; his mood lifted as he realized that he could buy it, furnish it himself, and live there with his father.*

I think both Joyce and Beckett would have appreciated that.

CHAPTER FOURTEEN

A mind of one's own: therapy with a patient contending with excessive intrusive identification and claustrum phenomena

Tara Harrison

This chapter chronicles the first years of therapy with a patient contending with both external and internal intrusive forces, leaving her struggling to form an authentic, thinking mind. I show how Meltzer's concepts of intrusive identification and claustrum phenomena have provided a crucial framework to help understand this patient's internal system.

Donald Meltzer initially used the term "massive projective identification" (1966, p. 17) to describe the excessive use of projective identification as conceptualized by Melanie Klein. He shifted to a qualitative view with the term "intrusive identification"—that is, an omnipotent phantasy of forceful intrusion into an external or, crucially, an *internal* object in order to control it, and eliminate its "otherness" (Meltzer, 1986b, p. 69, quoted in Fisher, 1999, p. 233). The aggressive quality of the projections has a significant impact on the internal containing function:

> . . . the violent nature of intrusive identification destroys the container, the place for maternal alpha function. The container is now transformed into a claustrum, a rigid prison brought about by the intrusive process either of active penetration or of being sucked in. [Gosso, 2004, p. 21]

The work with the patient described here demonstrates the severe impact of intrusive identification on internal object relations. It depicts the difficulties in trying to reach a patient whose inner world is rigidly encapsulated, so unlike maternal containment, "which wraps round and protects the baby, adjusting itself to its spatial and mental needs, and favouring creativity" (p. 21).

The patient, Olivia, was 35 years old at the start of our work, and lived in London. She described herself as having a chaotic life history, particularly during her university years when she developed an eating disorder, and was "acting out" (her term) in various ways. She linked the timing of her bulimia with moving away from home, and she spoke at great length about her intense relationship with her domineering mother.

According to Olivia, all the disturbing chaos was in the past. She had a grip on her eating disorder, and she was now in a better situation. Olivia was living with her long-term boyfriend, a GP. Their social circle was made up of doctors, psychologists, and psychotherapists, and she had learned a therapeutic language, albeit a rather clichéd version. She informed me that she had been "avoidant" or "regressed" or was "acting out", and she referred frequently to her boyfriend's diagnoses of her symptoms. During our initial meeting, Olivia told me that she was keen to use the couch right away. She had a friend, she said, who took years to get on the couch. Olivia described dinner parties where her friends would discuss their therapies and therapists. I wondered if Olivia felt that she too should have a therapy to bring to the table. Perhaps she felt she could appear accomplished at "being in therapy", having already established a sophisticated-enough defence to avoid real contact. Perhaps she brought into the consulting room, from the first session, her tendency to be what she would call "adaptive"—that is, her expectation that she would have to shape herself to the requirements of the therapy.

Intrusive identification in relation to the patient's external objects

Olivia's intrusive relationships were most clearly demonstrated in her presentation of two important people in her life: her mother and her fiancé.

Authoritative and charismatic, her mother, as described by Olivia, invaded Olivia with expectations and assumptions about who Olivia was. Olivia felt she had grown to fit the space imagined for her by her mother; if she revealed aspects of herself outside that shape, she felt the response from her mother was terrifying. Olivia came from a privileged background, and she had benefited from the family resources, having extra French lessons, going to a pony club, and so on. But every memory was associated with some sort of assault—her mother hitting her on the head with a riding boot on the way to pony club, for example. Her mother may have assaulted Olivia's head (invaded her mind), but she reportedly put Olivia "at the end of the corridor" as a baby, so that she didn't have to hear her constant crying.

Because Olivia spoke in psychological jargon, it was difficult to connect to her words, but I did think these descriptions described her paradoxical experience of feeling both invaded and neglected by her maternal object. She spoke of childhood illnesses and accidents, glandular fever, tonsillitis, a broken bone at only 18 months old. She had asthma as well as many allergies and intolerances to foods, which made life difficult for her. They were, perhaps, ways to get attention that she very much needed, but at great cost to herself. Strikingly, her mother had never been to Olivia's home: the assumption was that Olivia would travel to the village where her mother lived. "Mother's village" would become an important symbol for us throughout the therapy. Olivia's dreams were frequently located in her mother's village. In one dream, *Olivia is driving around her mother's village and she crashes the car, smashing her face against the steering wheel.* In another dream, *she drives around her mother's village and runs down two dogs that are killed and left at the side of the road.* It seems that she feels her mother's "management" of them has injured both her and her brother. Olivia's association to the dreams is that, if she is at the steering wheel, the results can be catastrophic. She is better as a passenger in a vehicle. I wondered if there was a road out of mother's village that could become available to her in her dream-life.

Olivia's fiancé was, as she portrayed him, another dominating force. A specialist in psychosomatic symptoms, he would provide absolute diagnoses of her symptoms and anxieties: "You are acting out", "You are suicidal", or "You're psychotic. I'm going to have you sectioned!" Olivia seemed to cling to his absolute diagnoses, however aggressively and impatiently they were put. She once fainted while he was away on a sporting trip. He diagnosed a "pseudo-faint because I was away". He may well have been along the right lines, since she certainly felt lost without the dominant figures in her life, but diagnosing Olivia substituted for understanding or containing her. Somehow it appeared to give Olivia a sense of being held, albeit rigidly. It seemed that Olivia had recruited a partner who maintained her mother's model of rather forceful communications and, like mother, seemed certain about who she is and what goes on inside her. Olivia, it appeared, perceived herself as a passive receptacle, condemned to accept the tyrannical management of an intrusive object.

From Olivia's point of view, these characters, so intrusive with their communications and projections, were impervious to any attempt *from her to reach them*. She reported that she would become increasingly more desperate, employing tears and tantrums to try and impact them, until she gave up and locked herself in her room with headaches and in despair. James Fisher describes the "not-good-enough mother who can neither recognize nor respond to the gesture of the infant", and he suggests that "*the substitution of her own gestures for those of the infant's* is a tyrannical move" (1999, p. 46; emphasis added). He goes on to describe the potential impact of this tyranny on the subject when he observes how "every false-self personality structure hides in it the tyrant, and one only has to observe such compliant persons when the tables can be turned" (p. 46). Olivia's reported tantrums and demands seemed to reflect Fisher's observation. I imagined Olivia's migraines as the pain of her banging her head against a brick wall—and I often had that feeling myself throughout the work!

Despite these colourful stories, the experience of actually being with Olivia in the consulting room was strangely hollow and empty. I often felt blank and dazed, followed by a feeling of panic that I would never be able to understand or help her.

Significantly, the assessor who first met with Olivia noted a similar experience, ending her report with this insightful note: "In case all this sounds a bit sunny and easy, I would like to put down a few thoughts about the countertransferential feelings I had with this patient. I normally see patients for assessment for an hour and ten minutes. With this young woman, I quite soon found my eyes straying to the clock and had an increasingly uneasy feeling that we were going to get through it all too quickly, that we would grind to a halt well before the 'end', and I wouldn't be able to think of anything more to say to her." Like the assessor, I would find myself looking at the clock worried that time was moving so slowly and wondering how would the session be filled.

Fisher, now reflecting on a paper by Michael Feldman (1989), continues thus:

> The infant confronted with an impenetrable mother or parental couple becomes increasingly desperate and this gives rise to two alternative patterns. Either the patient makes increasingly violent attempts to get through to this impenetrable object, or it withdraws

> to the blankness of a hopeless situation that it cannot face. Probably with most infants in such a situation, the former gives way to the latter. [Fisher, 1999, p. 46]

Over time I came to understand both the assessor's experience and mine as a countertransference experience of Olivia's blankness of mind. In contrast to the earlier "cry for help" tantrums, she had given up on having her projections and communications taken in, understood, and transformed by a penetrable, receptive object.

As we approached the first break, which fell quite early in the work, Olivia described her morning before she came to the session.

> Olivia: So this morning I was in a really bad mood. I really didn't want to come today. I had a tantrum in the bathroom. I was feeling ill and wanted to cancel the session. I was banging things in the bathroom and shouting. Nick knocked on the door and shouted, "It's all about the break, Livvy!" (*laughs*) . . . So I can see that I'm acting out about our break.
>
> TH (*gently*): It feels like I've been made redundant.
>
> Olivia: What do you mean?
>
> TH: Well, it's as though a therapy has already taken place—you are upset and you express this. It is recognized and interpreted as seemingly connected to our break—and all this before you get here!
>
> Olivia (*pauses for a moment*): Mmm . . . I think I can be quite avoidant of real contact. Nick says I have schizoid behaviours.

This snippet shows how hard it was to make contact with Olivia. She has an alternative system already established, with jargon in place of language and certainty instead of exploration. Olivia "knows" she should be disrupted by the break and that this should be "diagnosed" by an assured and certain therapist. Meltzer (1976a) called this kind of false-self version of therapy the "delusion of clarity of insight", and he linked it to intrusion into the head/breast compartment of the internal maternal object. Meltzer describes the internal mother's head/breast compartment as the source of richness, generosity, and insight. If in phantasy the internal object has been invaded and conquered, there is a shift in perspective—the resources, as Meltzer put it, get "vulgarized". Genuine search for knowledge becomes a rather grandiose possession of information. Through the intrusive processes, the patient is fused with the internal object. She has done away with any difference between them, including the difference of generations and of experience. This "pseudo-maturity" lacks genuine wisdom and relies on the delusion of mastery.

It was difficult to imagine a spontaneous exchange. Instead, we would have a hollow, empty version of a therapy that would at best maintain the status quo. Olivia portrayed her father as gentle and passive, but rather weak and disappointing. He features in the therapy more as an absent object or one with limited capacity to influence the external and internal dynamics. I think at some level she associated me with the gentle but impotent paternal object, and she relied on her fiancé's brutal but "exciting" form of therapy, finding me rather dull in comparison.

Internal situation

These relationships seemed to reflect Olivia's internal object relations, which also seemed to be characterized by tyranny and compliance.

We started to understand more about this through Olivia's positioning of her handbag in the consulting room. At the start of every session, she would place her handbag right next to my bag, even though it was quite awkward for her to get to and it meant we had to cross each other en route to the couch or chair: "It's as if you experience where I place my bag as an instruction for you. This is how you find a place for your bag." Olivia was initially puzzled by my observation. She could see that we crossed each other in an awkward way because of the bag, but she could not see that there could be somewhere more convenient for her to put her bag, a place that might suit her better. Already in the consulting room she felt like the passive receptacle for my instructive gesture. I wondered whether her bag stuck to mine indicated an attempt to attach adhesively. When projective identification fails, Meltzer hypothesizes that intrusive identification or adhesive identification can take its place. I wondered if there were times when Olivia unconsciously presumed that her objects, so unreceptive to her communications, had no space inside them, and so she would try to attach adhesively to the outside layer. It is possible that she would oscillate between attempts to get inside and attempts to attach to the outside of her object.

I think it was highly significant that, around this time, Olivia had started talking about two of her friends who had become pregnant. She had been quite scathing about their decision to have a baby and was quite sure that pregnancy was not for her. Yet just a few weeks later,

Olivia told me that she, herself, was newly pregnant. She described the conception as accidental and quite a shock. I found myself wondering if she had, quite unconsciously, experienced her friends' pregnancies as an instruction to become pregnant herself. And yet this would indicate a seriously confused internal system.

A little later in the therapy as Olivia's pregnancy developed, there seemed to be more evidence to support this theory. One of her friends suffered a miscarriage, and she told Olivia about this over a weekend. On the Monday morning, Olivia felt unwell: she felt "tightness" in her abdomen and strong sensations in her pelvic area. She became alarmed, got off the bus, and went to hospital, cancelling our session. During the course of the day at the hospital, perhaps as a response to her anxiety, Olivia underwent three internal examinations. At this point, she started to bleed, and by the end of the day it was Olivia who was dealing with a possible miscarriage. Eventually the light bleeding stopped and everything settled back down, but the pregnancy seemed to have been potentially endangered by the day's events. I was starting to understand this as a process whereby Olivia herself perceives an intrusive and instructive quality in her object's communications. She could not yet find her way to a kind of therapy in which we might be able to think together and make a distinction between her friend's pregnancy and her own. It is quite literally a con-fusion: a *fusion with* the identity and experience of the object, and there seems to be no choice about it. Any attempt to understand her is misconstrued as an instruction, and she is condemned to adjust to and even "suck in" the hostile communications. It is a very distorted version of introjection. It was a core issue in Olivia's psychopathology and put her, I think, in considerable physical and psychic danger.

Evidence of internal claustrum phenomena

Over the early months of her pregnancy, Olivia suffered from quite severe morning sickness. An acquaintance had informed her that morning sickness was an indication of ambivalence about the pregnancy. Olivia was deeply ashamed that she was "acting out" in this way. She thought she had to get a grip on the sickness—that is, on her ambivalence—and make sure it could not be seen.

Despite efforts to think with her about the credibility of such an absolute theory, Olivia clung to the premise that her ambivalence was a sign of being defective. She resisted the notion that mixed feelings about her pregnancy might be acceptable and we could think about them together. The need for certainty left her shifting from one stance ("I want this baby and I omnipotently became pregnant without even trying") to another ("I don't want a baby and everyone knows I don't because I am demonstrating it through my morning sickness"). She seemed to experience thinking as an internal act of violence, leaving her despairing. During a morning session, just before she was due for a scan at the hospital, Olivia spoke of her hatred of the scans: "They show what's inside you. I keep saying to the nurse, 'Only show the baby! Don't move it around . . . I don't want to see anything in there'." I asked her what the scan might show, and she answered with a shudder, "Oh one of my organs . . .".

I suggested that she was afraid that our therapy might reveal something that she feared was bad or unacceptable inside her. There was a pause before she went on to tell me about a dinner party that she had attended, where she had heard a story about an acquaintance who had discovered a "dead twin" inside her. It was a teratoma she was describing, I think: a tumour containing tissue or organ components such as hair, teeth, and bone. She has never been able to forget this image, Olivia said, because it resonated with her so powerfully.

Olivia started to describe a "creature" inside her. "It is a baby", she said, "but its face is old. Yes, it's old but it never matures or develops. It looks like Gollum from *The Lord of the Rings*. Gollum in the swamp . . . that's what's inside me." This was a very striking dream image indeed. Olivia was allowing us even deeper into her internal world. Meltzer describes an internal maternal object, built in phantasy, whose internal structural design borrows its form from the external counterpart, with an outside and inside with different chambers or compartments. Meltzer posits that a patient can "helter-skelter" through the compartments of the internal mother. And it seemed to me that Olivia was moving from the pseudo-maturity and superiority of certainty, so characteristic of the head/breast compartment, down into the darker, bereft world of the rectal compartment. Her primitive sensations are projected into the rigid, toxic rectal compartment of the internal mother. Here, no containment is available, only encapsulation. With no hope of the sensation being given language and symbolic meaning, it is a nightmare version of containment. I think back to Olivia's dream situated in her mother's village where she drives around in her car and smashes her face on the steering wheel. I can understand this now as a picture of Olivia feeling trapped inside a "compartment" (the car) of the maternal object (mother's village) where it is not possible to develop her own thinking, and thus her identity is severely deformed (her smashed, disfigured face). Now she provided us with the dream image of Gollum living in the swamp: a dream image, to my mind, of a primitive, infantile part projected into the rectal compartment of the internal mother. Meltzer imaginatively describes the shifts of perception that occur in this claustrophobic environment. It is "a world of assumption rather than thought, where right means either the law or precedent, where to be genuinely different means to be detected as an intruder . . ." (1992a, p. 92). It is a totalitarian and persecutory regime where spontaneity and uniqueness is prohibited. This describes the impression that I have gathered of Olivia's inner world. She is often in despair and exhausted—she seemed to be undergoing an almost constant internal assault from a persecutory regime. As far as one might be able to imagine the deeply unconscious world of internal object relations, it seemed that Olivia's internalized experiences and objects are fixed and rigidly managed. Olivia resists an authentic therapy, because she simply cannot imagine a creative, thoughtful container–contained dynamic that could liberate the internal objects to mature, develop, or combine. Reflecting on her dream image of the teratoma, I imagine fragments of infantile experience—part-objects and bizarre objects (beta-elements, in Bion's terms)—projected and paralysed in the claustrum, with little hope of transformation so that Olivia could have access to a richer and freer internal life.

Technical issues

During her pregnancy, Olivia became very frightened that she was going to lose her mind. Her anxieties seem to be connected to her partner Nick's history. His mother had become extremely disturbed during her pregnancy with him, and Nick was born in a psychiatric setting. During Olivia's pregnancy, he frequently described her as psychotic and requiring sectioning. Olivia experienced this as a sure prediction, and it caused her a huge amount of panic. Nick's excessive projections and Olivia's claustrum psychopathology are knotted together. I would present the possibility that an object, as James Fisher puts it, can "protect itself against intrusion, closing its orifices against an intrusive attempt to penetrate" (Fisher, 1999, p. 228), but Olivia found this concept difficult to really engage with.

Just as difficult for Olivia to acknowledge was the notion that her own lively, creative, and aggressive aspects—indeed, some of the much needed aspects that might propel her forwards—get split off and projected into her fiancé. She and Nick seemed to be caught in a "projective gridlock" (Morgan, 1995) that felt to Olivia like a version of togetherness and intimacy but is closer to collusion. It seemed immensely exciting at some level for Olivia to be at the mercy of such dominating objects, but the fixedness of their gridlock hampered progression in the therapy. The teratoma that Olivia imagines inside her seems to be a mass of fragments of identity. What belongs to whom? I suspect it is still too early to attempt unravelling, as that which is truly Olivia is still embryonic.

There were other challenges to the therapy. Olivia missed many sessions, and in this way the fragile link between us was broken. Any corresponding internal linking was impaired too, I think. Language would become jargon, and I would find my comments repeated back to me, with meaning drained. The insight was hijacked in the system of the claustrum, and in this way Olivia maintained control of the culture within the consulting room. Like Olivia, I felt unable to expand and develop outside preconceived expectations. I tried to find ordinary ways of putting things, but my non-psychological vocabulary caused suspicion that I must be underqualified and ineffective, rather than actually having a capacity to not know and to discover. Olivia was able to confess, at least, that Nick thought I was rather ineffectual.

I featured in a significant dream: *I am a small, dreamy "London-type" and Olivia discovers that I am a lesbian. I have a large, bossy wife from the countryside who dominates me.* I put it to her that she imagines I have an internal world like hers, dominated by a larger, managing aspect who comes from the countryside—a reference to "mother's village" and the intrusive maternal object, I think. As Meltzer observed, the patient assumes that "this interior world is all there is and the analyst is as much caught up in its net as is the patient" (1992a, p. 102). This would indicate that, stuck in the same swamp, I would be able to be of very little help to Olivia. She struggles to perceive me as an object that could help her, and I feel like I am banging my head against a brick wall to try to reach her. It is an important countertransferential situation, however difficult it is to bear. Perhaps the most hopeful aspect of the dream is that there is a "small me" who has a capacity for dreaming. I might be able to be uncertain, to explore, and to symbolize. Olivia may need to feel that I can enter her claustral world with her and for her, but that I can also exit and be able to think creatively. It might help her with the idea that she, too, could leave the claustrum.

Returning to her mother's village—the allure of the claustrum

After two years of working together, Olivia told me that she was moving many miles away, back to her mother's village. Indeed, her mother had given her a huge amount of money to help her buy a cottage in the village. Olivia felt she had no other option, since she found caring for her baby very difficult and she needed support. This was extremely discouraging, and I went through a period of despondency that things could never change for Olivia—a reflection of her doubt that there was any way out of her prison. Over the weeks that followed, I started to present, more actively, a symbolic "mother's village", not the actual, geographical one but the internal rigid trap of her earlier dreams. I started to wonder with her whether she could move back to her mother's actual village but resist the urge to settle back into the encapsulating system. Olivia would have to travel a significant distance to come to therapy.

To my surprise, Olivia maintained a tentative link with me and managed a once-weekly therapy. She decided to stop using the couch and sat on a chair. I felt encouraged by her rejection of the couch. It seemed that she was able to be more authentic about what she could truly manage, despite how that might appear. I think Olivia was starting to acknowledge and tolerate separateness between Nick and her. Nick's mother died during this period of the therapy. During a heated row, Nick cried out to Olivia, "You are dead inside." Olivia brought this to therapy as an example of something belonging to Nick that he needed to get rid of into her—and she was able to resist taking it in. This is hopeful since, as Meltzer put it, "the potentiality of a space, and thus the potentiality of a container, can only be realized once a sphincter-function has become effective" (Meltzer et al., 1975, p. 226). Olivia now has the challenge of differentiating herself from her baby. Her baby resembles her in appearance and shares her food allergies and other physical conditions, so there are considerable grounds for confusion of identities. Olivia's wish to be a receptive and responsive mother, and an advocate for her child in the external world, has urged her on in the work of separation and self-realization.

Her mother had left Olivia at the end of the corridor where her cries would not disturb her. Olivia has created a long corridor between us through her move back to her mother's village. But she travels the long distance, albeit sporadically, towards someone who wishes to listen and respond to her cries. As Olivia starts to create and protect a private internal space, she may be able to relate to her internal objects in a less intrusive, controlling way too. This work, done deep in the unconscious, relies upon a respectful, reciprocal, imaginative intimacy. Crucially, it must be intimacy established from the outside of her internal objects. If she can ease the rigid, intrusive culture in her unconscious life, her internal objects may be "free to come and go", to develop and combine—so that she would have access to more mature and creative internal resources (Cassese, 2002, p. 11). Olivia may discover she could bear to be uncertain, to have mixed feelings and to develop a mind of her own.

CHAPTER FIFTEEN

Battered women lose their minds

Cecilia Muñoz Vila & Nubia Torres Calderón

The material presented here comes from a three-year research project conducted by the Psychology Faculty of Javeriana University, Colombia, which took place in a shelter for battered women and their children, in Bogota. The authors of this chapter were supervisors of the project and thesis directors and were responsible for a research group of five students. The dissertations included the presentation of three individual psychotherapeutic process recordings, which were supervised and analysed using the *meditative review* method described by Bion (1963, pp. 99–100).

In total, we observed 40 women whose abusive relationships since childhood and currently with their spouses were described in detail in these protocols. As the stories of these battered women were reviewed, the research team had the impression that they were entering a territory of human misery and dehumanization that was common ground for these women, their aggressors, and their families, as well as for the neighbourhood they lived in. An atmosphere of despair and rage could be sensed by the research group, as if the psychic weave of the chronicles permeated the way they listened to the distressing stories born out of the presentations. The same thing happened when we reviewed the material for a second time, long after the original discussion.

The therapists working with these women were confused by the intensity of the drama in the accounts, and this made it difficult for them to understand the phenomena they were observing. The way these women had experienced their relationships persisted in their relationships with the staff and therapists in the shelter. The therapists either felt an urgency to do something immediately or were paralysed by a helplessness born of the terror and submission in the experiences of maltreatment and abuse. Rather than transference and countertransference, these stories seemed to generate actions and reactions in their listeners.

In cases where there had been early sexual abuse, there was denial and refutation, which prevented them grasping what was evident. Meanwhile, the students who worked in the shelter as psychologists or social workers were deeply affected by the suffering of these battered women, even when they had no direct contact with them; many broke their contracts and fled to protect themselves. This showed the impact on the therapists, who were in contact with experiences in which the annihilation of the self and the destructive urgencies of the id prevail and the tyranny and seduction of the object are simultaneous and become intolerable. Above and beyond this, as therapists, we are unlikely to be adequately prepared for such overwhelming situations.

Once the research team found a conceptual framework within which to understand the material, new questions and understandings arose: what makes a battered woman stay with her batterer and allow this vicious circle to be repeated for years? How can we understand these states of the mind? What conceptual frameworks can shed light on this phenomenon to generate therapeutic models specific to this population? How can we assist these women in their allotted two months in the shelter when we know that this time is too short to effect change in their social and psychic realities?

Throughout these three years, we found certain conceptual frameworks that accounted for the compulsion to repeat and to invite punishment. These battered women permanently function in a rotation of basic assumptions, as described by Bion (1961): going from dependence through a long process of fight and flight and ending up in pairing, which brings about the illusion of hope for a better future and the renewal of dependence. Dehumanization is also predominant as a form of existence, with the disappearance of social rules that enable the preservation of groups and communities.

Ultimately, this leads to individuals pursuing survival without regard to the needs of others.

Likewise, we found an imbalance in the influence of the psychic structures described by Freud as essential components of the psychic apparatus that lead to both an invasive pressure of the id and a destructive social reality. Thus the ego is left under the influence of objects in external reality and lives in fear of harming these objects or being punished by them if they are challenged. In this situation, the ego becomes defenceless against ill-treatment, and its functions deteriorate or become unable to develop.

Meltzer's concept of the dimensionality of psychic space (Meltzer et al., 1975) provided a helpful framework to think about the dynamic of battered and battering women and men, most of whom presented the one- and two-dimensional spaces that impaired the emergence of the internal world, the psychic space for meaning and symbolization. For the most part, they functioned in one dimension, in constant action–reaction and circumstantial attraction–repulsion. In the sensorial field they were two-dimensional: able to contact the outside world and experience physical sensations, but only capable of relating to others by imitating their sensorial qualities. Their existence is guaranteed by the presence of the other on the outside, which allows them some awareness of sensorial contact. Glances, words, sounds, skin contact, smells, and flavours experienced by the perceptive apparatus catch their attention and make them realize what nature and the social world have to offer. Often, the need for closeness takes precedence, impeding their capacity to consider the kindness or wickedness of the object. Similarly, the concepts of sensorial and structural dismantling described by Meltzer seemed to be present in many of these battered women. Another important finding was that the functioning of these women's families was gang-like or inverted.

Green (1986), focusing on Freud's psychic apparatus, reconsiders the supremacy of the id with the ego at its service, which inhibits the development of the Oedipus complex or its dissolution for the configuration of the superego; prohibition of incest is disregarded, and so life revolves around the fear and the threat of castration, resulting in random acts aimed at claiming possession over the other to ensure the existence of the powerful, unharmed penis. This dynamic is similar to the one described by Meltzer in his book *The Claustrum* (1992a).

The work that we present here stems from a wish to find humanity amidst the miserable life of many human beings living in a world dominated by destruction and death. It is based upon the work of therapists who tried to reach people who were both destroyed and destructive, by understanding their mental state. They remained side by side with them, as alive and available as they could be, in spite of their feelings of impotence, which they were only able to overcome in the discussion of their final reports. In this process, they came face to face with little girls who had been battered and abused and who went on to find groups or individuals who continued to maltreat them; these girls, filled with hatred, hopelessness, and rage, would take revenge and lead others to suffer the same ill-treatment and abuse that they had suffered.

The dehumanization of these battered women was evident. The environment in which they had survived evoked Turnbull's painful experience with the dehumanized tribe of the Ik, described in his book *The Mountain People* (1972). A life of scarcity and hunger had starved the tribe of all traces of sympathy, making them distrustful and cruel; they made fun of the difficulties of others and competed endlessly, even with their closest ones, for the morsel that would keep them alive in a hostile environment. This situation caused isolation in the families of the tribe and rupture in the relationships between husbands, wives, children—each one concerned only with their own survival. On the cover of the book, Margaret Mead wrote, "As Turnbull's writing weaves in and out between outrageous acts and his own outrage, he emphasizes again and again how fragile the structure of a society is." Turnbull suggested that the breakdown of social organizations and the deterioration of value systems permeates and disrupts the psychic functioning of human beings who grow and develop in these dehumanized social and cultural settings.

This would suggest that in order to survive, people will abandon their emotional, social, economic, and political ties; they will give up values, beliefs, and feelings related to love, hope, sympathy, esteem, help, cooperation, care, and protection, because they consider them an impediment to their survival. Society and communal life become dangerous and are replaced by a survival system devoid of human emotion and warm social interaction. It is undeniable that throughout history, some groups of people have assumed extreme positions of inhumanity towards other groups and built life styles that have perpetuated dehumanization. Violence in Colombia, for instance, testifies to the cruelty that dominant groups exert on populations that they attack, decimate, slaughter, and destroy in order to take over their land and increase their power.

Magdalena

Magdalena's breakdown

"Magdalena" was a 29 year-old prostitute who had taken refuge in a shelter for battered women and their children in Bogota. It was the second time she had sought therapeutic help. From her first session, she confronted us with the cruelty she had suffered and exerted since she was little. She told us how she had been abused by her brother-in-law, the father of her older sister, and a carpenter who used to give her money. She told the story of her relationship with a paramilitary man that made her the most wanted and expensive woman in the brothel. Things went sour when he demanded that she abort the child they had conceived "by mistake", arguing that he did not like to "leave a trace of his actions". When she refused, he sent hit-men to beat her up. They hurt her badly, but—as always—she felt nothing, alone with her "clouded mind". She was simply the woman who was abused by everyone, who felt nothing, because "it is not as terrible as people may think".

She described her current situation as the result of multiple experiences of work exploitation, poverty, starvation, and sexual abuse. When she reported her brother for raping her daughters and niece, she described him to the police as an "ill man, criminal, thief, and rapist". Her mother cursed her for this. The material of her stories was composed of dramatic adventures lived with indifference; her own experiences were felt to be someone else's. Her accounts were made up of scattered stories. Nevertheless, amid this violence, abuse, maltreatment, and attempted murder, two good figures appeared: her father, who had always taken care of her and loved her, and Miguel, her current boyfriend, who bewildered her with his unconditional kindness because she thought that, "in the end, all men are women abusers".

She would go from being the bad woman, condemned to poverty and filth, to being the great queen of the brothel, the one with the best income and largest number of clients. She claimed that she "never drank or sniffed anything" but told how she would "come home completely destroyed" or stopped by at her friend Miguel's place, so that other people would not see her like that: showing her worst face to the loved man and her best face to her abusers was a constant pattern.

As she shifted from being good, rich, and powerful to being bad, ugly, and poor, so her objects changed from good to bad at a glance: from great helpers to great abusers, from caring figures to battering figures. Her bad sister could suddenly become her good sister. The only constant was the endless sexual abuse: fathers and daughters, brothers-in-law and sisters-in-law, adults and children. The shelter and protection that she acknowledged they could give her could become the nastiest prison, with the worst conditions of abuse and maltreatment. She even thought of going back to the brothel, despite the death threats of her former client, because there she could at least make a living for herself and her daughters.

For Magdalena, neither sensations nor emotions helped her to differentiate between her experiences. Her stories lacked symbolization and meaning and were not organized in time and space; her only tense was present continuous and she alternated between idealized and denigrated persecutory places. In repeating herself, she conveyed the absence of an object capable of making sense of these contrasting experiences, with no one to mediate them.

Her disorganized sensory system seemed to have been damaged by violent intrusions, which may have ruptured her perceptive sensory matrix, making it difficult for her to discriminate, differentiate, relate, or transform her experiences. In such cases, the end result is a broken sensuality that makes women unable to feel, integrate, and make sense of their experiences and to generate meanings. Magdalena's internal reality, suffused with trauma, threats, and concrete images of finding a way out to a better future, oscillated, for no obvious reason, between being persecuted to persecuting, from abused to abusing. It was as though her body disappeared along with the possibility of perceiving and remembering her experiences or making any sense of them; she lost all sense of pleasure (Michel de M'Uzan, quoted by Green, 2002). Her sexuality became her profession, disassociated from her body, where the trauma was re-experienced time after time, masked by her attempts to listen to the men who visited her.

This sensory breakdown became more evident through the six sessions. The general feeling was that her discourse was falling to pieces and the association between events and words was unclear; no time, space, sensation, emotion, image, or bonds with objects remained long enough to become an organizing element. In her mind, everything appeared and disappeared: nothing was stable and nothing remained. For this reason, she would turn to her enemies for help, as if they could be her friends. Not even the scars of physical violence remained in her mind: she would see them and then forget them the next minute. One minute, she was a beauty queen; the next, she was bruised and bloody. With these alternating images, the essence of her existence was lost.

Magdalena told stories about repeated abuse by "ugly men", who gave her money that she would give to whoever needed it. Without body sensations, feelings, or clear memories that could link together and stay organized, she became simply a thing through which others would pass. Her stories suggested that the only way she could survive was by "clouding" her sensory apparatus. The ego was caught up in an expulsive movement from the inside of her body, where there were no differentiations, only abolitions. Since she could not build representations, everything was cloudy or void: she had nothing but perceptions, which moved back and forth between positive and negative, leaving her feeling disorientated and in need of someone to give her instructions. She was an ear that listened and an eye that saw, but she did not have "common sense" (Bion, 1963) at the core of her attention. She was a clear example of sensory dismantling and de-mentalization (Meltzer et al., 1975).

Magdalena's broken mind matrix

In Magdalena's case, it seemed that nothing remained of the two-way movement between container and contained that enables the development of thought, meaning, and mind itself. All she had were fragments, alternating in a disorganized manner, as pieces that appear and leave the sensory scene. These movements are erratic because of the lack of an organizing principle coming from the object or from the ego.

In addition, it is as if the two-way movements that facilitate integration by the discovery of a selected fact, which creates new constellations of elements, did not exist, and the only remnants in the mind were broken and disintegrated pieces of timeless experiences (Muñoz Vila, 2011). It is like a sensory collage, randomly built by bringing time, space, and objects together and apart. Good and bad characters alternate and change their status. Times alternate, and it becomes impossible to identify when a specific event takes place.

Magdalena seemed to pull her stories from up her sleeve until she ran out of energy and words. These were not coherent narratives but dispersed elements that came together by verbal contiguity or just by accident so that the qualities attributed to her objects as well as to her experiences was random. Bound up in discontinuous events, Magdalena seemed to use her stories as a second skin (Bick, 1968). In the absence of an internal space, the mechanisms of introjection and projection could not work, making it impossible for her to reduce her pain or develop her perceptual apparatus and her mental structure.

Final considerations

From what we can see, the non-mental functioning of battered women is the result of early experiences that damage the body and hinder the construction of an adequate psychic apparatus. These women were bombarded, from very young, with sensory experiences that exceeded their physical and mental capacities, and they had nobody to prevent this from happening. They had no object that could discriminate, differentiate, and set boundaries for this sensory and bodily experience, resulting in sensory dismantling and de-mentalization. All of them lacked an object that might act as a protective screen from the intrusive stimulation to which they were exposed: an object with the function of a boundary for the overflowing impulses, so they were not forced to eliminate their sensorial and mental apparatus.

The functions of Klein's "good object" and those of Winnicott's "good-enough mother" became clearer with Bion and Meltzer's work on the maternal function and its relation to the psychic apparatus, and the findings on infant observation published by Bick and Harris. The mother—or her replacement—receives the anxiety of the baby, contains it, thinks it, and returns it to the baby digested, creating the possibility of developing a thinking apparatus. This makes it possible for the sensory impressions of emotional experiences to be transformed into alpha elements, thoughts, connectors, and organizers of the experience of the world and its events as well as loving and destructive impulses.

It became clear that we were facing serious thinking disorders in the repetition of unrelated events in these women's stories. In *Explorations in Autism,* Meltzer differentiates between the secondary obsessional mechanisms related to motivational or defensive splitting, which aim for omnipotent control of objects to reduce anxiety, and the primary obsessional mechanisms that are more related to a "breach in the logic of cause and effect that leaps from the wish to its fulfillment without pause, to achieve the means of the transformation" (p. 186). He also focuses on the relation between the use of autistic and obsessional mechanisms and the impossibility of using introjection as "a means to establish identity" and for "coping with the separation from external objects". Existing merely in the sensory realm, dismantled and with a motor action–reaction ruled by attraction and repulsion, the self finds it impossible to develop or to differentiate between itself and the object. This highlights the absence of an internal world and the fragility of existence in the external world.

Meltzer also states that "judgment" may be defined as a mental act that, when verbally expressed, implies the presence of meaning and the possibility of communication in a symbolic form (Cassirer, 1955) through transformation (Bion, 1965). Thus, autistic and obsessional mechanisms attack the ability to perform mental acts, since they do not enable common sense or the attribution of meanings and symbols, also impeded by the absence of emotion. For Meltzer, the aim of the use of autistic and obsessional mechanisms in general is:

> rendering an incipient experience meaningless by dismantling it to a state of simplicity below the level of "common sense" so that it cannot function as a "symbolic form" to "contain" (Bion) emotional significance but can only, in its various parts, find articulations in a random and mechanical sort. [Meltzer et al., 1975, p. 217]

He adds that emotional experience empty of meaning cannot be used as a memory. In an emptiness of time and space, the remains are events "dotted with disarticulated fragments of recollection and image" (p. 217) shaped as thoughtless verbal pieces. According to Meltzer, these disarticulated segments suspend vital movement and impair emotional life and the integration of emotional and intellectual development.

At the end of his next chapter, "Dimensionality as a Parameter of Mental Functioning: Its Relation with Narcissistic Organization" (1975b), Meltzer explores two-dimensionality and the rejection of psychic reality, clarifying the confusion between the description of the deterioration of mental functions and the deterioration of the awareness of mental facts. He considers two-dimensionality to be not a state of consciousness, interest, or attention, but an organization of the self's perceptual processing of the objects and the "world"; nor is it a state of "thinness" of emotional life: rather, it describes how the self lives in a two-dimensional space where the only possible contact with one's objects is from surface to surface. It is a life with no inside world, where neither introjection nor mental acts are possible. This gave us a framework to conceptualize the impoverishment of the ego in battered women as the absence of an object that performs the containing function proposed by Bion, and Bick's "second skin" function (1968), essential for the constitution of the inside world and for the development of ego strength.

In the case of these battered women, their mothers were absent or unable to provide the maternal functions of perception, containment, and soothing of their children's anxiety due to their own difficult circumstances or, perhaps, because of their own personality disturbance. These mothers are like the mothers in the Ik tribe, who push their children into the world before they have been able to build the psychic apparatus to perform the functions of perception, attention, consciousness, judgement, and reflection in relation to the world and to themselves. These mothers do not assist in the introjection of a protective object, one that can comfort and alert them, enabling them to differentiate child from adult, good from bad, and self from object. They may tolerate, even encourage, aggression and incestuous sexual abuse. They also fail to provide the kind of integration that performs differentiating and protective functions of awareness and alertness. The absence of these objects and their functions leaves these battered women as sighted but deaf, in some cases, and able to listen but blind in others. They do not manage to articulate their experiences, a failure that further impedes a helpful building of their own mind. As a result, they remain trapped in an abusive situation, especially in a society in which maltreatment and destructiveness are part of daily life.

Concluding thoughts on the nature of psychoanalytic activity

Alberto Hahn

The content of our conference, as reflected in this book, bore witness to Donald Meltzer's enduring relevance, his inspiring ideas, and his attitude of profound respect for patients' relation to their internal and external world—in particular to the infantile parts of the self. During the conference, we heard repeated mention of Meltzer's legacy as a teacher and a thinker. The breadth of papers showed how important this influence remains, both in our clinical work and in our motivation to explore further the potential and the boundaries of his psychoanalytic insights.

It is in this spirit that I want to address myself briefly to some issues that have found their way into my own clinical work, the supervision of colleagues, and the process of teaching Meltzer's life's work, for over four decades. Meltzer wrote widely about the nature of the psychoanalytic processes he was observing, their theoretical connotations, and their clinical and technical implications, and I think that the foundations laid down in *The Psychoanalytical Process* (1967) 50 years ago remain a beacon that throws a shaft of light on the worlds of the two parties involved in every analytic process we engage in. This view, which argues that our internal world determines our outlook and creates the possibility of deploying our observational and analytic function on the process, seems to remain a permanent fundamental source of interest and scrutiny. Consequently, I could not conceive of the feasibility of developing an analytic relationship without an in-depth knowledge of the unconscious variables that shape our character and, in particular, our countertransference. This knowledge, which is part of what Meltzer liked to call our "equipment", seems to highlight questions about the nature of observation and the procedure that takes us ultimately to an understanding of unconscious communications.

In reading the many accounts of his clinical cases, one is struck by the sometimes mysterious ways in which Meltzer formulated his understanding in terms of part- or whole objects, of qualities of transference and internal object relations, and by his most vivid and idiosyncratic way of apprehending and transforming mental pain through the interpretation of states of mind that are always described in a sensitive and coherent way. This way of making sense of the internal experience carries the essence of the containing capacity (of which we so frequently talk) and is a stepping-stone for the integration of split-off parts of the self.

I also believe that the opportunity to develop intuitive work points to something more specific: it allows us to conceptualize our work as deeply personal for each one of us, and it gives our patients the opportunity to experience an intimacy with an object that is capable, through his own relations to his internal objects, of gaining access to deeper strata of his mind in order to have a view of the constellations of his own and the patient's unconscious phantasies.

In teaching Meltzer's work, I have noticed the slow and always puzzling and difficult process of learning that ensues for those who come to it with a different mind-set and a different theoretical framework. I am always struck first by the impact and then the inspiring conviction that arises from his theoretical papers, but I find that the area that creates a greater problem is the attunement to the clinical narratives that pepper his writings. This requires a decoding system that is extremely personal in that it is fed by our own analytic experience, our devotion to the method, and our capacity to not understand—as well as to understand—another human being. The O of the patient, as Bion formulates it, allows us to get close enough to the patient to foster the intimacy required for the development of the transference while at the same time understanding that the patient remains basically unknowable. This unknowability requires a state of "intuitive receptivity" in our free-floating attention, which allows us to deal with a multiplicity of uncertainties in the heat elicited by the transference–countertransference interaction. This receptivity draws our attention to our engagement or disengagement in this process, and it is my experience that an approximation of these states of mind with our "Negative Capability" is sometimes enough to bring about a mutative shift in our patient's emotionality. This provides the context in which it becomes possible to change, through introjective identification with the analytic qualities of an analyst who acquires the significance of an object in psychic reality with ego functions and other parental capabilities that promote and underpin the passage into a "depressive" view of the world.

It should be understood that by "shift" I am referring to internal changes brought about by understanding through empathy, as opposed to counterproductive attempts to pursue behavioural or symptomatic changes. In the last twenty years we have seen big changes in the practice of psychoanalysis. Those of us who follow the Kleinian tradition have witnessed a gradual distancing from some of the core values that we learned from our analysts and teachers. For example, unconscious phantasy and the understanding of part-objects have given place to new para-analytic theories; work with the infantile transference has been replaced by a discussion of the intersubjective relation between the patient and the person of the analyst in the here and now, with no reference to meaning or symbolizations; and the interpretation of dreams has fallen away as the "royal road to the unconscious", to be replaced by a more pragmatic understanding of the dream content with less reference to internal emotional links. Witnessing the tendency to trivialization or scotomization that affects the analyst's observational capacities is always a painful and dangerous experience, especially when it is compounded with a state of denial of the psychic reality of the suffering infant in the patient.

All clinicians have their own view about deviations from good analytic practice and, indeed, about what "good" means in this context. But it seems to me that we can compare that which we received in our training and the many years spent in clinical practice with that which is currently thought and practised by our young colleagues, and we should feel free to question whether the ideas, theories, and principles that underpin our view and theirs of current psychoanalytic practice are enriching our discipline or impoverishing the possibility of acquiring the knowledge that is due to our patients.

This book clearly addresses these questions, and at the conference it was heartening to hear Margaret Rustin, Maria Rhode, and Suzanne Maiello do so with exceptional clarity and wisdom.

As a member of the organizing committee, together with Catrin Bradley, Jonathan Bradley, and Margaret Cohen, I am very grateful to them and all the other contributors to the conference and to the book, as they confirm for us that we are following a tradition that keeps us on the right track in our individual, personal, and professional development. This is perhaps the best tribute we could have offered to the memory of Donald Meltzer on the 10th anniversary of his death.

REFERENCES

Abbott, E. A. (1884). *Flatland: A Romance of Many Dimensions*. London: Penguin, 1987.

Ames, L. S. (1946). The development of the sense of time in the young child. *Journal of Genetic Psychology, 18*: 97–125.

Anisfeld, L., & Richards, A. D. (2000). The replacement child: Variations on a theme in history and psychoanalysis. *Psychoanalytic Study of the Child, 55*: 301–318.

Barnes, J. (2015). Selfie with "Sunflowers". *London Review of Books*, 30 July, pp. 7–8.

Beckett, S. (1955). *Molloy*. London: Faber & Faber.

Beckett, S. (1958). *Endgame*. London: Faber & Faber.

Beckett, S. (1987). Exorcising Beckett. In: *The Paris Review: Playwrights at Work* (pp. 50–86). New York: Modern Library, 2000.

Beckett, S. (2006a). *Not I*. In: *The Complete Dramatic Works of Samuel Beckett*. London: Faber & Faber.

Beckett, S. (2006b). *Waiting for Godot*. London: Faber & Faber.

Bick, E. (1964). Notes on infant observation in psychoanalytic training. *International Journal of Psychoanalysis, 45*: 558–566. Reprinted in: M. Harris Williams (Ed.), *Collected Papers of Martha Harris and Esther Bick*. Strath Tay: Clunie Press, 1987.

Bick, E. (1968). The experience of the skin in early object relations. *International Journal of Psychoanalysis, 49*: 484–486. Reprinted in: M. Harris

Williams (Ed.), *Collected Papers of Martha Harris and Esther Bick*. Strath Tay: Clunie Press, 1987.

Bion, W. R. (1959). Attacks on linking. *International Journal of Psychoanalysis, 40*: 308–315. Reprinted in: *Second Thoughts* (pp. 93–109). London Heinemann; reprinted London: Karnac, 1984.

Bion, W. R. (1961). *Experiences in Groups*. London: Tavistock Publications.

Bion, W. R. (1962a). *Learning from Experience*. London: Heinemann; reprinted London: Karnac, 1984.

Bion, W. R. (1962b). The psychoanalytic theory of thinking. *International Journal of Psychoanalysis, 43*: 306–310. Reprinted as "A Theory of Thinking" in: *Second Thoughts* (pp. 110–119). London Heinemann; reprinted London: Karnac, 1984.

Bion, W. R. (1963). *Elements of Psycho-Analysis*. London: Heinemann; reprinted London: Karnac, 1984.

Bion, W. R. (1965). *Transformations: Change from Learning to Growth*. London: Heinemann; reprinted London: Karnac, 1984.

Bion, W. R. (1970). *Attention and Interpretation: A Scientific Approach to Insight in Psycho-Analysis and Groups*. London: Tavistock Publications; reprinted London: Karnac, 1984.

Bion, W. R. (1979). Making the best of a bad job. In: *Clinical Papers and Other Works* (pp. 321–331). London: Karnac, 1994.

Bion, W. R. (1980). *Bion in New York and São Paulo*. Strath Tay: Clunie Press.

Bion, W. R. (1991). *A Memoir of the Future*. London: Karnac.

Bion, W. R. (1997). *Taming Wild Thoughts*. London: Karnac.

Birksted-Breen, D. (1996). Phallus, penis and mental space. *International Journal of Psychoanalysis, 77*: 649–657.

Bloom, H. (1999). *Shakespeare: The Invention of the Human*. London: Fourth Estate.

Brentano, F. (1874). *Psychology from an Empirical Standpoint*. London: Routledge, 1995.

Briggs, A. (Ed.) (2012). *Waiting to Be Found: Papers on Children in Care*. London: Karnac.

Britton, R. (1989). The missing link: Parental sexuality in the Oedipus complex. In: R. Britton, M. Feldman, & E. O'Shaughnessy, *The Oedipus Complex Today: Clinical Implications*. London: Karnac.

Britton, R. (1994). The blindness of the seeing eye: Inverse symmetry as a defence against reality. *Psychoanalytic Inquiry, 14*: 365–378.

Caccia, O. (2007). La nascita della mente. In: S. Latmiral & C. Lombardo (Eds.), *Pensieri prematuri*. Rome: Borla.

Campbell, J. (2006). Homelessness and containment: A psychotherapy project with homeless people and workers in the homeless field. *Psychoanalytic Psychotherapy, 20* (3): 157–174.

Canham, H. (1999). The development of the concept of time in fostered and adopted children. *Psychoanalytic Inquiry, 19* (2): 160–172. Reprinted in: A. Briggs (Ed.), *Waiting to Be Found: Papers on Children in Care* (pp. 61–71). London: Karnac, 2012.

Cassese, S. F. (2002). *Introduction to the Work of Donald Meltzer.* London: Karnac.

Cassirer, E. (1995). *The Philosophy of Symbolic Forms.* Oxford: Oxford University Press.

Cecchi, V. (1990). Analysis of a little girl with an autistic syndrome. *International Journal of Psychoanalysis, 71*: 403–410.

Colarusso, C. (1979). The development of time sense: From birth to object constancy. *International Journal of Psychoanalysis, 60*: 243–251.

Coleridge, S. T. (1816). *The Statesman's Manual*, ed. R. J. White. London: Routledge, 1972.

de Sola, B. M. (1991). El amigo intimo de la adolescencia. Su lugar en el proceso psicoanalitico. *Psicoanalisis APdeBA, 13* (3): 565–583.

Descartes, R. (1641). *Méditations métaphysiques.* Paris: PUF, 2004.

Edel, L. (1980). The Genius and the Injustice Collector: A memoir of James Joyce. *The American Scholar, 49* (4): 467–487.

Ellmann, R. (1982). *James Joyce.* New York: Oxford University Press.

Emanuel, R. (2001). A-void: An explanation of defence against seeing nothingness. *International Journal of Psychoanalysis, 82*: 1069–1084.

Emanuel, R. (2012). An application of Bion's theory of thinking and transformation in hallucinations: An experience of supervision with Donald Meltzer. *Journal of Child Psychotherapy, 38* (3): 282–301.

Etchegoyen, H. (1991). *The Fundamentals of Psychoanalytic Technique.* London: Karnac.

Feldman, M. (1989). The Oedipus complex: Manifestations in the inner world and the therapeutic situation. In: R. Britton, M. Feldman, & E. O'Shaughnessy, *The Oedipus Complex Today: Clinical Implications* (pp. 103–128). London: Karnac.

Fisher, J. V. (1999). *The Uninvited Guest: Emerging from Narcissism towards Marriage.* London: Karnac.

Fisher, J. V. (2006). The emotional experience of K. *International Journal of Psychoanalysis, 87*: 1221–1237.

Fisher, J. V. (2009). The Macbeths in the consulting room. *Fort Da, 15* (2): 33–55.

Fisher, J. V. (2011). *The Proleptic Imagination.* Unpublished paper.

Freud, S. (1893a) (with Breuer, J.). On the psychical mechanism of hysterical phenomena: Preliminary communication. *Standard Edition, 2*: 1–17.

Freud, S. (1911b). Formulations on the two principles of mental functioning. *Standard Edition, 12*: 213–226.

Freud, S. (1914g). Remembering, repeating and working through. *Standard Edition, 12*: 147–156.

Freud, S. (1937d). Constructions in analysis. *Standard Edition, 23*: 257–270.

Freud, S. (1940a [1938]). *An Outline of Psycho-Analysis. Standard Edition, 23*: 144–208.

Gaiman, N. (2002). *Coraline.* New York: HarperCollins.

Gernsbacher, M. (2005). *Learning Communities and Learning Relationships: Older Children and Adults with ASD.* Panel presentation at the Annual Conference of the Interdisciplinary Council of Developmental and Learning Disorders, Tysons Corner, VA, 12 November.

Gerson, S. (2009). When the third is dead: Memory, mourning, and witnessing in the aftermath of the Holocaust. *International Journal of Psychoanalysis, 90*: 1341–1357.

Gittings, R. (Ed.) (1970). *Selected Letters of John Keats.* Oxford: Oxford University Press.

Gosso, S. (2004). Introduction. In: *Psychoanalysis and Art: Kleinian Perspectives.* London: Karnac.

Green, A. (1986). *On Private Madness.* London: Hogarth Press.

Green, A. (2002). *Time in Psychoanalysis: Some Contradictory Aspects.* London: Free Association Books.

Greenblatt, S. (2004). *Will in the World.* London: Jonathan Cape.

Grinberg, L. (1970). The problems of supervision in psychoanalytic education. *International Journal of Psychoanalysis, 51*: 371–383.

Grotstein, J. S. (2004). The seventh servant: The implications of a truth drive in Bion's theory of "O". *International Journal of Psychoanalysis, 85*: 1081–1101.

Haag, G. (2004). *Réflexions de psychothérapeutes de formation psychanalytique s'occupant de sujets avec autisme.* Available at: psydocfr.broca.inserm.fr/Techniques-psychotherapiques/Documentation/Archives/Haag0105.html

Harris, M. (1978). Towards learning from experience in infancy and childhood. In: M. Harris & E. Bick, *The Tavistock Model: Papers on Child Development and Psychoanalytic Training* (pp. 171–188). London: Harris Meltzer Trust, 2011.

Harris, M. (1980). Bion's conception of a psychoanalytical attitude. In: M. Harris & E. Bick, *The Tavistock Model: Papers on Child Development and Psychoanalytic Training* (pp. 45–50). London: Harris Meltzer Trust, 2011.

Herbart, J. F. (1824), *Psychologie als Wissenschaft neugegründet auf Erfahrung, Metaphysik und Mathematik*. Königberg: A. W. Unzer.

Highsmith, P. (1955). *The Talented Mr. Ripley*. New York: Coward-McCann.

Houzel, D. (1996). The family envelope and what happens when it is torn. *International Journal of Psychoanalysis, 77*: 901–912.

Houzel, D. (2001). The bisexuality of the psychic envelope. In: J. Edwards (Ed.), *Being Alive: Building on the Work of Anne Alvarez*. London: Routledge.

Houzel, D. (2014). Precipitation anxiety in the analysis of adult patients. In: J. L. Mitrani & T. Mitrani (Eds.), *Frances Tustin Today*. London: Routledge.

Hunter, M. (2001). *Psychotherapy with Young Children in Care: Lost and Found*. Hove: Brunner-Routledge.

Jackson, M. (2015). *Creativity and Psychotic States in Exceptional People: The Work of Murray Jackson*, ed. J. Magagna. London: Routledge.

Johns, G. (2010). *In the Dim Void. Samuel Beckett's Late Trilogy: Company, Ill Seen Ill Said and Worstward Ho*. Maidstone: Crescent Moon.

Joyce, J. (1914). *Dubliners*. London: Jonathan Cape.

Joyce, J. (1922a). *Ulysses*. London: Penguin, 1968.

Joyce, J. (1922b). *Ulysses: Annotated Students' Edition*. London: Penguin Classics, 1992.

Joyce, J. (1939). *Finnegans Wake*. London: Faber & Faber.

Joyce, J. (1984). *Giacomo Joyce*. London: Faber & Faber.

Kant, E. (1787). *Metaphysical Foundations of Natural Science*. Cambridge: Cambridge University Press, 2004.

Kaufmann, W. J. (1977). *The Cosmic Frontiers of General Relativity*. Boston, MA: Little, Brown.

Keats, J. (1884). La Belle Dame sans Merci. In: *The Complete Poems*, ed. J. Bernard. Harmondsworth: Penguin, 1973.

Kenner, H. (1962). *Flaubert, Joyce and Beckett: The Stoic Comedians*. London: Dalkey Archive Press.

Kiberd, D. (1992). Introduction. In: James Joyce, *Ulysses: Annotated Student* Edition (pp. ix–lxxx). London: Penguin.

Klein, M. (1929). Personification in the play of children. In: *The Writings of Melanie Klein, Vol. 1* (pp. 199–209). London: Hogarth Press, 1975; reprinted London: Karnac, 1992.

Klein, M. (1930). The importance of symbol-formation in the development of the ego. In: *The Writings of Melanie Klein, Vol.* 1 (pp. 219–232). London: Hogarth Press, 1975; reprinted London: Karnac, 1992.

Klein, M. (1932). *The Psycho-Analysis of Children. The Writings of Melanie Klein Vol. 2*. London: Hogarth Press, 1975; reprinted London: Karnac, 1998.

Klein, M. (1946). Notes on some schizoid mechanisms. In: *The Writings of Melanie Klein, Vol. 3* (pp. 1–24). London: Hogarth Press, 1975; reprinted London: Karnac, 1993.

Klein, M. (1957). *Envy and Gratitude. The Writings of Melanie Klein, Vol. 3*. London: Hogarth Press, 1975; reprinted London: Karnac, 1993.

Klein, M. (1961). *Narrative of a Child Analysis. The Writings of Melanie Klein, Vol. 4*. London: Hogarth Press; reprinted London: Karnac, 1996.

Klein, S. (1980). Autistic phenomena in neurotic patients. *International Journal of Psychoanalysis, 61*: 395–402.

Knowlson, J. (1996). *Damned to Fame: The Life of Samuel Beckett*. New York: Simon and Schuster.

Leibniz, G. W. (1714). *La monadologie*. Paris: Delagrave, 1880.

Lewis, W. (1927). An analysis of the mind of James Joyce. In: *Time and Western Man* (pp. 74–130). London: Chatto & Windus.

Liberman, D. (1976). The affective response of the analyst to the patient's communications. *International Journal of Psychoanalysis, 59*: 335–340.

Liegner, E., & Motycka, R. (2003). James Joyce's *Ulysses* revisited: Matricide and the search for the mother. *Modern Psychoanalysis, 28* (1): 143–160.

Lubbe, T. (2011). *A Kleinian Theory of Sexuality*. Available at: www.ipcp.co.za/wp-content/uploads/2011/06/Kleinian-Sexuality.pdf

Magagna, J. (2012a). A baby's "broken bridge" to the parents. In: *The Silent Child: Communication without Words*. London: Karnac.

Magagna, J. (2012b). Evolving patterns of parental containment of a young child communicating through not eating or speaking. In: *The Silent Child: Communication without Words*. London: Karnac.

McCourt, J. (2000). *The Years of Bloom: James Joyce in Trieste, 1904–1920*. Dublin: Lilliput Press.

Meltzer, D. (1960) (with Bick, E.). Lectures and seminars in Kleinian child psychiatry. In: *Sincerity and Other Works: Collected Papers of Donald Meltzer* (pp. 35–89), ed. A. Hahn. London: Karnac, 1994.

Meltzer, D. (1966). The relation of anal masturbation to projective identification. In: *The Claustrum: An Investigation of Claustrophobic Phenomena* (pp. 14–29). Strath Tay: Clunie Press.

Meltzer, D. (1967). *The Psychoanalytical Process*. London: Heinemann; reprinted Strath Tay: Clunie Press, 1970.

Meltzer, D. (1970). Positive and negative forms. In: *Sincerity and Other Works: Collected Papers of Donald Meltzer* (pp. 177–184), ed. A. Hahn. London: Karnac, 1994.

Meltzer, D. (1971). Sincerity: A study in the atmosphere of human relations. In: *Sincerity and Other Works: Collected Papers of Donald Meltzer* (pp. 185–284), ed. A. Hahn. London: Karnac, 1994.

Meltzer, D. (1973a). Identification and socialization in adolescence. In: *Sexual States of Mind* (pp. 51–57). London: Karnac, 2008.

Meltzer, D. (1973b). On the distinction ambisexual–bisexual. In: *Sexual States of Mind* (pp. 114–121). London: Karnac, 2008.

Meltzer, D. (1973c). Routine and inspired interpretations: Their relation to the weaning process in analysis. In: *Sincerity and Other Works: Collected Papers of Donald Meltzer* (pp. 290–306), ed. A. Hahn. London: Karnac, 1994.

Meltzer, D. (1973d). Terror, persecution, and dread. In: *Sexual States of Mind* (pp. 99–106). London: Karnac, 2008.

Meltzer, D. (1974). The role of pregenital confusions in erotomania. In: *Sincerity and Other Works: Collected Papers of Donald Meltzer* (pp. 330–334), ed. A. Hahn. London: Karnac, 1994.

Meltzer, D. (1975a). Adhesive identification. *Contemporary Psychoanalysis, 11* (3): 289–310.

Meltzer, D. (1975b). Dimensionality as a parameter in mental functioning: Its relation to narcissistic organization. In: D. Meltzer, J. Bremner, S. Hoxter, D. Weddell, & I. Wittenberg (Eds.), *Explorations in Autism: A Psycho-Analytical Study* (pp. 223–238). Strath Tay: Clunie Press.

Meltzer, D. (1975c). Aims, scope, and methods of the investigation. In: D. Meltzer, J. Bremner, S. Hoxter, D. Weddell, & I. Wittenberg (Eds.), *Explorations in Autism: A Psycho-Analytical Study* (pp. 3–5). Strath Tay: Perthshire: Clunie Press.

Meltzer, D. (1975d). Mutism in autism, schizophrenia and manic-depressive states: The correlation of clinical psycho-pathology and linguistics. In: D. Meltzer, J. Bremner, S. Hoxter, D. Weddell, & I. Wittenberg (Eds.), *Explorations in Autism: A Psycho-Analytical Study* (pp. 192–208). Strath Tay: Clunie Press.

Meltzer, D. (1975e). The psychology of autistic states and of post-autistic mentality. In: D. Meltzer, J. Bremner, S. Hoxter, D. Weddell, & I. Wittenberg (Eds.), *Explorations in Autism: A Psycho-Analytical Study* (pp. 6–29). Strath Tay: Clunie Press.

Meltzer, D. (1976a). The delusion of clarity of insight. *International Journal of Psychoanalysis, 57*: 141–146.

Meltzer, D. (1976b) (with Harris, M.). A psychoanalytic study of the child-in-the-family-in-the-community. In: *Sincerity and Other Works: Collected Papers of Donald Meltzer* (pp. 387–454), ed. A. Hahn. London: Karnac, 1994.

Meltzer, D. (1976c). Temperature and distance as technical dimensions of interpretation. In: *Sincerity and Other Works: Collected Papers of Donald Meltzer* (pp. 374–386), ed. A. Hahn. London: Karnac, 1994.

Meltzer, D. (1978). *The Kleinian Development*. London: Karnac, 2008.

Meltzer, D. (1981). Does Money-Kyrle's conception of misconception have a unique descriptive power? In: *Sincerity and Other Works: Collected Papers of Donald Meltzer* (pp. 496–513), ed. A. Hahn. London: Karnac, 1994.

Meltzer, D. (1983). *Dream-Life: A Re-Examination of the Psycho-Analytical Theory and Technique*. Strath Tay: Clunie Press, 1984.

Meltzer, D. (1986a). Concerning the perception of one's own attributes and its relation to language development. In: *Studies in Extended Metapsychology: Clinical Applications of Bion's Ideas* (pp. 175–186). Strath Tay: Clunie Press.

Meltzer, D. (1986b) (with Albergamo, M., Cohen, E., Greco, A., Harris, M., Maiello, S., et al.). *Studies in Extended Metapsychology: Clinical Applications of Bion's Ideas*. Strath Tay: Clunie Press.

Meltzer, D. (1989). Lecture to the APdeBA. *Psicoanálisis (APdeBA), 12* (1, 1990): 123–134.

Meltzer, D. (1992a). *The Claustrum: An Investigation of Claustrophobic Phenomena*. Strath Tay: Clunie Press.

Meltzer, D. (1992b). *Supervision in the Grupo Psicoanalítico Barcelona: Case of Christian*. Unpublished paper.

Meltzer, D. (1997). Concerning signs and symbols. *British Journal of Psychotherapy, 14* (2): 175–181.

Meltzer, D. (1999). Clinical dialogues with DM: Graciela. *Psicoanalisis (APdeBA), 21* (1/2): 119–146.

Meltzer, D. (2000). A review of my writings. In: M. Cohen & A. Hahn (Eds.), *Exploring the Work of Donald Meltzer*. London: Karnac.

Meltzer, D. (2002) (with the Psychoanalytic Group of Barcelona & Mack Smith, C.). *Psychoanalytic Work with Children and Adults: Meltzer in Barcelona*. London: Karnac.

Meltzer, D. (2003) (with Castellà, R., Tabbia, C., & Farré, L.). *Supervisions with Donald Meltzer: The Simsbury Seminars*. London: Karnac.

Meltzer, D. Bremner, J., Hoxter, S., Weddell, D., & Wittenberg, I. (1975). *Explorations in Autism: A Psycho-Analytical Study*. Strath Tay: Clunie Press.

Meltzer, D., & Harris, M. (1998). Elsa: Fear of the adolescent community. In: *Adolescence: Talks and Papers by Donald Meltzer and Martha Harris*. London: Karnac, 2011.

Meltzer, D., & Harris, M. (2011). *Adolescence: Talks and Papers by Donald Meltzer and Martha Harris*, ed. M. Harris Williams. London: Karnac.

Meltzer, D., & Harris Williams, M. (1988). *The Apprehension of Beauty: The Role of Aesthetic Conflict in Development, Art and Violence*. Strath Tay: Clunie Press.

Milton, J. (1644). *Areopagitica: A Speech for the Liberty of Unlicensed Printing*. London: Hunter, 1819.

Minghella, A. (Dir.) (1999). *The Talented Mr. Ripley* [Film]. Hollywood, CA: Paramount.

Mitchell, J. (1996). Sexuality and psychoanalysis: Hysteria. *British Journal of Psychotherapy, 12*: 473–479.

Mitchell, J. (1998). Trauma, recognition and the place of language. *Diacritics, 28*: 121–133.

Money-Kyrle, R. (1968). Cognitive development. In: *Man's Picture of His World and Three Papers* (pp. 209–228). London: Harris Meltzer Trust, 2014.

Morgan, M. (1995). The projective gridlock: A form of projective identification in couple relationships, In: S. Ruszczinski & J. Fisher (Eds.), *Intrusiveness and Intimacy in the Couple*. London: Karnac.

Mukhopadhyay, T. R. (2000). *The Mind Tree*. New York: Arcade.

Mukhopadhyay, T. R. (2008). *How Can I Talk if My Lips Don't Move?* New York: Arcade.

Muñoz Vila, C. (2011). *Reflexiones psicoanalíticas*. Bogotá: Pontificia Universidad Javeriana.

Muñoz Vila, C. (2014). *Clínica psicoanalítica. Doce estudios de casos y algunas notas de técnica*. Bogotá: Pontificia Universidad Javeriana.

Nemas, C. (2000). Development is beauty, growth is ethics. In: M. Cohen & A. Hahn (Eds.), *Exploring the Work of Donald Meltzer*. London: Karnac.

Nemas, C. (2016). Courage and sincerity as a base for reverie and interpretation. In: D. Blue & C. Harrang (Eds.), *From Reverie to Interpretation: Transforming Thought into the Action of Psychoanalysis* (pp. 131–144). London: Karnac.

Oates, J. C. (2015). Inspiration and obsession in life and literature. *New York Review of Books*, 13 August.

Oelsner, M., & Oelsner, R. (2005). About supervision: An interview with Donald Meltzer. *British Journal of Psychotherapy, 21* (3): 455–461.

Ogden, T. H. (2005). *This Art of Psychoanalysis: Dreaming Undreamt Dreams and Interrupted Cries*. London: Routledge.

O'Shaughnessy, E. (2015). The absent object. In: *Inquiries in Psychoanalysis:*

Collected Papers of Edna O'Shaughnessy (pp. 19–31), ed. R. Rusbridger. Hove: Routledge.

O'Toole, F. (2015). Beckett in love. *New York Review of Books*, 2 April.

Pontalis, J.-B. (2011). *Al margen de las noches*. Buenos Aires: Paidos.

Pozzi Monzo, M., Micotti, S., & Rashid, S. (2015). The mutism of the mind: Child and family therapists at work with children and families suffering with selective mutism. *Journal of Child Psychotherapy, 41*: 22–40.

Rey, H. (1979). Schizoid phenomena in the borderline patient. In: J. LeBoit & A. Capponi (Eds.), *Advances in the Psychotherapy of the Borderline Patient*. New York: Jason Aronson.

Rey, H. (1994). *Universals of Psychoanalysis in the Treatment of Psychotic and Borderline States*, ed. J. Magagna. London: Free Association Books.

Rhode, M. (1997). Going to pieces: Autistic and schizoid solutions. In: M. Rustin, M. Rhode., A. Dubinsky, & H. Dubinsky (Eds.), *Psychotic States in Children*. London: Karnac.

Rhode, M. (1999). Echo or answer? Towards the development of ordinary speech in three children with autistic spectrum disorder. In A. Alvarez & S. Reid (Eds.), *Autism and Personality*. London: Routledge.

Rhode, M. (2000). On using an alphabet: Recombining separable components. In: J. Symington (Ed.), *Imprisoned Pain and Its Transformation: A Festschrift for H. Sydney Klein*. London: Karnac.

Rhode, M. (2004). Different responses to trauma in two children with autistic spectrum disorder: The mouth as crossroads of the sense of self. *Journal of Child Psychotherapy, 30*: 3–20.

Rhode, M. (2008). Joining the human family. In: K. Barrows (Ed.), *Autism in Childhood and Autistic Features in Adults*. London: Karnac.

Rhode, M. (2013). The physicality of words: Some implications of Donald Meltzer's writings on language. *International Journal of Infant Observation, 16*: 270–285.

Ricks, C. (1993). *Beckett's Dying Words*. Oxford: Oxford University Press.

Rios, C. (1985). Las identificaciones en la adolescencia. *Psicoanálisis (APdeBA), 7* (3): 499–515.

Rosenfeld, D. (2001). Psychotic addiction to video games. In: P. Williams (Ed.), *A Language for Psychosis: Psychoanalysis of Psychotic States* (pp. 149–174). London: Whurr.

Rustin, M. E., & Rustin, M. J. (2000). Beckett: Dramas of psychic catastrophe. In: M. Cohen & A. Hahn (Eds.), *Exploring the Work of Donald Meltzer* (pp. 152–172). London: Karnac.

Rustin, M. E., & Rustin, M. J. (2002). *Mirror to Nature: Psychoanalysis, Drama and Society*. London: Karnac.

Sabbadini, A. (1988). The replacement child. *Contemporary Psychoanalysis, 24*: 528–547.

Schwarz, D. R. (1987). *Reading Joyce's Ulysses.* London: Macmillan.

Selick, H. (Dir.) (2009). *Coraline* [Film]. Universal City, CA: Focus Features.

Shelley, P. B. (1891). *A Defense of Poetry*, ed. A. S. Cook. Boston, MA: Ginn & Company.

Silver, D. (1983). The Dark Lady: Sibling loss and mourning in the Shakespearean sonnets. *Psychoanalytic Inquiry, 3* (3): 513–527.

Sorensen, P. (2000). Observations of transition facilitating behaviour—developmental and theoretical implications. *Infant Observation: International Journal of Infant Observation and Its Applications, 3* (2): 46–54.

Staehle, A. (2007). Zwischen Kuscheln und Beißen. Anfang einer Analyse mit einem elektiv mutistischen Kind. *Kinderanalyse, 1*: 20–40.

Tamm, C. (2014). *Autistic Functioning and Language Development.* Unpublished PhD dissertation, University of East London.

Thoreau, H. D. (2009). *The Journal: 1837–1861.* New York: New York Review of Books Classics.

Thurston, W. P., & Weeks, J. (1984). The mathematics of three-dimensional manifolds. *Scientific American, 251* (1): 108–120.

Trilling, L. (1967). James Joyce in his letters. In: *The Moral Obligation to Be Intelligent: Selected Essays* (pp. 450–476). Evanston, IL: Northwestern University Press, 2000.

Trowell, J., & Kolvin, I. (1995). A follow-up study of selectively mute children as adults. *Bulletin of the Association of Child Psychology & Psychiatry.*

Truckle, B. (2006). *Blue in Blue.* Unpublished paper.

Turnbull, C. (1972). *The Mountain People.* New York: Simon & Shuster, 1987.

Tustin, F. (1966). A significant element in the development of autism: A psycho-analytic approach. *Journal of Child Psychology and Psychiatry, 7*: 53–67.

Tustin F. (1972a). *Autism and Childhood Psychosis.* London: Hogarth Press; reprinted London: Karnac, 1995.

Tustin, F. (1972b). Psychotic depression. In: *Autism and Childhood Psychosis.* London: Hogarth Press; reprinted London: Karnac, 1995.

Tustin, F. (1981). *Autistic States in Children.* London: Routledge.

Tustin, F. (1984). The growth of understanding. *Journal of Child Psychotherapy, 10*: 137–149.

Tustin, F. (1986a). The rhythm of safety. In: *Autistic Barriers in Neurotic Patients* (pp. 268–285). London: Karnac.

Tustin, F. (1986b). A significant element in the development of psychogenic autism. In: *Autistic Barriers in Neurotic Patients* (2nd revised edition, pp. 76–93). London: Karnac, 1994.

Tustin, F. (1990). *The Protective Shell in Children and Adults.* London: Karnac.

Tustin, F. (1994). The perpetuation of an error. *Journal of Child Psychotherapy, 20* (1): 3–23.

Weininger, O. (1992). Elective mutism in children: A Kleinian approach. In: *Melanie Klein: From Theory to Reality* (pp. 133–150). London: Karnac.

Wilkinson, B. (2012). Phil Brown, *Il Avalit* [Book review]. *Times Literary Supplement,* 14 September.

Williams, G. (1997). *Internal Landscapes and Foreign Bodies.* London: Duckworth.

Williams, M. H. (2003). Conversations with internal objects: Family and narrative structure in Homer's *Odyssey*. *British Journal of Psychotherapy, 20* (2): 219–235.

Williams, M. H. (Ed.) (2008). A post-Kleinian model for aesthetic criticism. *PsyArt. An Online Journal for the Psychological Study of the Arts.* Available at: http://psyartjournal.com/article/show/harris_williams-a_post_kleinian_model_for_aesthetic_critl

Williams, M. H. (Ed.) (2010). *A Meltzer Reader*. London: Karnac.

Williams, M. H. (Ed.) (2015). *Art and Analysis: An Adrian Stokes Reader.* London: Harris Meltzer Trust.

Winnicott, D. W. (1951). Transitional objects and transitional phenomena. In: *Through Paediatrics to Psycho-Analysis.* London: Tavistock Publications, 1958; reprinted London: Karnac, 1984.

Winnicott, D. W. (1952). Anxiety associated with Insecurity. In: *Through Paediatrics to Psycho-Analysis.* London: Tavistock Publications, 1958; reprinted London: Karnac, 1984.

Winnicott, D. W. (1960). The theory of the parent–infant relationship. In: *The Maturational Processes and the Facilitating Environment.* London: Hogarth Press, 1965; reprinted London: Karnac, 1990.

Winnicott, D. W. (1963). The mentally ill in your caseload. In: *The Maturational Processes and the Facilitating Environment.* London: Hogarth Press, 1965; reprinted London: Karnac, 1990.

Winnicott, D. W. (1974). Fear of breakdown. In: *Psycho-Analytic Explorations,* ed. C. Winnicott, R. Shepherd, & M. Davis. London: Karnac, 1989.

Winterson, J. (2011). *Why Be Happy When You Could Be Normal?* London: Vintage.

Woolf, V. (1929). *A Room of One's Own.* New York: Harcourt Brace, 1989.

Yeats, W. B. (1989). *Poems*. London: Macmillan.

INDEX